TAIWAN'S POLITICS IN THE 21ST CENTURY

Changes and Challenges

TAIWAN'S POLITICS IN THE 21ST CENTURY

Changes and Challenges

Edited by

Wei-Chin Lee

Wake Forest University, USA

World Scientific

NEW JERSEY • LONDON • SINGAPORE • BEIJING • SHANGHAI • HONG KONG • TAIPEI • CHENNAI

Published by

World Scientific Publishing Co. Pte. Ltd.

5 Toh Tuck Link, Singapore 596224

USA office: 27 Warren Street, Suite 401-402, Hackensack, NJ 07601

UK office: 57 Shelton Street, Covent Garden, London WC2H 9HE

British Library Cataloguing-in-Publication Data
A catalogue record for this book is available from the British Library.

TAIWAN'S POLITICS IN THE 21ST CENTURY
Changes and Challenges

ISBN-13 978-981-4289-08-5
ISBN-10 981-4289-08-6

Typeset by Stallion Press
Email: enquiries@stallionpress.com

Printed in Singapore by World Scientific Printers.

Contents

Acknowledgments

In editing this volume, I owe a great deal to many people. Chapter authors are certainly on the top of my list of appreciation. Without their willingness and cooperation at every stage of the preparation process, this volume would have been an impossible task. I would also like to thank Max Phua, Executive Director of the World Scientific Publishing Company, for his initiative and invitation to publish a book to detail and explain Taiwan's political development in the first decade of the 21st century. Two senior editors, Pauline Chan at the beginning and followed by Venkatesh Sandhya, have been very helpful throughout the whole process. They all have my heartfelt thanks for their suggestions and encouragement. I am also very grateful to Emily Young, who has done a marvelous job wading through all chapters, offering perceptive suggestions, and pointing out errors. Naturally, any mistakes and errors in the volume remain to be the editor's sole responsibility. Moreover, Dean's Office of the College of Arts and Science at Wake Forest University deserves our appreciation for its funding to allow the completion of the manuscript. The Political Science Department of Wake Forest University has been extremely supportive at every stage of the process in any way to facilitate the preparation of this book. Last, but not least, my deepest appreciation goes to my wife Cristina Yu and daughters Rae-Yao and Rae-Ling. They have made all phases of this project more manageable.

About the Authors

Lu-huei Chen (National Chengchi University, Taiwan): Lu-huei Chen is a research fellow of the Election Study Center, National Chengchi University, Taipei. He received his PhD in Political Science, Michigan State University, in 1999. His research on Taiwan's democracy, election, political trust, and cross–strait relations has appeared in various scholarly journals, including *Journal of Election Studies, Issues and Studies, Taiwan Democracy Journal, Japanese Journal of Electoral Studies,* and *Social Science Quarterly.*

Cal Clark (Auburn University, USA): Cal Clark is a Professor of Political Science and the Director of the MPA Program at Auburn University. He has previously taught at New Mexico State University and the University of Wyoming and has been a Visiting Professor at Chung Yuan Christian and Tunghai Universities in Taiwan. He is the co-author of *Taiwan's Development*, *Women in Taiwan Politics*, and *Comparative Development Patterns in Asia* and the co-editor of *Beyond the Developmental State*, *The Evolving Pacific Basin*, and *Democracy and the Status of Women in East Asia*. He has served as the President of the American Association for Chinese Studies.

John Fuh-sheng Hsieh (University of South Carolina, USA): John Fuh-sheng Hsieh is Professor of Political Science at the University of South Carolina. His teaching and research interests include rational choice theory, constitutional design, electoral systems, electoral behavior, political parties, democratization, and foreign policy.

Shu Keng (National Chengchi University, Taiwan): Shu Keng is an Associate Professor at the Graduate Institute of East Asian Studies, National Chengchi University, Taiwan. He is also the Director of Taishang Research Resources of the University, the Executive Editor of *Chinese Political Science Review* (CPSR), and the editor of *East Asian Studies.* His research areas include cross–strait relations, government–business relations, and Chinese political economy.

Chyungly Lee (Institute of International Relations, National Chengchi University, Taiwan): Chyungly Lee is a research faculty in the Institute of International Relations and an adjunct Associate Professor of the College of Social Science and the College of Communication in National Chengchi University. She received her PhD from the Department of Government and Politics, University of Maryland, in 1995. Her major publications and researches cover topics of Asia–Pacific security multilateralism, regionalism in Asia, conflict prevention in East Asia, and nontraditional security issues.

Wei-chin Lee (Wake Forest University, USA): Wei-chin Lee is Professor of Political Science at Wake Forest University. He has been a visiting professor at National Sun Yat-sen University in Taiwan and Kansai Gaidai University in Japan. His books include *Taiwan* (1990), and *Taiwan in Perspective* (edited, 2000), and *Sayonara to the Lee Teng-hui Era: Politics in Taiwan, 1988–2000* (edited, 2003). His articles on arms transfer, civil–military relations, political economy, ocean politics, and military security have appeared in numerous scholarly journals. His recent publications include "The Greening of the Brass: Taiwan's Civil–Military Relations Since 2000", *Asian Security*, 2007, and "Yours, Mine, or Everyone's Property? China's Property Law in 2007", *Journal of Chinese Political Science*, 2010.

Guoli Liu (College of Charleston, USA): Guoli Liu is Professor of Political Science at the College of Charleston. He received his BA and MA degrees from Peking University and a PhD in political science from the State University of New York at Buffalo. His main teaching and research interests are comparative politics and international relations. He served as President of the Association of Chinese Political Studies, and Vice President of South Carolina Political Science Association. His edited books include *Chinese Foreign Policy in Transition* (Aldine Transaction, 2004), (with Weixing Chen) *New Directions in Chinese Politics for the New Millennium* (Edwin Mellen, 2002), (with Lowell Dittmer) *China's Deep Reform: Domestic Politics in Transition* (Rowman and Littlefield, 2006), and (with Quansheng Zhao) *Managing the China Challenge: Global Perspectives* (Routledge, 2009).

Shelley Rigger (Davidson College, USA): Shelley Rigger is the Brown Professor of East Asian Politics at Davidson College in Davidson, North Carolina. She has a PhD in Government from Harvard University and a BA in Public and International Affairs from Princeton University. She has been a visiting researcher at National Chengchi University in Taiwan and a visiting professor at Fudan University in Shanghai. Rigger is the author of two books on Taiwan's domestic politics. *Politics in Taiwan: Voting for Democracy* (Routledge, 1999) and *From Opposition to Power: Taiwan's Democratic Progressive Party* (Lynne Rienner Publishers, 2001). She has published articles on Taiwan's domestic politics, the national identity issue in Taiwan–China relations and related topics. Her current research studies the effects of cross–strait economic interactions on Taiwan people's perceptions of mainland China. Her monograph, *Taiwan's Rising Rationalism: Generations, Politics and 'Taiwan Nationalism'* was published by the East West Center in Washington in November 2006.

Huo-yan Shyu (Academia Sinica, Taiwan): Huo-yan Shyu is a Senior Research Fellow at the Institute of Political Science, Academia Sinica, and a Joint Professor of Political Science at National Taipei University. His areas of specialization include comparative politics, voting behavior, and political psychology. He is the author of over 50 articles, book chapters, and other publications both in English and Chinese.

Alex Tan (University of Canterbury, New Zealand): Alexander C. Tan is Associate Professor of Political Science at the University of Canterbury in Christchurch, New Zealand. He is also Associate Director of the New Zealand Contemporary China Research Centre and a Senior Fellow of the John Tower Center for Political Studies, Southern Methodist University, Dallas, TX. He has published and written widely in the areas of comparative political parties and comparative political economy of the Taiwan and other advanced industrial democracies.

T.Y. Wang (Illinois State University, USA): T.Y. Wang is Professor of Political Science at Illinois State University. He is currently the co-editor of the *Journal of Asian and African Studies* and was the Coordinator of the Conference Group of Taiwan Studies (CGOTS) of the American Political Science Association. Professor Wang's research focuses on Taiwanese national identity, cross–strait relations, U.S. policy toward China and Taiwan, and research methodology. He has published articles in such scholarly journals as the *American Political Science Review*, *Asian Survey*, *International Studies Quarterly*, *Journal of Peace Research*, *Political Research Quarterly*, and *Social Science Quarterly*. His most recent publications include "The Rise of China and its Emerging Grand Strategy", *Journal of Asian and African Studies* (Special issue editor, 2008), *Quantitative Analysis in Political Science* (in Chinese) (Beijing: China Renmin University Press, 2007) and "Political Tolerance in Taiwan: Democratic Elitism in a Polity under Threat", *Social Science Quarterly* (with Lu-huei Chen, 2008). Professor Wang has been frequently invited to conduct lectures and present papers in China, Taiwan, and the United States.

Joseph Wong (University of Toronto, Canada): Joseph Wong is an Associate Professor of Political Science at the University of Toronto, where he holds a Canada Research Chair in political economy. He is also the Director of the University's Asian Institute. Wong received his PhD from the University of Wisconsin–Madison in 2001. His books include *Healthy Democracies: Welfare Politics in Taiwan and South Korea* (Cornell University Press, 2004) and *Political Transitions in Dominant Party Systems: Learning to Lose* (Routledge, 2008). Wong recently finished a book on biotechnology innovation in Taiwan, Korea, and Singapore.

Quansheng Zhao (American University, USA): Quansheng Zhao is Professor of international relations and Director of Center for Asian Studies at American University in Washington, DC; serving as Director of the Division of Comparative and Regional Studies for three terms (1999–2008). He is also Guest Professor at Beijing, Qinghua, and Fudan Universities in China, and Korea University in Korea, and Coordinator for the Global Forum of Chinese Political Scientists. Professor Zhao received his BA from Beijing University and MA and PhD from the University of California at Berkeley. After a one-year post-doctoral research at Harvard University, he served for many years as Research Associate at Harvard's Fairbank Center for East Asian Research. He was also a visiting professor in numerous academic institutions. A specialist in international relations and comparative politics focusing on East Asia, Dr. Zhao is the author of *Interpreting Chinese Foreign Policy* (Oxford University Press, winner of the Best Academic Book Award by the Ministry of Culture of the Republic of Korea), and *Japanese Policymaking* (Oxford University Press/Praeger, selected as "Outstanding Academic Book" by *Choice*). He is editor or co-editor of *Managing the China Challenge: Perspectives from the Globe*, *Future Trends in East Asian International Relations*, and *Politics of Divided Nations: China, Korea, Germany, and Vietnam*. His books have been translated into Chinese, Japanese, and Korean. Professor Zhao has previously taught at Tufts University's Fletcher School of Law and Diplomacy and at Old Dominion University. He has held several distinguished year-long visiting positions (research or teaching) at the University of Tokyo, Harvard University, United States Institute of Peace, Hong Kong University of Science and Technology, and East–West Center in Hawaii.

Chapter

1

Taiwan's Politics in the 2000s: An Introduction

Wei-Chin Lee

Democratic transition and consolidation have not been easy tasks for most non-Western societies. However, Taiwan's navigation from an authoritarian regime to democracy in the 1990s was characterized by its peaceful nature and therefore attracted immense international media attention and generated widespread academic studies. In 2000, when Chen Shui-bian won a three-way presidential election, Taiwan was rightly proud of its smooth regime change from the long-term governing Kuomintang (Nationalist Party, KMT) to the then opposition party, Democratic Progressive Party (DPP). Although it is fair to say that Chen Shui-bian's victory and the DPP's ascent to power opened a new page of Taiwan's political development, the initial triumphant sentiment did not last very long. Chen's government constantly faced political disputes with opposition parties and diplomatic challenges from China. In the aftermath of a failed assassination plot against Chen and his campaign partner on the eve of the 2004 presidential election, lingering public suspicion resulted in frequent legitimacy crises during his second presidential term. Meanwhile, unending accusations of "pay-for-appointment" corruption scandals and incessant media revelations of his family's financial improprieties raised questions regarding his political integrity and fitness for office. A massive demonstration of "red shirts" in 2006 almost toppled him down. Consequently, the election of Ma Ying-jeou in the 2008 presidential election was to some extent a Taiwanese majority's self-emancipation and relief: They were free at last from the tedium of both Chen's over-employment of ethnicity in campaigning and endless political disputes in governance during the "A-bian" era. At the end of his presidency in May 2008, Chen, his family members, and political associates soon faced several major corruption and embezzlement charges in court. The image of his arrest in handcuffs was an ironic reminder of his 2000 campaign pledges to roll back "black and gold" (corruption and gangsterism) politics of the previous administration. After all, Chen had always prided himself on being a "clean" leader immune to the KMT's web of corruption in 2000.

Surely, as Shelley Rigger (2001, 957) has ascertained, it is a daunting task for Chen and the DPP to dismantle some of the roadblocks affecting the quality of Taiwan's democracy. Still, it is a chagrin to witness a party, which loudly enunciated campaign slogans of "happiness and progress" in the past and gained the euphoric endorsement of a great number of intellectuals, social elites, and independent voters, devolve into a less competitive position. Could it be that the DPP's emphasis on ideological and symbolic politics had no way to win Taiwan's conservative and pragmatic majority votes? What have both parties done in the 2000s to reverse their fates? Meanwhile, with the DPP's shrinking size in Taiwan's political landscape after 2008, what will be the future development of Taiwan's party politics in the coming decade?

Before responding to these questions above, we should not forget that the KMT's catastrophic defeat in the 2000 presidential election also prompted serious doubts among the public and pundits about the possibility of its resurgence as a formidable contending force in Taiwan's politics, although some scholars cautioned to not draw any swift conclusions about the demise of the KMT (Hsieh, 2001, 943).

Hence, the result of the 2008 presidential election offers an opportunity to examine the resurgence of the KMT and the demise of the DPP.

Following their inquisitive endevors in 2001 in *China Quarterly*, John Hsieh and Shelley Rigger revisit their former topics in this volume to examine Taiwan's party politics. After eight years away from political governance in Taiwan, the KMT's incredible comeback with a strong showing in elections prompted John Hsieh to explore the reasons behind the KMT's potential invincibility in the near future. Given the KMT's impressive results in 2008 in both the legislative election and the presidential race, one wonders whether the KMT will achieve the "happily ever after" effect in the years to come. By delineating the cleavages underpinning the party structure in Taiwan, Hsieh probes Taiwanese voters' preferences and choices among a variety of issues, such as national identity, welfare, economic performance, environmental protection, clean government, and Taiwan's international status. As expected, national identity remains both the dominate cleavage among voters and a crucial variable in determining Taiwan's party strength of the KMT and the DPP. Since a majority of people supports the *status quo* position advocated by the KMT, the KMT will continue to be a seemingly invincible force in Taiwan. The institutional setting of the electoral system, which has changed from a single nontransferable vote (SNTV) system to a new mixed member plurality-PR model at parliamentary election (Reilly, 2007), additionally consolidates the KMT's formidable position. The new electoral system has given the KMT a built-in advantage in seat gains in comparison to its vote shares in the 2008 legislative election. Hsieh's parsimonious explanation of the electoral wonder will be of great interest to anyone who has been fascinated by the surprising electoral results in 2008.

On the other hand, although the 2000 electoral victory awarded the DPP with the highest prize — the presidency — the win also foreordained the DPP's demise since then. Thus, Rigger investigates why and how the DPP became weaker organizationally and further divided ideologically by the end of the Chen presidency than it was at its beginning. Encountering internal challenges (e.g., intraparty factionalism, disputes over party platforms, and advocacy for ethnic justice) as well as external changes (e.g., China's powerful rise, U.S. strategic adjustment, and East Asian regional changes), the DPP's ideological aspiration for Taiwan independence has hampered the DPP's expansion of its electoral base to secure a confident majority of voters. As Rigger plows through various issues embattled within the DPP in her rich and reflective analysis, the party's adoption of a Leninist organizational structure mixed with its democratic spirit in policy deliberation and often led to grueling debates within the party itself. These intraparty disputes seriously affected the party's unity and political momentum. Later, the charges and scandals against Chen, his family members, and DPP associates drained the DPP's energy and political capital. Facing accusations, Chen's defiant and provocative acts further dragged the DPP along his Via Dolorosa. This put the DPP in constant defense and embarrassment during Chen's second term. Finally, the DPP's major strategic mistake in accepting the single-member district (SMD) plurality system undercut its vote share and seat gains, as evidenced in the result of the 2008 legislative election.

This is not to claim that electoral system changes should bear the full responsibility of the reconfiguration of Taiwan's political landscape. The conventional expectation is that elections usually paper over divisions in the society. Taiwan's elections in the 2000s apparently contest such a noble notion, when sensational campaigning and identity slogans were heatedly shouted and exchanged in political campaigns. Most of the last decade has been overly burdened with frequent claims of the correlation between partisanship and ethnicity, even though generational shifts in demography, immigration, and marital inter-ethnicity have made ethnicity hold less crucial weight in party identification (Corcuff, 2002). Hence, national identity continued to carry an unbearable weight in partisanship and electoral campaigns and made any rational policy debates in Taiwan almost impossible. In such a divided society based on the controversy of national identity, public sentiment and emotion runs high, and suspicion rules party politics. Should one be asked to come up with one unique feature of Taiwan's political development in the 2000s, it is widely agreed that a dichotomy of "love Taiwan or don't love Taiwan" has consumed almost every political act and debate.

In a divided society like Taiwan, it would be valuable to see how the public, not just political elites, responds to multifarious socio-political measures and the level of Taiwanese people's confidence and trust in democracy as "the only game in town" throughout the twist and turns process of democratic consolidation. Because there is no perfect formula to guarantee equal realization of all individual and group interests, democracies require a sufficient level of public trust in socio-political institutions to minimize political confrontations and conflicts between different constituencies over the allocation of collective goods and the passage of collectively binding decisions (Tilly, 2007, 80–105; Warren, 1999). Trust is the key to any meaningful collective action in democratic consolidation. Therefore, Huoyan Shyu's timely study answers our curiosity about the Taiwanese level of trust in democratic institutions.

Based on the available date sets of the Asian Barometer Survey in the 2000s and a meticulous design in methodology, Shyu aims to test the relationship between several independent variables, such as the individual's socio-demographic background, partisanship, perception of corruption, political satisfaction with democratic governance, and economic evaluation, and the dependent variables of trust in democratic institutions and support for democracy.[1] His chapter generates plentiful and interesting findings regarding Taiwanese trust in various socio-political institutions. With a wealth of data, Shyu's study confirms that Taiwanese support for democracy remains unwavering, though the level of their support may reach various degrees in multiple dimensions. Beyond doubt, as Shyu concludes, both well-established and nascent democracies will face voluminous globalization challenges that cannot be easily solved by an emphasis on public trust in a political institution. Any future study of democratic transition and consolidation should expand its research to the polity's capability and quality of governance to ensure the regime stability and sustainability for democratic consolidation (Hyden *et al.*, 2004, 26, 27; Shin, 2008, 114–120).

Since political institutions are frequently called upon to monitor and regulate economic activities, state-market relations have been a fascinating and important topic with respect to the study of governance.

In particular, robust economic performance matters for the sustainability and maturity of democracies (Przeworski *et al.*, 2000, 128; Diamond, 1999, 78). A latecomer in economic development, Taiwan's economy has achieved unprecedented accomplishments since the end of World War II with the state actively "intervening" in market operation and "guiding" the course of development. Similar to Japan, Singapore, and South Korea, Taiwan has been one of the textbook cases symbolizing the importance of the "development state" in economic development. The question is: will the once acclaimed developmental state continue to play a decisive role in an increasingly globalized and integrated economy?

Japan's "lost decade" in the 1990s has raised doubts about the wisdom of the development state. Moreover, as evidenced by the 1997 Asian Financial crisis, the close business–government relation and intensive state intervention in the financial sector have contributed to a moral hazard in that financial institutions might engage in unsound lending, investment distortion, and crony capitalism (Krugman, 1998; Wan, 2008, 171–192; Wade, 2000; Beeson, 2007, 143–160). The lesson appeared to demand a free and full operation of market force with minimum governmental regulations for economic sustainability. However, the 2008 worldwide financial catastrophe and various governmental rescue and bailout plans have implicated the opposite by emphasizing the importance of the state in enforcing more government regulations, supervision, and participation in market operation in order to resuscitate the ailing national and global economy. The debate has shifted to the efficacy and fairness of various state policy options, rather than remaining concentrated on the necessity of governmental intervention. Thus, if the state is an indispensable player in economic development, the Taiwanese government's experience in tackling previous economic challenges could offer valuable lessons for other countries.

This is where Cal Clark, Alex Tan, and Joseph Wong cut in. Clark and Tan examine Taiwan's political economy by delineating the key features of Taiwan's developmental experiences. Compounded by an identity indigenization movement for democratic transition in the early 1990s, Taiwan's relative lack of a give-and-take norm in policymaking among various political forces has resulted in constant political gridlocks, politicization of financial institutions, and contentious party competition. Small and medium enterprises (SMEs), a main pillar of Taiwan's economic success from the 1960s to 1980s, began to feel the mounting pressures of market competition from China and other newly industrializing countries in the mid-1990s. In addition, SMEs felt underpowered in an increasingly globalized knowledge-based economy, which demands substantial investment, innovation, and R&D capability for high-value-added products.

Even so, Yun-han Chu's study (2007) has shown how the resourcefulness and shrewdness of Taiwan's economic bureaucrats helped build up a shock-absorbing strategic capability, unmatched by any other East Asian country, sail through regional economic crises, and facilitate industrial sector-wide collective action for a transition to a knowledge-based economy in the context of globalization and democratization in the 1990s. However, as Clark and Tan's chapter has demonstrated in their lucid description of Taiwan's financial reforms in the 2000s, prerogatives and authority formerly held by economic technocrats prior to the 1990s gradually shifted to politicians as a result of democratization. This gave politicians leeway to gain political favors with promises of economic benefits to fulfill the interests of their constituencies. Policy debates became more tedious and complicated as parties struggled to reach a compromise. Ultimately, it affected Taiwan's timely responses to shifting economic circumstances and lessened its competitive capability.

Moreover, as Clark and Tan clearly testify, the bickering over Taiwan's national identity continued to be a political stigma, causing many economic enterprises to calculate carefully their political risks in Taiwan before venturing into China's market during Chen's era. How to minimize malapropos and unwanted intervention of politicians in the management of national economy and industrial policy will be perennial issues for Taiwan's healthy economic development in the future.

Indeed, tough global competition is not an insoluble problem to Taiwanese industry, which has been quite resilient and versatile in mobilizing resources and finding a way out of any economic predicament.

According to Wong, instead of waiting patiently for the transfer of production technology from leading economies in a pecking order similar to the flying geese analogy, Taiwan has stepped up its innovation capability to look for different revenue streams in science-based industries, especially the biotechnology industry, in order to reap "the first mover advantages" by moving up the technology value chain. The challenging task for a development-oriented state like Taiwan is how to cope with the abundant uncertainties inherent in the brave new world of science-based industry. Rarely could one find available and reliable market referents in science-based industries to confidently project its market value and profitability. State bureaucracy dispenses various forms of assistance — value-enhancing "developmental rents" — to encourage economic growth and industrial structural transformation (Jomo, 2003; Khan, 2000, 136–141). In other words, the current Taiwanese "developmental state" tries to chart uncertain territory, and its future economic prospects depend on the collective governmental and industrial efforts to navigate through technological, economic, regulatory, and political uncertainties.

However, as Wong perceptively describes, Taiwan's science-based industries, including the bio-technological sector, have attempted to use Taiwan as a springboard, leaping into China's resources and markets. In 2008, well over 60% of China's high-tech products were manufactured by Taiwanese companies (GIO, 2008, Chap. 7). An example of their close collaboration is the recent report of remarkable achievement of "Chaiwan" (China and Taiwan) in the production chains and marketing networks in information technology. This has made South Korean manufacturers concerned over their future market shares (Digital Chosunilbo, 2007; UD, 2009). This rare window of opportunity for Taiwan's industrial sectors to cross the Taiwan Strait immediately sparked loud dissenting views from those who deeply worry that economic integration may constrain Taiwan's future political chances of independence. The repeated efforts in "de-Chineseness" policies in juxtaposition with obvious emphasis on "Taiwanese subjectivity" (*Taiwan zhutixing*) in the 2000s have aggravated such concerns over the detrimental consequences of economic interactions with China (Lee, 2005).

Such grave concerns of negative spillover effects derived from economic interactions are not uncommon. A quick and brief glimpse of Taiwan's Mainland Affairs Council's Statistic Monthly will reveal Taiwan's heavy and asymmetric dependency on China. The mainland is Taiwan's largest trading partner, absorbing 40.7 percent of Taiwan's total exports in 2007. Conservative estimates of Taiwanese cumulative investments in China exceeded US$100 billion at the end of 2007, along with more than one million Taiwanese professionals and their family members residing in China (GIO, 2008, Chaps. 6 and 9). Paradoxically, the rapid progress of cross–strait economic interactions has not generated an equally positive effect in Taiwan–China political exchanges. Taiwan's ruling DPP party elites and their supporters feared that intensive economic integration may dilute the substance of Taiwanese indigenous identity and undermine Taiwan's capability to deter and resist China's aggression. China will have more leverage to extract further political concessions from Taiwan.[2] Concurrently, cross–strait economic ties naturally create winners and losers within Taiwan and provide politicians, especially anti-China candidates, with an opportunity to mobilize the resources and support for electioneering. In the end, rather than embracing the idea of comparative advantage, Chen's government insisted on maintaining restrictions on trade with and investment in China.

Certainly, Chen's "de-Chineseness" policy should not bear the full blame for the cross–strait stalemate. Beijing's monopoly of the "one China" domain in international discourse and naming has put Taiwan in an awkward situation. Taiwan has encountered China's excruciating demand in a high-handed manner to subscribe to the "one China" principle with almost no input, whatsoever, into the definition of "China". Such an exclusionist approach only propagates Taiwanese apathy toward China or hostility toward the "one China" principle. Either situation does not serve China's policy objective well. It only adds fuel to political spoilers' justification for the cause of Taiwan independence.

Here enters the unique contribution by Wang, Chen, and Keng, and to see how individual values and affective identity, economic self-interests, and perception of China's security threat influence

Taiwanese views of cross–strait economic exchanges based on survey data collected in Taiwan in 2007. Contrary to previous findings of the overriding effect of identity-based symbolic politics, their study indicates that Taiwan's continuous democratization has witnessed the diminishing effect of identity politics. Their study shows that Taiwanese with a higher threat perception of China tend to support Ma Ying-jeou's policy expanding economic interactions to ease cross–strait tensions. As Taiwanese society becomes increasingly democratic with free flowing information and unrestrained expression of individual views, Taiwanese people become more and more rational and realistic in analyzing the various policy options for cross–strait relations.

Undoubtedly, any of Taiwan's attempts to reduce cross–strait tension requires Beijing's reciprocal support. Zhao and Liu elaborate Beijing's conciliatory policy toward the Ma government after eight years of unpleasant and tense political stalemate with the DPP regime under Chen Shui-bian. In dealing with the Taiwan issue, China has envisioned two different scenarios: economic-integration-based unification and Taiwan-independence-led war. While Beijing hopes to strengthen and deepen cross–strait economic integration for its ultimate goal of unification, it has maintained the military solution as the last resort to deter Taiwan from taking risky moves toward independence. Particularly during the second term of Chen's presidency, Taiwan's relentless drive for independence by means of referendums and UN membership applications not only halted meaningful Taiwan–China dialogs but also compelled China to seriously consider different scenarios of Taiwan-independence-led war (Center of Taiwan Studies, 2007). Moderate tones and pragmatic signals returned after Taipei's change of guard in May 2008. Robust economic growth and a China-friendly international environment have made Beijing more confident in shifting from preparing for the worst case scenario to finding policies for tension-reduction and conflict prevention in cross–strait relations. Certainly, stable cross–strait relations will allow China to concentrate on its regime stability.

The shift from a tempestuous atmosphere to a conciliatory environment across the Taiwan strait is a remarkable sign of change, even though numerous obstacles and challenges are expected ahead. It is true that China could behave exactly as the Melian Dialog described ages before, "the strong can do whatever it wants to do", in an asymmetric cross–strait balance. However, one should not forget Rousseau's famous line — "the strongest man is never strong enough to be always master, unless he transforms his power into right, and obedience into duty" (1967, Book I, Sec. 3). This implies that even an aspiring hegemon like China needs to rely on something other than brute force and coercive mechanisms to rope in the weaker counterpart in any institutional arrangement (Ikenberry, 2003, 51–54). By settling for fewer short-term benefits and enlarging the mutual zone of acceptance in cross–strait relations, China may need delicate maneuvers to reap long-term gains and provide Taiwan with sufficient incentives for a mutually agreeable framework of conflict resolution. As Bush (2005) has keenly observed, without an extremely attractive deal, why should a democratic, *de facto* independent Taiwan accept China's unification offer? Thus, China must refrain from exercising its power in indiscriminate and impudent ways in cross–strait interactions. China's willingness and ability to do so will allow Taiwan to feel a sense of empowerment for dialogs and negotiations. Moreover, the "degree of stickiness" between both polities may increase with the constant and deepening economic integration process as referred in Zhao and Liu's chapter.

Still, Wei-chin Lee's piece contends that China's unwillingness to face squarely Taiwan's changing political landscape and the new social construct based on Taiwanese identity apparently convinced Chen Shui-bian to take a series of bold moves to demand Taiwan's international space and unfortunately strained the United States–Taiwan relations in the 2000s. Frankly speaking, regardless what option — independence, unification, or status quo — that Taiwan decides to pursue, the United States is unlikely to be a bystander in terms of stability and security in Taiwan and East Asia. Although there is no formal bilateral treaty governing their bilateral relations, the push and pull between entrapment and abandonment in any alliance arrangement have been vividly shown in the United States–Taiwan interactions. Chen constantly wedged an identity-based foreign policy to express

Taiwan's dissatisfaction with the shrinking international space within the "one China" domain. With Taiwan's relatively diminishing economic and military power in comparison with China's growth of national capability and international status, Taiwan feared U.S. abandonment or weak support of Taiwan's cause. Eventually, Taiwan may one day be forced to accept a preferred solution to the sovereign dispute on Beijing's terms. Undeniably, Chen's policy is also a politically calculated act aimed at turning international denial of Taiwan's legitimate international status into domestic campaigning issues for vote gains. Furthermore, in Chen's view, material gains from economic interactions with China cannot offset the loss of Taiwan's political identity. Chen's policies, unfortunately, provoked U.S. concerns that Taiwan's move could trap the United States in a risky conflict with China. As a result, Taiwan's active identity-based pursuit and high expectation for international support simply tilted the Taiwan–United States–China triangular relations to China's favor by the end of Chen's presidency.

The deterioration of United States–Taiwan relations in the 2000s also accompanied Taiwan's limited participation in Asia–Pacific region. There is a proliferation of free trade agreements proposals, ranging from the Association of Southeast Asian Nations' initiative like ASEAN+1 (China) in 2010, to ASEAN+3 (China, Japan, and South Korea) in 2012, and the pending arrangement ASEAN+6 (China, Japan, South Korea, New Zealand, Australia, and India) for intra-regional trade in East Asia. The regret is that Taiwan has been excluded from most of the negotiation and bargaining processes of East Asian schemes of meso- or mega-regionalism (Hatsuse, 1999). The exclusion certainly constrains Taiwan's economic capability in maintaining its competitive edge in trade (Dent, 2005). Thus, Chyungly Lee has provided readers with a great service by looking into cases of Taiwan's limited — but fruitful — involvement in pan-Asian economic cooperation through Asia–Pacific Economic Cooperation (APEC), indirect participation in pan-Asia–Pacific security cooperation through the Council for Asia–Pacific Security Cooperation (CSCAP), and interest in a series of state-led East Asian integration process. Beijing's nod remains the key to Taiwan's regional involvement and participation. Consequently, Chyungly Lee explores a variety of alternatives for Taiwan's advancement of regional participation in light of the new dynamics of cross–strait interactions after 2008. Taiwan's desire to expand its participation in regional integration schemes relies on its skillful negotiation with China. Apparently, Taiwan's noble claims of democratic and liberal values fail to move beyond the geopolitical reality of China's recent rise.

Generally speaking, Taiwan has achieved a significant benchmark in democratic consolidation if one accepts the idea that political power has been alternated twice between rivaling parties through contested elections, and all political elites appear to accept democracy to be "the only game in town" (O'Donnell, 1996a,b; Gunther *et al.*, 1996; Przeworski 1991; Przeworski *et al.*, 2000, 18–32). The canvass of these chapters reveals that Taiwan's politics in the first decade of the 21st century has been driven by the competing and converging process of the following issues: the progression or regression of cross–strait exchanges; the ups or downs of the United States–Taiwan relations; the confrontation or conciliation between political parties in domestic bargaining; the rigidity or multiplicity of the constructive process of identity; and finally economic growth or stagnation.

It would be a mistake to treat each of these issues individually without mastering the intricacies of the other. These multiple issues interact and intertwine with each other and make Taiwan's politics complicated and sometimes volatile. For example, during Chen's era, cross–strait relations have become an inevitable element in Taiwan's domestic politics. As long as China is unwilling to accept Taiwan independence without a war and the U.S. geopolitical principle is against Taiwan independence, a substantial majority of pragmatic voters have a realistic sense of the extreme adversity of Taiwan's status change. These pragmatists contrast with Taiwan independence supporters who insist on their inalienable right to self-determination. Such a realistic understanding among voters existed in the 1990s (Marsh, 2002) and continued in the 2000s as several chapters in this volume testify. This understanding finally became a key factor to the regime change in the 2008 presidential election. In sum, each issue examined can be examined as an independent variable as well as a dependent variable.

The intertwining nature of these issues illustrates that future challenges to Taiwan are quite formidable. First, Taiwanese political elites have to deal with the recurring tension between international interests and domestic politics and reach acceptable and workable trade-offs between collective demands from below and individual power consideration. However, in a patronage-soaked party system like Taiwan, politicians may rely on access to public resources and cronyism to foster a broad base of political clientelism. As part of a legacy of traditional political practice in Taiwan, clientelist linkages and patronage politics are unlikely to be eradicated. The challenge is how to significantly constrain patronage-based political practices to prevent corruption. One remedy is to enhance the level of accountability and transparency in the political process, both of which are essential ingredients to political legitimacy and democratic governance. These institutional enhancements for checks and balances may slow the policy process. Nevertheless, if one accepts Socrates' belief in a good life being equivalent to a just and honorable life as stated in his dialog with Crito, corruption scandals in the past decade may be lessened in the future with increased transparency and accountability (Plato, 2004, 37).

An equally critical challenge to Taiwan is the specter of national and state identity. Even with an increasing level of socio-economic interactions and intermarriages between ethnicities and nationalities in recent years, the heavy dose of ethnicity in construing identity beliefs has continued in party bickering and electoral campaigns in the last decade. One noticeable phenomenon at the end of Chen's era has been the diminishing return of political benefits of identity cards in voting results. In truth, unrestrained application of identity politics has impeded civic equality by promoting stereotypes of opponents without recognizing the complicated, multi-layered nature of individual identity affiliation. In the end, a staunch self-righteous attitude of one's political correctness in identity assertion and an unwillingness to tolerate divergent views may halt Taiwan's democratic consolidation. The future challenge for all Taiwan's political leaders is how to separate ethnicity from state identity and minimize the misuse and abuse of Taiwanese nationalism.

Of course, Taiwan is unlikely to avoid the issue of state identity in cross–strait interactions. A recent official poll about citizen's political identity affiliation has shown that 64.6 percent of Taiwanese residents consider themselves "Taiwanese", in contrast to the 18.1 percent of "both Taiwanese and Chinese" and only 11.5 percent of "Chinese" (Research, Development, and Evaluation Commission, 2009). Thus, China's policy toward Taiwan remains a third challenge to Taiwan's political development.

China's adamant stand on the "one China" policy will continue to face Taiwan's resistance. However, the economic logic of cross–strait interactions has been too powerful and attractive for Taiwan to ignore, and Taiwan's economic vitality has been closely tied to China. As expected, the degree of asymmetric interdependence may accelerate with Ma's lifting of numerous trade and investment restrictions in the future. While the pursuit of economic profits is never in doubt, increasingly inseparable relations and continuous integration will gradually reframe one's self-identities and self-interests along the repeated interactions. The challenge is: will Taiwan be able to maintain a clear separation between politics and the economy in its interactions with China? Stated differently, given Taiwan's economic closeness with China, is Taiwan capable of holding its political ground of *de facto* independence? If reality illuminates the impossibility of such distinction, is Taiwan ready to paddle back the tide of integration even at the expense of huge non-salvageable economic losses? On the other hand, if the impression of China's "political hostage taking" is looming large in the process of integration, is Taiwan ready to face the music and tackle a serious cross–strait political agenda?

Undoubtedly, China is taking a similar risk of identity reformulation with more and more Taiwanese economic and cultural penetration into the mainland. Along the winding and grinding process of economic integration, inevitably China has to face the practice of "altercasting", or a mirror-like identity reformulation. In other words, Taiwan's social constructs may eventually influence and alter the conception of the "the other" (i.e., China). Once the process begins, it will be difficult to undo and unwind the logic of economic integration that has been institutionalized and thickened over the years. Nevertheless, as a relatively weak party in the asymmetrical interdependence, Taiwan will have to look far and think hard about the prospect for an acceptable cross–strait solution.

Thus far, Ma's decision to resume the "1992 Consensus" has not been a surprise to all parties involved in the dispute. Serving as Taiwan's Mainland Affairs Council's senior vice chairman and spokesman and one of the members involved in the November 1992 negotiations in Hong Kong that led to the consensus, Ma has consistently claimed that such an oral consensus of "one China, different interpretations by each side" did exist (Ma, 2003, 44). China has tacitly confirmed his recollection.[3] Legally speaking, Ma reasons that the "one China" principle is merely a faithful fulfillment of the ROC constitution and should not be unconscionably extrapolated to be making concessions to the PRC. In his view, cross–strait talks will achieve meaningful progress only when the "one China" issue has been resolved, shelved, or at least managed. Although both sides have a different reference to the meaning of "China", the implicit bargain in the "one China" principle can potentially reach a sub-optimal, yet agreeable, solution. When all is said and done, Ma argues that Taiwan's expansion of international space will occur upon the mutual understanding of "agree to disagree" embedded in the "1992 Consensus" (Ma, 2003, 55, 59).

Ma's adherence to the "1992 Consensus" — the closest point of convergence on both sides — becomes the key to reviving dialogs and consultations to overcome the cross–strait stalemate of the past eight years. At this moment, Ma's three-no policy (no unification, no independence, and no use of force to resolve the cross–strait dispute) seems to work well in the delicate situation of the Taiwan–the United States–China triangular relations for peaceful, meaningful interaction. Therefore, Ma's peace initiative in exchange for Taiwan's international space offers China an opportunity to move forward a constructive, cooperative relationship. Never has the word "opportunity" been so clear and timely. Ma's policy seems to reflect current conjunctures of Taiwan's political development and fit well into the distinctive material circumstances, public sentiments, and political leader's initiatives across the Strait.

Ma's cross-strait initiative certainly requires US support. The United States is an inevitable third party to back up Taiwan's legitimate demands, bargaining strength, and requests for faithful fulfillment of deals. With the United States reiterating security guarantees for a peaceful solution across the Taiwan strait, it would be difficult for Taiwan to cut the security cord with the United States to agree to Beijing's conditions (Bush, 2005, 177). The tumultuous second half of Chen's years seemed to make the United States less resistant in its criticism of Taiwan independence move, especially considering the big picture of China's weight in international politics and economy. Does this imply that the United States is more deferential toward China than before? When both the United States and China see eye to eye on the Taiwan issue, will this mean the abatement of the U.S. commitment to a peaceful resolution of the Taiwan issue? Accordingly, a fourth challenge to the Ma government is how to gain firm and forceful U.S. support in the complicated Taiwan–United States–China triangular relationship. Even so, moving unnecessarily closer to either the United States or China definitely invites the other party's uneasiness and suspicion and affects Taiwan's external policies. In essence, Taiwan's balancing act requires political leader's careful maneuvering.

Consequently, leadership matters in either foreign policy or domestic governance. In contrast to Ma's less passionate temperament and no-drama style in governance, Chen's feisty Give-'Em-Hell comments frequently generated opposing reactions. The presidency, to Chen, is less an office than a performance. That being said, with his unique qualities of resilience in career setbacks and calculative skills in domestic politicking, Chen Shui-bian is a worthy opponent to all contenders. He beat all the odds to accomplish a political unthinkable by winning loyalty from his supporters, conjuring his opponents within the party to follow his lead, and at last achieving a stunning victory against a powerful KMT electoral machine in 2000.

In retrospect, besides Chen's over-zealous incitement of ethnicity-based national identity to create strife and division within the society, perhaps the saddest aspect of Chen's political demise — as the reports of Chen's financial improprieties and corruption scandal rolled out with no immediate and appropriate closure on sight — was how often political leaders fall into the trap that Lord Acton famously identified: "All power corrupts; absolute power corrupts absolutely". If ever there was a Greek tragedy that could be applied in a politician's life in Taiwan, Chen's presidency was it.

Chen's stunning success in politics apparently changed Chen. The career so fully engulfed in power and money that he seemed to forget some basic values of democracy for clean government and responsibility to the people. We saw him cheerfully accept the public mandate, dazzled with the political responsibility bestowed upon him in the 2000 presidential election. And then we saw him sorrowfully escorted to court with handcuffs in 2008. As Chen frequently reiterated, the world is watching Taiwan's amazing democratic achievement. Unfortunately, he was the one manifestly presenting his own personal drama to provide all political observers and practitioners with a valuable lesson that democracy should not be a convenient mechanism for grabbing the resources of the public. His fall into disgrace also demonstrates the indispensability of institutional design to uphold the principle of justice in any democratic society by treating leaders and commoners equally in front of law.

Even with Chen's tarnished legacy, the development in the 2000s is an ultimate and unmistaken testimony to Taiwan's decade-long vitality of democratic consolidation. In the end, Taiwan's conviction in democracy has been reconfirmed by the second regime alternation in 2008, if we agree that the value of democracy is to have an effective and peaceful translation of citizens' collective will through the electoral process. Indeed, democracy will be sustained with people's constant consent. Each electoral victory is only people's contingent consent, which does not equal a blank check to any elected leader (Tilly, 2007, 94, 95). One valuable admonition of Taiwan's democratic consolidation is that the long and gradual process of democratic consolidation requires watchful eyes in political governance. Without careful examination of political leaders' decisions and behavior, democratic consolidation may be like waiting for Godot: in the end, the great man may never come. The Chen Shui-bian era came to its conclusion in 2008, but Taiwan's process of democratic consolidation surely never ends.

REFERENCES

Beeson, M (2007). *Regionalism and Globalization in East Asia*. New York: Palgrave Macmillan.

Bush, R (2005). Taiwan faces China: Attraction and repulsion. In *Power Shift: China and Asia's New Dynamics*, Shambaugh D (ed.), pp. 170–186. Berkeley, CA: University of California Press.

Center of Taiwan Studies, Beijing University, and Global Forum of Chinese Political Scientists (2007). In *Taiwan Haixia weiji de yufang yu guanli* (The Prevention and Management of Taiwan Strait Crisis). Conference Proceedings (in Chinese). Center of Taiwan Studies, Peking University, and Global Forum of Chinese Political Scientists. September.

Chan, S (2009). The political economy of Détente: Taiwan's economic integration with China. In *Paper presented as the Taiwan–China Conference*, Southern Methodist University, Dallas, TX, April 16–17, 2009. <smu.edu/tower/us-taiwan-china09.htm>.

Chu, Y-H (2007). Re-engineering the developmental state in an age of globalization: Taiwan in defiance of neoliberalism. In *Neoliberalism and Institutional Reform in East Asia*, Woo MJ-E (ed.), pp. 91–121. New York: Palgrave Macmillan.

Corcuff, S (2002). *Memories of the Future: National Identity Issues and the Search for a New Taiwan*. Armonk, NY: M.E. Sharpe.

Dent, CM (2005). Taiwan and the new regional political economy of East Asia. *China Quarterly*, 182, 385–406.

Diamond, L (1999). *Developing Democracy: Toward Consolidation*. Baltimore, MD: The Johns Hopkins University Press.

Digital Chosunilbo (2007). Rise of 'Chaiwan' threatens Korea's tech industry. August 1. <english.chosun.com/w21data/html/news/200708/200708010016.html>.

Gowa, J (1994). *Allies, Adversaries, and International Trade*. Princeton, NJ: Princeton University Press.

Grieco, JM (1990). *Cooperation Among Nations: Europe, America, and Non-tariff Barriers to Trade*. Ithaca, NY: Cornell University Press.

Gunther, R, PN Diamandouros and H-J Puhle (1996). O'Donnell's 'Illusions': A Rejoinder. *Journal of Democracy*, 7(4), 151–159.

Hatsuse, R (1999). Regionalism in East Asia and the Asia–Pacific. In *Globalism, Regionalism and Nationalism: Asia in Search of Its Role in the Twenty-first Century*, Yamamoto Y (ed.). Maldern, MA: Blackwell Publishers.

Hsieh, JF-S (2001). Whither the Kuomintang? *China Quarterly*, 168 (December), 930–943.

Hyden, G, J Court and K Mease (2004). *Making Sense of Governance: Empirical Evidence from Sixteen Developing Countries.* Boulder, CO: Lynne Rinner Publishers.

Ikenberry, GJ (2003) State power and the institutional bargain: America's ambivalent economic and security multilateralism. In *US Hegemony and International Organizations*, Foot R, SN MacFarlane and M Mastanduno (eds.), pp. 49–70. New York: Oxford University Press.

Jomo, KS (2003). Rethinking economic discrimination. In *Paper presented at National Economic Association and American Economic Association*, January 4–5, Washington, DC. <siteresources.worldbank.org/INTDECINEQ/Resources/AERdraft.pdf>.

Khan, MH (2000). Rent-seeking as process. In *Rents, Rent-seeking and Economic Development: Theory and Evidence in Asia*, Khan MH and JK Sundaram (eds.), pp. 70–144. New York: Cambridge University Press.

Krugman, P (1998). What happened to Asia? In *A conference paper in Japan.* January. <web.mit.edu/krugman/www/DISINTER.html>.

Lee, W-C (2005). Taiwan's cultural reconstruction movement: Identity politics and collective action since 2000. *Issues and Studies*, 41(1), 1–51.

Ma, Y-J (2003). Cross–strait relations at a crossroad: Impasse or breakthrough? In *Breaking the China–Taiwan Impasse*, Zagoria DS (ed.), with the assistance of C. Fugarino, pp. 39–65. Westport, CT: Praeger.

Marsh, R (2002). National identity and ethnicity in Taiwan: Some trends in the 1990s. In *Memories of the Future: National identity issue and the Search for a New Taiwan*, Corcuff S (ed.), pp. 144–159. Armonk, NY; M.E. Sharpe.

Plato (2004). *Dialogues of Plato Containing the Apology of Socrates, Crito, Phaeto, and Protagoras.* Translated by Benjamin Jowett. New York: Kessinger Publishing.

O'Donnell, G (1996a). Illusions about consolidation. *Journal of Democracy*, 7(2), 34–51.

O'Donnell, G (1996b). Illusions and conceptual flaws. *Journal of Democracy*, 7(4), 160–168.

Prezworski, A (1991). *Democracy and the Market: Political and Economic Reforms in Eastern Europe and Latin America.* New York: Cambridge University Press.

Prezworski, A, ME Alvarez, JA Cheibub and F Limongi (2000). In *Democracy and Development; Political Institutions and Well-Being in the World, 1950–1990.* New York: Cambridge University Press.

Government Information Office (GIO), ROC (2008). *The Republic of China Yearbook 2008.* Taipei: Government Information Office.

Papayoanou, IA (1999). *Power Ties: Economic Interdependence Balancing, and War.* Ann Arbor, MI: University of Michigan Press.

Reilly, B (2007). Democratization and electoral reform in the Asia–Pacific region: Is there an 'Asian model' of democracy?" *Comparative Political Studies*, 40(11), 1350–1371.

Research, Development, and Evaluation Commission, Executive Yuan (2009). 'Minzhong de zhengzhi taidu ji zuqun guantian' minyi diaocha (Public Opinion Report of "People's Political Attitudes and Ethnic Viewpoints"). May 1–2. <www.rdec.gov.tw/np.asp?ctNode=12141&mp=100>.

Rigger, S (2001). The democratic progressive party in 2000: Obstacles and opportunities. *China Quarterly*, 168 (December), 944–959.

Rousseau, J-J (1967). *The Social Contract and Discourse on the Origin of Inequality*, edited and with an introduction by Lester G. Crocker. New York: Washington Square Press.

Shin, DC (2008). The third wave in East Asia: Comparative and dynamic perspectives. *Taiwan Journal of Democracy*, 4(2) (December), 91–131.

Tilly, C (2007). *Democracy*. New York: Cambridge University Press.

United Daily (UD) (2009). Shuipa Chaiwan? (Who Is Afraid of Chaiwan (China + Taiwan)?) June 1. <udn.com/NEWS/OPINION/OPI1/4936897.shtml>.

Wade, R (2000). Wheels within wheels: Rethinking the Asian crisis and the Asian model. *Annual Review of Political Science*, 3, 85–115.

Warren, ME (1999). Democratic theory and trust. In *Democracy and Trust*, Warren ME (ed.), pp. 310–345. New York: Cambridge University Press.

Wan, M (2008). *The Political Economy of East Asia*. Washington, DC: CQ Press.

Xu, S (2003). The 1992 consensus: A review and assessment of consultations between the association for relations across the Taiwan strait and the straits exchange foundation. In *Breaking the China-Taiwan Impasse*, Zagoria DS (ed.), pp. 81–102. Westport, CT: Praeger.

ENDNOTES

1. Readers interested in the Asian Barometer Survey can visit the project's Web site (www.asianbarometer.org) for details.
2. Theoretical analysis on the relationship between trade and security, please see Chan (2009), Papayoanou (1999), Gowa (1994), and Grieco (1990).
3. English texts of the communications and exchanges about the "1992 Consensus" between Taiwan and China can be found in Xu (2003, 96–101).

Part I

Political Development

Chapter

2

Is the Kuomintang Invincible?

John Fuh-Sheng Hsieh

For Taiwan's Kuomintang (Nationalist Party, KMT), 2008 was a very good year. In January, it won a landslide victory in the Legislative Yuan (Parliament) election, and in March it scored another victory in the presidential race. Once again, it won control over both executive and legislative branches of government after having lost the governing power to the Democratic Progressive Party (DPP) for eight years.

Given its impressive showings at the polls, will the KMT be able to continue its dominance in Taiwan politics for many years to come? More specifically, who supports the KMT? Is that support shallow or deep-rooted? Does the KMT benefit from the institutional arrangements currently in place? How likely will it be challenged by other political forces, notably the DPP? These questions will be addressed in this chapter. In the first section, a brief introduction to the transformation of the KMT from an authoritarian ruling party to a player in democratic politics will be provided. This will be followed by a discussion of the cleavages underpinning the party structure in Taiwan, which largely determines the relative strengths of the various political forces on the island. The next section looks into the institutional arrangements that may benefit or cost the KMT in the political game. The final section concludes.

THE TRANSFORMATION OF THE KMT

The KMT had continuously ruled Taiwan since the mid-20th century. In 1945, Taiwan, formerly a Japanese colony, was returned to China after Japan was defeated in World War II. China's KMT government under the leadership of Chiang Kai-shek then engaged in a bloody civil war with the Chinese Communist Party (CCP). Finally, in 1949, the Nationalist troops lost the war and moved to the island of Taiwan. For about four decades afterwards despite remarkable socioeconomic development, the KMT imposed authoritarian rule over the island.[1]

For quite some time, the KMT government was controlled by a handful of mainlanders who accompanied the Nationalists to the island. In the early 1970s, Chiang Ching-kuo, Chiang Kai-shek's son and designated successor, started the Taiwanization process by recruiting many more native Taiwanese to work for the party and the government. At about the same time, a group called *Tangwai* (literally "outside the party") formed in opposition to the minority mainlanders' rule. They enjoyed some popular support and proved to be a formidable political force pressuring the KMT regime to make significant changes.

In 1986, the DPP was formed out of the *Tangwai* movement, and — albeit considered illegal at the time — was nonetheless tolerated by the Chiang Ching-kuo government, paving the way for the development of a democratic party system in Taiwan. Almost at the same time, Chiang pledged his support for political reform and lifted the martial law the following year. He passed away in 1988 and was succeeded by Lee Teng-hui, a native Taiwanese, to be President of the Republic of China (ROC). Lee sped up the democratization process, leading eventually to the establishment of a full-fledged democracy in Taiwan.

Transforming from an authoritarian ruling party to a player in democratic politics represented an extraordinary makeover of the

KMT. Indeed, right after losing the civil war on the mainland, the KMT in Taiwan reorganized itself in line with the Leninist model. Although a quasi-Leninist party at best (Meaney, 1992), the KMT did turn out to be a stronger organization capable of penetrating various parts of the state and society.

However, even though the KMT had previously maintained authoritarian rule, it allowed local elections beginning as early as 1950. The elections were held at the village, township, county, and provincial levels. Beginning in the late 1960s, elections for parts of the national legislatures were also held. These elections were not truly free and fair; yet, occasionally, they turned out to be quite competitive as witnessed by the victory of Kao Yu-shu, a non-KMT politician, to defeat KMT candidates in the Taipei City mayoral elections in 1954 and 1964. As a result of these elections, the KMT gradually transformed into an election machine of some sort. Thus, when democratization started, the KMT was reasonably well prepared to participate in electoral politics, much more so than many former authoritarian ruling parties in other parts of the world in adapting to democratic reform.

Indeed, the KMT's showings in elections had been quite remarkable. It was able to acquire about 50–60 percent of the popular vote in parliamentary elections prior to the mid-1990s. In 1993, a group of young turks split from the KMT to form the New Party (NP), to protest, among other things, President Lee's position on the national identity issue. The KMT's vote shares dwindled afterwards, but the pan-KMT camp — the KMT and the parties split from it — continued to win close to 50 percent of the vote.

The devastating blow came in 2000. In the presidential election of that year, the KMT split. James Soong, a KMT-turned independent, competed against Lien Chan, the official KMT nominee, and Chen Shui-bian, the DPP candidate. Chen won the race with only 39.3 percent of the vote. Shortly after the election, Lee was forced to leave the KMT and later helped form the Taiwan Solidarity Union (TSU), which became a close ally of the DPP's. James Soong also formed his own party, the People First Party (PFP), which maintained close ties with the KMT and the NP.

After its defeat, the KMT started a new round of reorganization to shed its Leninist legacy and to further transform itself into an election machine. However, such reform did not reverse the party's misfortunes at the polls, at least at the beginning. In the presidential election of 2004, Chen Shui-bian, the incumbent president, managed to get reelected due largely to the assassination attempt on the president and his running mate on the eve of polling day, an event which undoubtedly attracted many sympathy votes for the DPP ticket. He won by a very slim margin (Hsieh, 2004).

In 2005, a constitutional amendment was passed to change the electoral system for the Legislative Yuan elections from the single nontransferable vote (SNTV) to the mixed-member majoritarian (MMM) system consisting of 73 seats elected by the single-member district (SMD) plurality system and 34 seats by proportional representation (PR) plus six seats reserved for the aborigines elected by SNTV.[2] The new electoral system was used for the first time in January 2008. The KMT emerged the decisive winner by winning 57 out of 73 seats (or 78.1 percent) with 53.5 percent of the vote in the SMD part of the election and 20 out of 34 seats (or 58.8 percent) with 51.2 percent of the vote in the PR portion. It also captured four out of six aboriginal seats with 54.9 percent of the vote. Out of a total of 113 seats, the KMT won 81 seats (or 71.7 percent) in the new parliament. Together, the KMT and its allies controlled three-quarters of the seats. This was indeed a very impressive victory for the KMT.

In the presidential election held two months later, KMT's Ma Ying-jeou scored another victory by gaining 58.45 percent of the vote. As a consequence, the KMT is now able to control both executive and legislative branches of government, reversing the divided government situation that had haunted the society in the previous eight years.[3]

Overall, as a former authoritarian ruling party, the KMT has been quite successful in transforming itself into a player in democratic politics. What, then, are the factors contributing to its success? In particular, who supports it? Why? These are the questions to which we now turn.

WHO SUPPORTS THE KMT?

An individual may support a political party for a variety of reasons. He/she may, for instance, support a party because he/she likes the leader or leaders of the party or because he/she prefers the party's positions on certain issues. Generally, for a party to survive for an extended period of time, it cannot rely only upon individual leaders or ephemeral issues; rather, it needs to find niches on some long-standing issues on which the society is often divided.

Indeed, division of some sort is inevitable in any society. The workers, for example, prefer higher wages so as to support their families, but factory owners would like to cut labor costs so that their products can be sold to the market at lower prices. Such a conflict of interests is natural. Sensing this, some politicians may form a party to appeal to the workers, while others may organize another party to attract the support of factory owners. In their seminal work on the development of political parties, Lipset and Rokkan (1967) argued that political parties in Western democracies were born out of two major events in history: the National Revolution resulting in state–church and center–periphery cleavages, and the Industrial Revolution leading to the emergence of class and rural–urban cleavages. Such cleavages underpin the party structure in the West even up to now (Lijphart, 1999). One caveat: In the past several decades, a number of new issues, such as environmentalism, have emerged, which have molded or remolded the party structure in some Western democracies (Dalton, 2008).

In contrast, Taiwan is very different from most Western democracies. Many of the above-mentioned cleavages are either irrelevant or not particularly important in shaping the party configuration in Taiwan. The most salient cleavages in Taiwan are ethnicity and national identity which are often highly emotional. In this sense, Taiwan is a divided society (Hsieh, 2008).

At the time when Taiwan started to democratize, ethnicity did play an important role for the democracy movement in mobilizing popular support to pressure the KMT regime to change. The democracy movement, to a certain extent, represented the expression of grievances on the part of some native Taiwanese against the minority mainlanders' rule (Hsieh, 2000). Nonetheless, as Taiwan became democratic, political power was soon transferred to the native Taiwanese. Ethnicity thus lost part of its salience. Instead, national identity became the dominant issue in Taiwan politics (Hsieh and Niou, 1996a,b; cf. Lin *et al.*, 1995).

National identity refers to people's attitudes toward the future relationships between Taiwan and mainland China. In Taiwan, some people insist that Taiwan is different from China and should be separated from China for good; some others believe that Taiwan and the mainland are integral parts of a larger China and should be reunited sooner or later. There are still others who stand somewhere in between, representing what may be called the status quo, that is neither independence nor unification. Currently, the official name of Taiwan remains the ROC; the Constitution is still the one that was adopted on the mainland in the 1940s; and the national flag and the national anthem are the same as the ones used in China before the end of the civil war. That is, the status quo contains a certain degree of Chineseness. However, Taiwan has not been ruled by the Chinese government in Beijing since 1949. It has been able to maintain *de facto*, if not *de jure*, independence. The controversies over the national identity issue have dominated Taiwan politics for many years.

Table 1 shows the results of the logistical regression analysis based upon the Taiwan Election and Democratization Studies (TEDS) Survey for the 2008 presidential election regarding the significance of the various cleavages in affecting Taiwanese voters' preferences toward the two major political groupings, the pan-KMT camp and the pan-DPP camp.[4] The dependent variable is the voters' inclination to support the pan-KMT camp as against the pan-DPP camp. The independent variables include four potential cleavages which may affect voters' partisan preferences. These four variables — more welfare vs. less welfare, environmental protection vs. economic growth, independence vs. unification, and reform vs. stability — are measured in the same way. On each issue, respondents were asked to pick a score between 0 standing for more welfare, environmental protection, independence, and reform and 10 for less welfare, economic

Table 1: Logistic Regression for Leaning Toward the Pan-KMT Camp.

	Toward the Pan-KMT camp	
Variable	*B*	S.E.
Intercept	–4.045**	0.740
Less welfare	–0.029	0.025
Less environment	0.088**	0.031
Unification	0.499**	0.100
Stability	0.088**	0.028
Clean government	1.283**	0.391
Minnan Taiwanese	–0.745	0.549
Mainlanders	1.373	0.921
Minnan × unification	0.068	0.111
Mainlanders × unification	0.198	0.207
Female	0.472**	0.156
Older	0.089	0.070
Better educated	0.228**	0.073
Number of cases	1.126	
Nagelkerke R^2	0.492	

Source: Taiwan Election and Democratization Studies 2008P Survey.
The reference category is the pan-DPP camp.
* Indicates $p < 0.10$.
** Indicates $p < 0.05$.

growth, unification, and stability to represent their most preferred position.[5] In addition to these four issues, a valence issue, namely, the clean government issue, along with several demographic variables is also included.[6]

Since the four major issues are measured in the same way, their coefficients can be compared. Obviously, national identity is the dominant issue in Taiwan. Not surprisingly, those who are further away from independence tend to support the pan-KMT camp. And those who prefer economic growth to environmentalism as well as stability to reform are also inclined to back the pan-KMT camp. Interestingly, those who care about the clean government issue tend to lean toward the pan-KMT camp as well. This may have a lot to do with the scandals involving many DPP officials, including President

Chen Shui-bian himself. Women and the better educated tend to support the pan-KMT camp, too. All variables involving ethnicity are not significant.

Thus, national identity is indeed the dominant cleavage underpinning the party configuration in Taiwan. To visualize the voters' tendency to support one party or the other, I regroup voters' attitudes toward the national identity issue: those who pick a score between 0 and 4 are reclassified as independence supporters; a score 5 qualifies as status quo supporters; and a score between 6 and 10 is identified as a unification supporter. As can be seen from Table 2, those who are in favor of Taiwan independence tend to support the pan-DPP camp while those who prefer unification or the status quo are inclined to support the pan-KMT camp. Since, as shown in many surveys, a majority or close to a majority of the population in Taiwan support the status quo, the pan-KMT camp has a clear edge over the pan-DPP camp. Herein lies the real strength of the KMT or the pan-KMT camp.

The reason that the status quo supporters tend to back the KMT or the pan-KMT camp is clear and simple. The status quo as symbolized by the official name of the country, the Constitution, the national flag, and the national anthem is defined by the KMT, not by the DPP. These are the very symbols that many independence supporters want to tear down.

The KMT's strength also derives from its performance as Taiwan's ruling party in the second half of the 20th century. It was

Table 2: Respondents' Attitudes Toward the National Identity Issue and Their Party Identification.

	Pan-DPP Camp	Pan-KMT Camp	Total
Independence	316 (82.9%)	65 (17.1%)	381 (100.0%)
Status Quo	168 (31.5%)	366 (68.5%)	534 (100.0%)
Unification	36 (13.4%)	233 (86.6%)	269 (100.0%)
Total	520 (43.9%)	664 (56.1%)	1184 (100.0%)

Source: Taiwan Election and Democratization Studies 2008P Survey.
Note: Cell entries are row percentages.

able to achieve an economic miracle and to maintain Taiwan's security despite diplomatic setbacks since the 1970s. These achievements have given the party the credibility to rule in the eyes of some residents on the island.

Of course, the KMT has its weaknesses, too. For a long time, it was depicted as a "black-and-gold" party. It controlled a huge number of party-owned enterprises, including some print and electronic media. It spent a large amount of money in elections, and many of its candidates bought votes in the races. Such an image continues to hurt it, although ironically, as Table 1 shows, the DPP also suffers from such charges now, probably more so than the new KMT under President Ma. But this may continue to be a problem for the KMT, and it is likely to haunt it again and again in the years to come. Additionally, the KMT's old image of being a mainlanders' party has caused some problems for the party. However, given the diminishing significance of ethnicity in Taiwan politics, the damage done to the KMT has diminished.

It is true that ethnicity and national identity are closely related. As can be seen from Table 3, Minnan Taiwanese, who constitute about three-quarters of the total population, are more likely than others to favor Taiwan independence, but close to a majority of Minnan Taiwanese actually support the status quo. By contrast, mainlanders are overwhelmingly in favor of either the status quo or unification,

Table 3: Ethnicity and National Identity.

National identity Ethnicity	Independence	Status quo	Unification	Total
Minnan	450	611	211	1,272
Taiwanese	(35.4%)	(48.0%)	(16.6%)	(100.0%)
Hakka	49	99	48	196
Taiwanese	(25.0%)	(50.5%)	(24.5%)	(100.0%)
Mainlanders	14	110	77	201
	(7.0%)	(54.7%)	(38.3%)	(100.0%)

Source: Taiwan Election and Democratization Studies 2008P Survey.

Note: Cell entries are row percentages.

and very few of them support independence. Hakka Taiwanese stand somewhere in between.[7] Yet when it comes to politics, it is national identity rather than ethnicity that counts. For instance, if a Minnan voter believes that Taiwan and the mainland should be reunited, it is likely that he supports the pan-KMT camp. Or if a mainlander insists that Taiwan should seek permanent independence from China, it is quite likely that she supports the pan-DPP camp. It is national identity rather than ethnicity that, more often than not, determines a voter's partisan attachment.

In summary, the KMT has been doing very well in elections. It derives strength mainly from its unique position on the national identity issue, the dominant cleavage underpinning the party configuration in Taiwan. Its past performance as Taiwan's ruling party also gives it certain credibility in the eyes of some voters. Since the distribution of voters on the national identity issue has been quite stable over the years (Hsieh, 2002), and there is no reason to believe that it will change drastically in the foreseeable future, the KMT will continue to be a formidable force in Taiwan politics.

THE INSTITUTIONAL SETTING

Although the KMT's unique position on the national identity issue makes it a formidable political force in Taiwan, institutional arrangements also determine how formidable it is. Under certain institutional arrangements other political forces may stay in the game, and the KMT has to accommodate the presence of these forces. But under some arrangements these political forces may be wiped out or be significantly weakened, leaving the KMT in a truly dominant political position. One such institutional arrangement that will determine the fortunes of the various political forces is the electoral system.

Prior to the 2008 Legislative Yuan election, Taiwan had long used at all levels of government the SNTV for legislative elections and the SMD plurality system for the election of executive offices. The SMD plurality system is used in districts with only one seat up for grabs. Each voter has only one vote, and the candidate who receives more votes than others (not necessarily a majority of votes) wins. The

SNTV can be seen as an extension of the SMD plurality system to multimember districts in which each voter has, as in the case of the SMD plurality system, only one vote, and the top several vote-getters get elected.

In the study of electoral systems, it is a well-known fact that the SMD plurality system favors two-party competition unless the votes received by third parties are concentrated in specific areas. William H. Riker dubbed this Duverger's Law (Duverger, 1954; Riker, 1982). This system favors two-party competition because third-party supporters often turn away from their preferred party and instead choose the lesser evil of the big two so as not to waste their votes on the candidate of the third party. Moreover, this system also "encourages parties which repeatedly lose to merge with each other so as to capture a combined total of votes larger than the total received by the party which repeatedly wins" (Downs, 1957, 123, 124). Moreover, since there is only one seat available in each district, it is a waste of resources for candidates and parties to enter the race unless the candidate/party stands a chance of being in one of the top two slots (Cox, 1997). Generally, under such a system the large parties, particularly the largest one, will get huge bonuses (i.e., higher seat share than vote share) across districts, and the third parties are at a significant disadvantage by winning far fewer seats than votes in proportional terms. As a consequence, only two parties may survive.

The SNTV functions quite differently. As the district magnitude (i.e., the number of seats to be elected) gets larger, the chances increase for third-party candidates to get elected. In general, in an SMD, a candidate receiving 50 percent of the vote plus one is sure of winning. In a two-member district, a candidate getting 33.3 percent of the vote plus one will win no matter what, and so on. That is, a candidate who is able to garner $1/(M + 1)$ of the vote plus one will win for sure, where M stands for the district magnitude. Thus, a party supported by only 25 percent of the electorate may not be viable in an SMD, but it may have a good chance of winning in a large district. In other words, the SNTV displays a certain degree of proportionality by reducing the bonuses enjoyed by large parties and by giving small parties "fair" shares in elections. The larger the district magnitude, the more proportional it is. This is the case in Taiwan prior to the 2008 Legislative Yuan election.

In a sense, the KMT has "suffered" from the SNTV. Its bonuses have been reduced, and the system has encouraged its rank and file to split from the party. Thus, we have witnessed the fragmentation of the party system in Taiwan, particularly on the pan-KMT side, since the mid-1990s (Hsieh, 2002).

Although the SNTV had bolstered third parties in legislative elections before 2008, it has been difficult for third parties to run successful campaigns in elections for executive offices. As a result, these elections have often become a two-way competition between the two camps led by the KMT and the DPP. The holding of executive elections has thus put the brakes on further fragmentation of the party system in Taiwan.

Under the MMM system used for the 2008 Legislative Yuan election, the situation changed dramatically. Nearly two-thirds of the seats were elected by SMD plurality system with the rest mainly by PR. Such a system discriminates against the small parties. First, it was very difficult for any third parties to win seats in the SMD plurality part of the election unless they cooperated with one of the large parties. Second, even the PR portion of the election has not made the life of many third parties easier since it requires that a party must receive at least five percent of the popular vote — a very high threshold — to be allocated any seats in this part of the election. In fact, the small parties were almost completed wiped out in 2008. The KMT has been greatly helped by the new rule as the incentives to split from the party have diminished significantly.

Furthermore, the KMT — or more precisely the unified pan-KMT camp — also benefits from the rule change since it is the larger of the two major political groupings in Taiwan. In the SMD part of the election in 2008, the KMT and the DPP received 53.5 and 38.2 percent of the popular vote, respectively, which do not deviate much from the distribution of votes between the two major camps in previous elections. However, the KMT won 78.1 percent of the seats as against the DPP's 17.8 percent. To some extent, this is not too surprising, since under the SMD plurality system the largest party often benefits more.[8] However, it is a bit surprising that the DPP performed significantly worse than what would normally be expected. Under the new system, the KMT does enjoy some built-in advantages, and it will be very difficult for any other party, including the DPP, to challenge it unless the KMT were to implode from within.

Does this mean that the KMT is invincible? In the Legislative Yuan elections, that may be the case. However, in the presidential races, the DPP may still have some chance of winning. Ironically, if we read the ROC Constitution carefully, it is obvious that it provides essentially for a parliamentary form of government. The highest administrative organ in the country is the Executive Yuan (cabinet), not the presidency; the Executive Yuan headed by the premier is responsible to the Legislative Yuan, not to the president; the Legislative Yuan can bring down the Executive Yuan with a vote of no confidence, although the president may dissolve the Legislative Yuan after a no confidence vote is passed — the premier may also initiate the dissolution under the circumstances; and as promulgating laws and issuing mandates, the president has to get the countersignature of the premier or the countersignatures of the premier and the ministers concerned. Even though the president is now directly elected by the general public and can appoint the premier on his/her own, all of the above-mentioned stipulations indicate that the governing power resides in the hands of the Executive Yuan and the Legislative Yuan, not the president.[9] If this is how the system functions, and since the KMT will most likely continue to control the Legislative Yuan, it will remain the ruling party for many years to come.

However, the actual practice in Taiwan has often deviated from what the Constitution stipulates. Before the year 2000, given that the KMT controlled both the presidency and the Legislative Yuan, it did not create serious problems. But when the DPP won the presidency in 2000 and 2004 while the KMT or the pan-KMT camp continued to control the Legislative Yuan, serious stalemate ensued. This may happen again in the future. It also implies that, given the precedents, the presidency remains a big prize. And given the many idiosyncratic factors that may influence such races, no possibility can be ruled out *a priori*. That is, there is no guarantee that the KMT will remain invincible.

CONCLUSION

This chapter has examined the transformation of the KMT from an authoritarian ruling party to a player in democratic politics. In the past, its strength has often been underestimated by scholars and laymen alike. The stereotype of the party as authoritarian, anachronistic, and corrupt indeed leads many to believe that it has no future. But things have turned out quite differently; the KMT has been doing well in elections.

It is true that the party has made some changes, but the most significant advantage it enjoys derives from its unique position on the national identity cleavage, the dominant issue shaping Taiwan's party configuration. Adding the built-in advantages in the new electoral system for the Legislative Yuan elections, the KMT will continue to dominate Taiwan politics for many years unless it implodes from within. Nonetheless, even though it may win the Legislative Yuan elections easily under normal circumstances, there is no guarantee that it will always win the presidential races. It is invincible, but only to a certain extent.

REFERENCES

Copper, JF (2009). *Taiwan: Nation-State or Province*, 5th edn. Boulder, CO: Westview.

Cox, GW (1997). *Making Votes Count: Strategic Coordination in the World's Electoral Systems.* Cambridge: Cambridge University Press.

Dalton, RJ (2008). *Citizen Politics: Public Opinion and Political Parties in Advanced Industrial Democracies*, 5th edn. Washington, DC: CQ Press.

Downs, A (1957). *An Economic Theory of Democracy.* New York: Harper & Row.

Duverger, M (1954). *Political Parties: Their Organization and Activity in the Modern State.* Trans. by North, Barbara and North, Robert. London: Methuen.

Hsieh, JF-S (2000). East Asian culture and democratic transition: With special reference to the case of Taiwan. *Journal of Asian and African Studies*, 35, 29–42.

Hsieh, JF-S (2002). Continuity and change in Taiwan's electoral politics. In *How Asia Votes*, Hsieh JF-S and D Newman (eds.), pp. 32–49. New York: Chatham House.

Hsieh, JF-S (2004). The march surprise: Taiwan's presidential election of 2004. Annual Conference of the American Association for Chinese Studies in Williamsburg, Virginia.

Hsieh, JF-S (2008). Democracy in a mildly divided society. In *Democratization in Taiwan: Challenges in Transformation*, Meernik J and P Paolino (eds.), pp. 11–24. Aldershot, UK: Ashgate.

Hsieh, JF-S (2009). The origins and consequences of electoral reform in Taiwan. *Issues & Studies*, 45, 1–22.

Hsieh, JF-S and EMS Niou (1996a). Issue voting in the republic of China on Taiwan's 1992 legislative yuan election. *International Political Science Review*, 17, 13–27.

Hsieh, JF-S and EMS Niou (1996b). Salient issues in Taiwan's electoral politics. *Electoral Studies*, 15, 219–235.

Lijphart, A (1999). *Patterns of Democracy: Government Forms and Performance in Thirty-Six Countries.* New Haven, CN: Yale University Press.

Lin, T-M, Y-H Chu and MJ Hinich (1995). Conflict displacement and regime transition in Taiwan: A spatial analysis. *World Politics*, 48, 453–481.

Lipset, SM and S Rokkan (1967). Cleavage structures, party systems, and voter alignments: An introduction. In *Party Systems and Voter Alignments: Cross-National Perspectives*, Lipset SM and S Rokkan (eds.). New York: The Free Press, pp. 1–64.

Meaney, CS (1992). Liberalization, democratization, and the role of the KMT. In *Political Change in Taiwan*, Cheng T-J and S Haggard (eds.), pp. 95–120. Boulder, CO: Lynne Rienner.

Rigger, S (1999). *Politics in Taiwan.* London and New York: Routledge.

Riker, WH (1982). The two-party system and Duverger's law: An essay on the history of political science. *American Political Science Review*, 76, 753–766.

Taagepera, R and MS Shugart (1989). *Seats and Votes: The Effects and Determinants of Electoral Systems.* New Haven, CN: Yale University Press.

Tien, H-M (1989). *Great Transition.* Stanford, CA: Hoover Institution Press.

ENDNOTES

1. For a detailed account of Taiwan's political development, see Tien (1989), Rigger (1999), and Copper (2009).
2. For the rationale behind the electoral reform, see Hsieh (2009).
3. From 2000 to 2008, the DPP controlled the executive branch while the KMT or the pan-KMT camp maintained a majority in the Legislative Yuan.
4. The Taiwan Election and Democratization Studies Surveys are sponsored by Taiwan's National Science Council. The coordinator of this multi-year project is Chi Huang, and the principal investigator of the survey for the 2008 presidential election is Ching-hsin Yu. The survey was conducted in June–August 2008 with a sample size of 1,905.

5. In the survey, the original wordings for the question on social welfare are 0 for "maintaining the current level of social welfare" and 10 for "expanding social welfare". I reverse the scores so as to make it consistent with other issues where 0 stands for the left/reform position while 10 for right/conservative.
6. There are no questions in the survey tapping directly the clean government issue. What is done here is to use the questions asking the respondents to pick the most and the second most important issues in the election. A dummy variable was constructed pitting those who choose clean government as either the most or the second most important issue (1) against all others who do not (0).
7. According to the TEDS 2008P survey, Minnan Taiwanese, Hakka Taiwanese, and mainlanders constitute, respectively, 74.9, 11.5, and 11.1 percent of the population. There are also a small number of aborigines in Taiwan.
8. The cube law, a well-known proposition in the literature, states that the ratio of seat shares received by the two political parties is the cube of the ratio of vote shares between them under the SMD plurality rule (Taagepera and Shugart, 1989).
9. Indeed, in many parliamentary democracies such as Austria, Iceland, Ireland, and Portugal, the president who is essentially a figurehead is also directly popularly elected. Also, in many parliamentary systems like the United Kingdom, the head of state can legally appoint anyone to be the prime minister without an investiture vote in parliament.

Chapter

3

The Democratic Progressive Party: From Opposition to Power, and Back Again

Shelley Rigger

On 28 September 1986, Taiwan passed a critical milestone on the road to democracy when a group of political activists founded the Democratic Progressive Party (DPP). The DPP was the first organized party to challenge the Kuomintang's long-standing political monopoly. Its founders did not wait for the single-party authoritarian state to give its blessing; they birthed their party in open defiance of martial law. It was a courageous act, undertaken at a moment of great uncertainty and risk. It forced Taiwan's authoritarian regime to choose: continue to repress opposition and postpone democratic reform; or accept the DPP's *fait accompli* and the competitive political system it would usher in.

To its credit, the KMT-dominated regime under President Chiang Ching-kuo chose the latter path. The DPP's founders were not prosecuted, and the party offered its first slate of candidates in legislative elections held three months later. For a party with only a few months' history, the Democratic Progressives did well, winning about 20 and 25 percent of the vote in National Assembly and legislative elections, respectively. Although the party system remained lop-sided for many years — KMT candidates retained a strong majority of electoral support well into the 2000s — the DPP's founding ended the era of one-party politics in Taiwan.

Since those early days, the DPP has remained the Kuomintang's largest and most potent challenger. Of the scores of start-up parties that have entered politics since 1986, none has come close to it in electoral support, political influence, or grassroots organization. Nonetheless, the DPP has fallen short of its founders' expectations in an important respect: their party still does not run neck-and-neck with the KMT. Since the late 1990s, the DPP's vote share has hovered around 40–45 percent of the electorate. It has broken that barrier only once, in 2004, when President Chen Shui-bian won reelection with 50.02 percent of the vote. The party's vote share is respectable and establishes its *bona fides* as the island's main opposition party, but it is not enough to put the DPP in power — or even seriously threaten a united KMT (Fig. 1).

DPP leaders, activists, and politicians are keenly conscious of this "glass ceiling" on the party's vote share, and they are determined to break through it. They want their party to be a peer competitor to the KMT, to reliably command a vote share that compels regular alternation in government and maintains a legislative presence that can check and balance governments led by others. But as of 2009, the DPP was still struggling to achieve peer competitor status with the KMT. In the first decade of the 21st century the party's vote share stayed within its historical limits, and its share of elected offices actually declined. The 2008 legislative elections left the Democratic Progressives with the smallest legislative delegation since 1992. Many interacting factors — some internal to the party, others originating outside the DPP — have contributed to its two-steps-forward, one-step-back development.

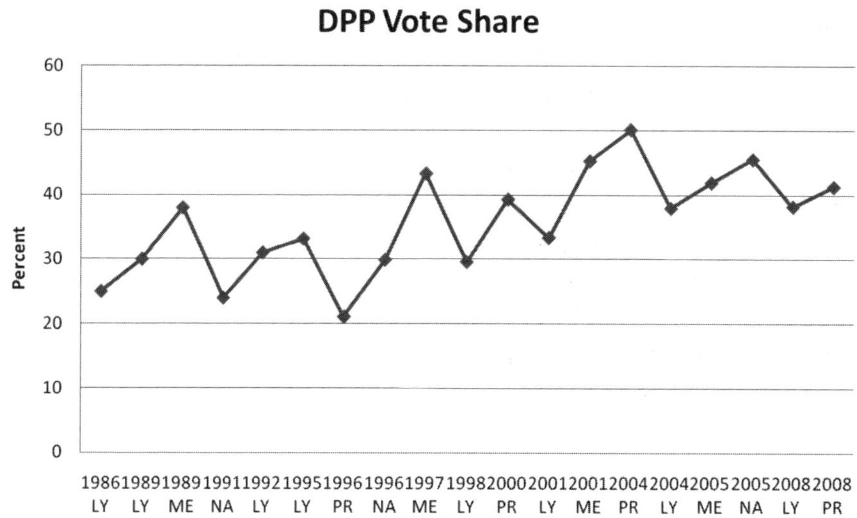

Figure 1. LY, legislative yuan; ME, municipal executive; NA, national assembly; PR, presidential.

EXTERNAL CHALLENGES

Perhaps the most intractable force working against the DPP in its effort to become a peer competitor to the KMT is the KMT itself. The "Third Wave" democratic transitions have shown that authoritarian parties can be very durable. The KMT is hardly alone in leading its country through decades of authoritarianism and then out-performing its rivals in democratic elections. Authoritarian parties that are flexible enough to accommodate demands for democratic reforms and adjust their behavior to newly-democratic institutions can win free elections.

The KMT possesses several virtues that have contributed to its success in post-transition political competition. First, it has deep roots in Taiwan society. In the four decades prior to the democratic transition, the KMT invested vast resources in cultivating grassroots participation and popular support. The most effective mechanism it employed was local elections, which were held continuously throughout the authoritarian period. As early as the 1940s, the KMT allowed

Taiwanese to elect village, township, municipal, and provincial officials. In 1969, the ROC opened a limited number of national legislative seats to direct election, and in the 1990s all legislative and executive posts were turned over to popular election.

From the beginning, Taiwanese competed fiercely to win elected offices, but because opposition parties were outlawed, the competition took place *within* the KMT. The opportunity to seek and hold office under the KMT banner was an enticing prospect for ambitious individuals. Successful local politicians brought their personal support networks with them into the party, giving the party a strong grassroots presence. To this day, the KMT dominates grassroots politics; in the 2005 township executive elections, the KMT won five times as many seats as the DPP.

To maintain a strong popular base the KMT cultivated a second important virtue: ideological flexibility. When international developments made the prospect of unification remote, the KMT downplayed unification in favor of economic development. When economic development made Taiwanese society complex, the KMT diversified its positions. When the DPP offered popular new ideas such as a national health insurance scheme, the KMT adopted those positions as its own — and because it was in power, it got the credit when they were implemented. Most recently, when popular support for unification had all but disappeared, KMT president Ma Ying-jeou promised "Three Nos" — no independence, no unification, and no war.

A third KMT virtue is the party's record of successful economic management. It was under the Kuomintang that Taiwan grew from an agricultural backwater to become a world leader in high-tech manufacturing. In 1950, the United States' per capita GDP was more than ten times that of Taiwan, but by 2008, the gap had shrunk to the point where the U.S. figure was just 1.5 times that of Taiwan. The first five decades of KMT rule saw enormous improvements in living standards, educational opportunity, and public health, convincing many Taiwanese that it is uniquely competent and capable of governing.

Taiwan's political institutions further reinforce the KMT's political dominance. In their eagerness to move the democratic transition forward, DPP politicians accepted rules for the new system that disadvantaged their party. In the lingo of transition theory, they accepted a bad pact. The new system's deficiencies included institutional problems — such as an ineffectual legislature and an unsettled balance of power between the legislature and the executive — and political problems, such as the KMT's enormous financial advantage, which allowed its candidates to spend massive amounts on their campaigns — even to the point of paying for votes.

Among the most consequential choices in Taiwan's reform process was the decision to retain single, non-transferable voting in multi-member districts. Under this electoral formula (known as SNTV), candidates from a given party compete against one another in any district where that party believes it can win more than one seat. As the number of districts in which the DPP aspired to win multiple seats increased, individual DPP politicians were forced to run against their party brethren. In large districts, where the number of votes needed to win was small, single-issue voters tended to favor pro-independence "fundamentalists". Party unity suffered.

In the 1990s, the DPP took up the cause of electoral system reform. Party analysts blamed SNTV elections for all sorts of distortions in the political system, from party fragmentation to corruption, and they argued that single-member district elections would reduce these complications. This reform also seemed like a good strategic move for the DPP. Over the course of the decade, the DPP found itself gaining ground in executive elections (in 1997, the DPP won 12 out of 21 municipal executive posts in Taiwan, and its vote share in head-to-head contests always exceeded its share in SNTV races). The party's arguments in favor of reform proved persuasive, and constitutional reforms adopted in 2005 replaced SNTV elections for the national legislature with a two-vote system in which 73 seats are now filled by single-member, first-past-the-post district elections and 34 by a party list proportional representation process.

The DPP championed electoral reform for two reasons. First, party leaders were convinced it was the right thing to do for Taiwan's democracy. Second, they believed (at least in the mid-1990s when they started their reform campaign) that single-member district elections would be easier to win. The basis for that belief was the party's strong performance in executive elections; it was reinforced in 2000 when Chen Shui-bian won the most important executive election of all, the presidency.

The party's logic rested on three observations: First, the DPP was most successful in head-to-head electoral combat in which its candidates could criticize their KMT opponents directly, while emphasizing the programmatic and stylistic differences between parties. Second, because the DPP was smaller and more unified, it could exploit divisions within the KMT — divisions the KMT could finesse in SNTV elections, but not in single-seat races. Third, election results were breaking along regional lines, with the Democratic Progressives running very strong in the south. Single-seat elections, they anticipated, would amplify that strength.

When the first legislative election under the new rules took place in January 2008, it was a disaster for the DPP. While there was evidence that some voters who had chosen DPP candidates in past elections turned against the party in 2008, the disproportionality of the new system clearly worked against the DPP.[1] DPP candidates won 38 percent of the vote, but only 27 out of 113 legislative seats, or 24 percent.

None of the factors predicted to benefit the DPP worked as expected in 2008. Head-to-head partisan combat when Chen Shui-bian's administration was imploding made it harder, not easier, for DPP candidates to attract votes. The system's strong incentives for party unity disciplined the KMT and its allies, leaving few splits for Democratic Progressive candidates to exploit. And even in its "southern stronghold" the DPP did far worse than expected.[2] The DPP came close to its traditional "glass ceiling", averaging 40 percent of the vote in the 21 municipalities where it nominated candidates, but given the disproportionality built into the new electoral rules, the party's seat share was dismal. The PR portion of the ballot added a few seats to the party's total, but the DPP's share of PR votes — 37 percent — was unexpectedly low.

A final external challenge facing the DPP is one that lies entirely beyond the party's control: the rise of China. China's increasing international power and influence are convincing many in Taiwan and elsewhere that the quest for independence is a lost cause. Even though most DPP politicians take nuanced positions on the issue, the party as a whole has not yet persuaded voters that it can protect and advance Taiwan's interests better than its competitors. Political scientist Hsu Szu-chien has detailed how the rise of China changes the economic, political and strategic context in which Taiwan pursues its interests:

> Simply put, as far as Taiwan independence thinking is concerned, the rise of China is an inconvenient truth. For Taiwan, China's national power is overwhelming.... If we continue to use an outdated world view to deal with China we will drive Taiwan deeper into a corner, making its future even gloomier and the realization of Taiwan independence even more remote (Hsu, 2009).

Hsu urged the DPP to develop a "new discourse on cross–strait relations" — a pragmatic strategy for maintaining Taiwan's political independence by avoiding both naïve optimism and fatalistic defeatism. Without such a development, he argued, the DPP will be marginalized.

INTERNAL CHALLENGES

The DPP's organizational predecessor was a congeries of opposition political figures and dissident intellectuals calling itself the *Dangwai* (outside-the-party) movement. The individuals who participated in the *Dangwai* came from many economic, ethnic, social, and political backgrounds, but they shared a desire to replace the Kuomintang's authoritarian party-state with a democratic system in which all of Taiwan's inhabitants would have an equal voice.

Beyond these two issues — democratization and ethnic justice — the DPP's founders shared few common opinions. To hold the party together in the absence of a broad ideological and programmatic consensus, the party developed rules and structures to accommodate and synthesize a wide range of views and opinions. In the 1980s and 1990s, this approach worked well, but after Chen Shui-bian became president in 2000 — and especially after his reelection in 2004 — the mechanisms for intraparty negotiation began to fail.

In the 1970s, the *Dangwai* movement combined two loosely organized camps with differing strategic approaches. The politicians in the moderate camp believed the best way to increase the opposition's influence and bring about democratization was to stand for election and use their power as elected officials to reform the ROC's authoritarian practices. Other *Dangwai* activists believed direct action to be the most efficient route to democratization. Known initially as the "Alliance of *Dangwai* Writers and Editors", this more militant group later adopted the name "New Tide" (*Xin Chaoliu*). Although they were at times critical of their election-oriented peers, more often than not, New Tide worked alongside the moderates, and their strategies ultimately proved complementary.

When the *Dangwai* activists founded the DPP, they kept its platform narrow, focusing on political reform and ethnic justice. Organizationally, they adopted a Leninist structure modeled on the KMT, but it was poorly suited to Taiwan's democratic institutions and the Democratic Progressives' collective personality. In the end, the arranged marriage of the KMT's organizational structure and the *Dangwai's* democratic outlook produced an odd and unwieldy beast: a Leninist party without discipline, ideology, or centralized authority.

The apparent similarity between the DPP's original organizational structure and that of the KMT and the CCP disguised a crucial difference: all of the DPP's leadership organs were constituted by genuinely democratic selection processes. The most democratic of these, ironically, was the process for choosing the party's top leader. Until 2002, the DPP party chair was elected directly by the party's members, with strict term limits and other restraints. To make matters worse, the rules put formal authority in the hands of individuals whose actual political influence was limited. For DPP politicians, influence within the party is a product of the elected offices one holds. Yet until President Chen Shui-bian took over the chairmanship in 2002, few DPP chairs had held elected office during their tenure as chair. Kuo Cheng-liang described the result:

> As a matter of fact, according to the party charter, the party central office, the party caucuses and the municipal executives' alliance all enjoy equal status, with none under the jurisdiction of any other. In the event of a conflict within this power structure, the only way to make a decision is through discussion and compromise. However, in actual operation, with the exception of a few special cases, the party center invariably yields to the decision of the party caucuses and the municipal executives' alliance (Kuo 1998, 161).

One reason the party's organizational problems were so severe was the lack of consensus on political strategy — a problem that has tended to reinforce ideological disputes within the party. Even before the DPP was founded, the strategic differences between New Tide and other factions had begun to take on an ideological coloration centering on Taiwan's relationship with Mainland China. In the early 1990s, a third force entered the debate: pro-independence activists returning from exile. Under the intense political repression of the 1940s, 1950s, and 1960s, scores of Taiwanese political activists went into exile, where they founded the Taiwan Independence Movement. By the 1980s, the political climate on Taiwan had eased enough that pro-independence sentiments began to be heard — quietly — on the island itself. In 1991, the government ceased enforcing the blacklist that had kept pro-independence activists out of Taiwan, opening the door for them to enter politics.

While the early DPP included supporters of unification, the returning exiles, along with many New Tide activists and some moderates, saw Taiwan independence as a logical extension of the party's quest for democracy. In their view, independence would solve two problems: it would eliminate the KMT's political monopoly (since the KMT's legitimacy rested on unification as a national goal) and it would assure the political ascendancy of Taiwan's native-born majority. The DPP's first platform reflects a compromise between independence advocates and skeptics; it calls for self-determination for Taiwan.

Despite the DPP's efforts to put forward a more nuanced platform, most KMT politicians and pundits insisted "self-determination" was a euphemism for independence. At the time, at least, this criticism was unfair: the only goal that enjoyed true consensus in the DPP was to avoid a settlement of the cross–strait dispute by the Chinese Communist Party and the Kuomintang without input from the Taiwanese people. As Robert Sutter wrote in 1988,

> For moderate members of the DPP, self-determination means greater political power for the majority of Taiwanese, to be accomplished by equitable campaigns, open elections, and divestment of KMT business interests. Other members of the DPP assert — at least implicitly — that the Taiwanese electorate would abandon the goal of reunification if given a choice. In this view, self-determination could be seen as a veiled call for Taiwan independence (Sutter 1988, 49).

Pro-independence forces continued to press their case, and the party changed its position in 1991, approving a New Tide-sponsored proposal to insert a pro-independence plank into the party platform. The new plank was also a compromise: It combined the party's aspiration for independence with a procedural element emphasizing democracy:

> Based on the principle of popular sovereignty, the establishment of a sovereign, independent and self-governing Republic of Taiwan and promulgation of a new constitution should be carried out by all residents of Taiwan through a national referendum (Resolution of the DPP National Party Congress, 13 October 1991).

The 1991 resolution proved to be a workable compromise that stabilized the party's position and created a foundation for unity. Its success points to the value of another quirky DPP institution: formal factions. The New Tide faction was a tight-knit organization based on well-defined ideological and strategic logics, but other factions cared little for ideology. They were networks of politicians held together by their shared ambition to hold leadership positions within the party and secure nomination to elected office. They worked with the party center to formulate candidate lists for district and at-large elections; faction leaders secured their share of the party's political spoils and made sure the DPP did not take policy positions unacceptable to their members' constituents. In a pinch, they used the party chair as a negotiator to resolve intra-factional conflicts and arrive at party-wide compromises. In short, factions provided a work-around for the party's bulky Leninist institutions.

Because DPP factional politics were both ideological and interest-oriented, they allowed for multi-dimensional negotiating strategies that produced complex, sturdy compromises. Thus, the transparent, competitive and (relatively) democratic factionalism that had its heyday in the 1990s was an important source of strength and unity for a DPP divided on many issues. The 1991 Independence Plank compromise is but one example of factions helping the party hold together — and advance its interests — in the face of thorny ideological quarrels.

The 1991 compromise did not end the debate over independence within the DPP. Two years later, Chairman Hsu Hsin-liang announced, "The DPP cannot unilaterally declare Taiwan independence. Whether or not the Taiwan independence platform plank will become national policy will depend upon objective international conditions" (Kuo, 1998, 72). Two years later, a new party chair, Shih Ming-teh, expanded this interpretation when he stated, "If the DPP becomes the ruling party, we will not need to, nor will we, declare independence" (Kuo, 1998, 72). "Will not need to", he implied, because Taiwan — under the name "Republic of China" — already was independent. This innovation — essentially "discovering" independence as opposed to declaring it — was so successful that the KMT adopted similar rhetoric.

The struggle over independence reemerged in 1996, when the DPP chose Peng Ming-min to represent it in Taiwan's first direct presidential election. Throughout the campaign, DPP battled with Peng over his insistence that independence should be the centerpiece of his campaign. In the end, he won only 21 percent of the vote, a significant decline from the DPP's previous electoral performance that many observers interpreted as a clear rejection of his pro-independence line. Beijing's missile tests in the Taiwan area just prior to the presidential election also helped to cool DPP leaders' ardor for independence. As political scientist Chu Yun-han wrote, "an unexpected consequence of the recent showdown in the Taiwan Strait was the convergence of the DPP's reading of the island's structural constraints and realm of possibilities with that of the KMT. A growing number of DPP leaders have recognized that there is no realistic chance for Taiwan pursuing de jure independence in the foreseeable future" (Chu, 1997, 255). Even New Tide began to rethink its approach, eventually settling on a pragmatic line in which formal independence would be deferred to the future, while in the near term Taiwan would embrace economic opportunities in mainland China. (By 2005, New Tide had become a leading voice for moderation on China policy.)

In 1997, the most radical independence hardliners left the DPP to form their own party, freeing the DPP to adopt a more centrist position on the independence issue. In 1999, the party adopted the "Resolution Regarding Taiwan's Future", which reads in part, "Taiwan is a sovereign and independent country ... Taiwan, although named the Republic of China under its current constitution, is not subject to the jurisdiction of the People's Republic of China. Any change in the independent status quo must be decided by all residents of Taiwan by means of a plebiscite" (Resolution of the National Party Congress, 8 May 1999). This resolution marked a new consensus. The DPP would no longer seek to change the status quo by shifting to independence; on the contrary, it would defend the status quo against a shift from independence under the ROC to unification. In 2002, the party adopted this Resolution as equivalent to a platform plank, effectively supplanting the pro-independence plank adopted in 1991.

The Democratic Progressives' evolving position on the independence issue reveals the party's ideological fractiousness, but its ability to hold together and work through deeply-held differences of opinion points to its resilience. As we have seen, the main coordinating mechanism within the DPP was factionalism. Although they emerged originally from the debate over strategy, factions persisted — and proliferated — because they performed a useful function. And because the DPP was, until 2000, an opposition party, eliding differences of opinion on issues among and within factions was relatively easy.

Unfortunately, not all issues are amenable to factional negotiations, and the DPP has found itself at an impasse on a number of important questions. Where consensus was unreachable, the party's inclination was to take no action (Rigger, 2001, 95). As the DPP's access to political power increased, the haphazardness of factionalism as a coordinating mechanism became more problematic. Ignoring issues on which the fractious party could not find consensus turned out to be a terrible way to govern a country. Thus, in the hope of improving the party's functioning as a resource for elected officials, party leaders began to look for ways to unify the party's governmental influence with its organizational center.

Beginning in the mid-1990s, DPP leaders began to address the party's limitations through a process of institutionalization dubbed "internalization" (*neizaohua*). The term captures the concept of a party whose leadership and centers of influence originate within the ranks of the party's representatives in government. Initially, internalization emphasized the role of DPP legislators in setting party policy; the idea was that in parliamentary systems, party leaders are drawn from the ranks of the parties' parliamentarians. In 2000, the DPP adjusted the definition of internalization to accommodate an unexpected development: the party's capture of the presidential office.

From the beginning, the DPP's ultimate goal was to become Taiwan's ruling party. Until 1999, that prospect seemed remote; the party's vote share was sufficient to give it a respectable minority in the legislature and a healthy share of municipal executiveships, but it consistently fell short of a majority. But as the 2000 presidential election approached the DPP faced an exciting prospect: a KMT split.

The Kuomintang nominated former vice president Lien Chan, giving him access to the national party's massive resources. Opposing Lien was James Soong (Soong Chu-yu) a career KMT politician with strong backing from local KMT activists. When the party nominated Lien, Soong decided to run anyway. Both Lien and Soong were resourceful, serious, and determined. The possibility that they might divide the KMT vote, allowing Chen Shui-bian to win, electrified the Democratic Progressives. The party threw itself behind its candidate with unprecedented enthusiasm and unity. In the end, the result was just as they had hoped: Chen 39 percent; Soong 37 percent; Lien 23 percent.

THE PERILS OF SUCCESS: THE DPP IN THE CHEN SHUI-BIAN ERA

Chen's victory in the 2000 presidential election carried the DPP from political exile to the center of executive power. The KMT and its allies (known as the "Blue Camp") retained a strong legislative majority, and Chen's first cabinet included many non-DPP officials; nonetheless, the presidential victory rocketed the DPP to national prominence and altered the public's perception of the party. No longer could one dismiss the Democratic Progressives as insignificant, and the discovery that the sky did not fall in the first days after his inauguration hurt the credibility of those who had promised apocalyptic results were the DPP to come to power.

Chen's presidential win was a huge boon to the DPP, but it also exacted a price. The party's experiences after March 2000 forced it to reassess many of its core positions, and Chen's sudden elevation to the top office wreaked havoc with the party's decision-making process. On the policy front, the DPP struggled to shed the burden of its past support for *de jure* independence and reopen dialog with Beijing while remaining true to its Taiwan-centric ideology. It also discovered the necessity — and difficulty — of compromising with other political parties. The 2001 legislative elections demonstrated the power of unity, as a coordinated and cooperative campaign strategy made the DPP the largest party in the legislature. Even so, it fell short of the majority it needed to support Chen's initiatives.

Chen Shui-bian's presidency upset the complex distribution of power within the party. The new president controlled more political resources than the rest of the party combined: power of appointment, access to mass media, control over the budget process, legislative initiative, and a national electoral mandate. The center of gravity within the party moved overnight from the legislative caucus to the presidential office. This sudden shift destabilized decision-making in the party and government. To govern Taiwan effectively, Chen needed to reconstitute his party's decision-making process.

Reforming the DPP's Institutions, 2000–2002

To bolster its authority, the presidential office sought to broaden DPP participation in decision-making by convening a nine person policy coordination committee. The nine individuals were the key players in the executive and legislative branches and the DPP central party office. Its goals were to harmonize dissonant voices, stabilize the DPP's position in the legislature, and enable President Chen to lead the country more effectively.

The nine-person group was an interesting experiment in ad hoc institution-building, but it did not cure Taiwan's political ills. In theory the group forced Chen to consult regularly with important co-partisans, but in practice it functioned mainly as a venue for Chen to tell the others what he planned to do. Recognizing its failure, the DPP central office soon resumed its efforts to identify internal reforms capable of strengthening the party's role as an instrument for governing.

In the spring of 2002, the DPP launched an internalization reform effort. DPP politicians holding top government posts took the top party jobs. The hope was that synchronizing party and state power would allow the DPP to execute its policy-making role more effectively, promote cooperation among DPP legislators, and encourage coordination between the DPP legislators and the presidential office and cabinet. A unified and decisive DPP would have a better chance of pushing through its proposals in the legislature and attracting KMT defectors.

The reforms overhauled the selection process for the DPP's Central Executive and Central Standing Committees. In both cases, the intent was to unify the party's actual political power with its internal decision-making by putting the highest-ranking DPP elected officials into party leadership. During a DPP presidency, the executive branch was to dominate; when the DPP did not hold the presidential office, the focus would shift to the legislative caucus and the alliance of municipal executives. The most widely publicized element of the reform program was the decision to have the president serve as party chair. The provision brought the DPP into line with parties in parliamentary systems, but it sparked a backlash.

Chen Shui-bian assumed the party chairmanship on 21 July 2002, attracting criticism from media and political elites. The most common line of attack recalled Chen's promise two years earlier that he would distance himself from his party and serve as a "president of all the people". This contradiction led a leading conservative to remark, "Two years ago during the presidential election, President Chen promised he wouldn't meddle with his party's affairs during his presidency, yet now not only has he meddled with the party's affairs, he's gone one step further to become the party's chairman" (James Soong, quoted in *Taipei Times*, 22 July 2002).

Chen's ascent raised uncomfortable memories of the era of single-party Kuomintang-led authoritarianism, when party and state were fused under a series of powerful presidents who served concurrently as KMT chairmen. While accusations that Chen was seeking to reestablish party-state fusion clearly were overdrawn, even some of the president's DPP comrades wondered whether the move might be a step backward for Taiwan's democratization efforts. DPP Legislator Ker Chien-ming declined the offer of a party leadership post, saying, "It seems strange that the head of state should boss legislators around" (*Taipei Times*, 16 July 2002).

The DPP Under Chairman Chen Shui-Bian

These organizational reforms rationalized the DPP's decision-making and improved coordination between the presidential office and the party headquarters, but they did little to reduce the party's internal divisiveness. The presidential office wanted the party to be an instrument of its policy priorities, but party members were reluctant to surrender their independence. Over the course of Chen Shui-bian's eight-year presidency, tension between these two positions intensified, driven by debates over ideology and strategy; by the end of his presidency, the party's hard-won unity was again in tatters.

There was never any doubt that Chen Shui-bian and his vice president, Annette (Hsiu-lian) Lu would be the DPP candidates in 2004, but what strategy the party should use — continuing the moderate approach chosen in 2000, or leaning more toward the pro-independence side of the spectrum — was uncertain. After three years of being frozen out by both the KMT and the Beijing government, despite many goodwill gestures and statements, Chen Shui-bian was in no mood for more of the same. His 2004 presidential campaign tried to mobilize the party's Sino-skeptical base and paint the KMT-led legislature as obstructionist and unreasonable.

At the heart of Chen's 2004 electoral strategy was a plan to hold a referendum on the same day as the presidential voting. Party strategists believed a referendum on a symbolic issue would energize DPP supporters and increase Chen's vote share. Initially, Chen hoped to use the referendum to carry out a campaign promise: ratifying a new constitution for Taiwan. DPP politicians were coy about the relationship between a new constitution and Taiwan independence, but Beijing was adamant that a new constitution — even one that did not explicitly change Taiwan's name or territory — would be a significant gesture toward formalizing Taiwan's independence, something China was determined to prevent by any means necessary. Ultimately, pressure from the US compelled Chen to drop the new constitution in favor of more anodyne questions, but the referendum debate reinforced the widespread feeling that Chen's second term would have a strong pro-independence flavor.

Not everyone in the DPP was comfortable with this shift, but Chen's reelection — which he won with 50.02 percent of the vote, breaking the "fifty percent barrier" for the DPP for the first time — seemed to prove him right. That claim was put to the test nine months later, in the legislative elections of December 2004. If the DPP could deny the Blue Camp a majority, it would break the legislative deadlock. Once again, the DPP faced a strategic conundrum: emphasize Taiwan nationalism and independence, or try to appeal to centrist voters opposed to *both* independence and unification?

The DPP approached the legislative election with confidence. Chen's reelection in March energized his party, not least because it represented the DPP's first majority vote share win in national elections. It also sparked a meltdown in the Pan-Blue leadership that many thought would hogtie the Blues' legislative effort. But against the DPP's expectations, Blue Camp legislators were able to pull together their campaigns despite the disarray in their leadership. They coordinated their nominating strategy to minimize internecine conflict and protect Blue incumbents.

As the elections drew near, DPP headquarters tried to lower expectations, predicting a narrow win for the DPP and its allies (collectively known as the "Green Camp"), but admitting a DPP majority was unlikely. As it turned out, the KMT-led Blue coalition retained its majority. Part of the reason for the DPP's poor showing was its nominating strategy. Several multi-member districts that could have elected DPP legislators failed to do so because the Democratic Progressives' votes were divided among too many nominees. Nor was the DPP able to persuade its erstwhile ally, the Taiwan Solidarity Union, to share "Green" votes with the DPP.

Although they were important, these strategic and technical factors alone do not explain the DPP's setback. Chen Shui-bian's domineering leadership also hurt. As the campaign heated up, the president played an increasingly public role, brushing aside the candidates themselves. Flush with his own victory nine months earlier, Chen imposed the same issue positions on the legislative election that he had used in the presidential campaign. His stump speeches scoffed at U.S. advice not to antagonize China. He revived his proposal for a new constitution, and went even further, implying Taiwan should change its national flag and announcing his intention to rename government agencies to stress "Taiwan".

After the election, Chen Shui-bian followed DPP tradition and resigned from the party chairmanship to take responsibility for the poor outcome. Politically, it was the right move, but it defeated the purposes of the 2002 reforms. The reforms were intended to merge party and state leadership and encourage continuity, but Chen's resignation installed a revolving door on the chairman's office. Between July 2004 and January 2008, no fewer than six different politicians occupied that office. Even Chen Shui-bian himself served a stint from

October 2007 to January 2008. The revolving chairmanship was symptomatic of the overall failure of party reform to resolve the tension between strong leadership and intraparty democracy.

Party in Freefall

The 2005 municipal elections were essentially a replay of the 2004 legislative race. Chen used his bully pulpit to take over the campaign, to disastrous effect. The Democratic Progressives dropped three executive seats, falling from nine to six. The Blue Camp increased its share to 16 out of 23, with the KMT capturing 14. The losses capped a year of bruising setbacks for the DPP. In the summer, Lien Chan and James Soong each visited China, and the friendly reception they were given boosted the Blues' fortunes. Then, in early fall, a corruption scandal erupted around one of Chen Shui-bian's closest aides.

The scandal came at the worst possible moment. With few policy accomplishments to boast of, the DPP was hoping its reputation as a corruption-fighter would provide a foundation for its campaign strategy in the municipal elections. Now it was facing a scandal to rival the KMT's worst embarrassments — and the KMT had just chosen an anti-corruption standard bearer, Taipei mayor Ma Ying-jeou, as its chair. With public confidence in Chen's government collapsing, critics within the DPP began to raise their voices. In October, a group of young politicians declared their intention to launch a "New DPP Movement" to promote to self-reflection and reform. The idea was received enthusiastically in many quarters, but Chen mobilized his party allies to crush it, silencing the young generation. Meanwhile, party elders were already jockeying for the presidential nomination in 2008 — a dynamic that further eroded trust and unity in the DPP. Chen remained uncompromising, determined not to become a lame duck with less than half his term gone.

The party's disappointing performance in the 2005 municipal elections sharpened the confrontation between moderates and ideologues. Chen's critics implored the president to consider a more liberal line on cross–strait economic ties; his 2006 New Year address seemed a calculated rebuke. The speech hammered away at hardline themes: consolidating Taiwan consciousness, tightening controls on cross–strait economic ties, and promoting a new constitution. It reversed Chen's previous policy on cross–strait economic relations, stressing the risks of economic engagement and demanding the government act as a "gatekeeper". He followed up on the speech by unveiling a reshuffled cabinet larded with Sino-skeptics.

Chen's speech surprised many observers because it ran counter to the dominant trends in public opinion and among political elites. The party's own internal post-election report listed failure to reach out to centrist voters through moderate policy positions as a key factor in the December defeat. In a party chair election held in early 2006, party members rejected pro-independence candidates in favor of a more moderate choice. New Tide legislator Lee Wen-chung said publicly that most party members believed the Chen Administration was taking the party — and the nation — in the wrong direction. He told the *Taipei Times*, "The government must face the reality that China is rising economically and politically. The nation must respond to the situation and try to reposition itself in an era of globalization". Lee also took on the president's ruling style, saying, "I just don't think it is right for the president to continue the one-person decision-making model and leave everyone else out of the loop, especially in the wake of the party's resounding defeat in the December 3 local elections". (*Taipei Times*, 10 January 2006).

Electing a new party chair had little effect on the president. On February 27, Chen announced that the National Unification Council and Guidelines would "cease to function". Chen used this gesture to thumb his nose at Beijing — and Washington — and pander to pro-independence hardliners in Taiwan. As Chen's popular support continued to plummet, frustrated Blue Camp lawmakers proposed legislation to force the government to permit cross–strait flights. The Blues lined up enough votes to pass the bill, but DPP legislators used obstructionist tactics aimed at running out the clock on the legislative session; at one point, a DPP legislator prevented action by stuffing the printed bill in her mouth and chewing it up. Clearly, inter-party and inter-governmental relations were reaching new lows.

In May, the president's son-in-law was taken into custody on charges that he used his relationship with the president to engage in insider trading. After years of swirling allegations, always denied, prosecutors had linked wrongdoing to Chen's family. In response to the charges — and the growing chorus of criticism aimed at his hard-line policies and erratic behavior — Chen announced on May 31 that he would turn over most of his duties to Premier Su Tseng-chang.

The gesture failed to pacify Chen's Blue Camp opponents, who promptly launched another recall petition. Although the Blue Camp held a majority, the recall motion (and two more that followed) fell short of the required two-thirds threshold. Chen was battered but still in office. The recall campaign briefly unified the DPP, but a few weeks later, a group of DPP-linked academics circulated a petition asking Chen to resign. Then, former DPP chairman and pro-democracy martyr Shih Ming-teh launched his own movement to demand Chen's resignation; by September, thousands of demonstrators were taking part in Shih's "Red Shirt" demonstrations.

The shift from Blue to Green calls for Chen's resignation divided the DPP and further eroded public support for the embattled president. In late July, the party decided to enforce unity by banning factions. The proposal was aimed mainly at New Tide, the strongest faction, and the one most critical of Chen. Criticism of New Tide — long a staple of DPP infighting — had reached new heights. An item posted on a Deep Green website captured the tone of this discourse, comparing New Tide to an invasive and destructive pest:

> When Chen Shui-bian started cooperating with New Tide it was like when fish breeders introduced the apple snail: with its tight-knit organization and extreme discipline, New Tide took over the DPP administration and elected offices at lightning speed. Like snails coating every body of water in Taiwan, from the smallest creek to the biggest river to every last pond and pool — from the presidential office to the Executive Yuan to the Legislative Yuan and even at the county level, you could see New Tide in every important post ("Antiseptic becomes Carcinogenic").

New Tide tried to fight back against these attacks, arguing that diversity was a DPP strength. New Tide leader Tuan Yi-kang warned: "The DPP's factions are by no means the cause of disorder. Policy flip-flops and power struggles are the crux of the problems ... Without the existence of factions, the DPP will lose a mechanism for communication and coordination. Will it be a good thing for the DPP to have gangs existing in the party that have no [formal] organization?" (*Taipei Times*, 24 July 2006). New Tide's efforts failed; factions were banned.

In November, prosecutors charged Chen's wife with embezzling government funds. They said they had evidence to charge the president himself, were it not for the immunity conferred by his office. Chen's legal woes presented a terrible dilemma to other DPP politicians. On the one hand, there was little affection for the president among DPP officials, many of whom viewed him as stubborn and self-centered, more concerned about his own future than his party's. On the other hand, most DPP supporters believed the attacks on Chen were unfair. In their view, the Blue Camp never accepted the voters' verdicts in 2000 and 2004, and instead used every trick imaginable to overturn the election results. For DPP politicians, allowing the Blues to drive Chen out of office was anathema, but allowing Chen to drag the entire DPP down with him was an equally unattractive prospect. Caught in this vise, some DPP lawmakers asked Chen to take a voluntary "leave of absence", a partial solution that satisfied no one.

And, as always, there was an election to worry about: in early December, residents of Taiwan's two largest cities elected mayors and city councilors. For the DPP, it was a do-or-die moment. Both of its nominees were long-time heroes of the democratic movement with credentials as moderate and pragmatic administrators. In Taipei, Frank Hsieh's 41 percent vote share was hard-fought and respectable, although not enough to win the post. In Kaohsiung, the New Tide-linked DPP candidate Chen Chu squeezed past her opponent, reviving the DPP's hopes in southern Taiwan — and fueling more anti-New Tide hysteria.

A year before the crucial 2008 elections, the DPP's predicament was stark. The embattled president had taken a sharp fundamentalist turn, pleasing his core supporters but alienating centrist voters. DPP politicians were torn between following his unpopular line and breaking with the president — at the risk of being labeled fellow-travelers of the Blues. The new electoral rules under which the next round of legislative elections would be held drastically increased centrist voters' influence on the election outcome, but "Deep Green" hardliners were determined to punish DPP moderates — a resolve they demonstrated to devastating effect in the DPP primary.

DPP primary elections use a two-stage procedure that combines party member voting with public opinion polling. The polling component ensures the nominees are acceptable to centrist voters, but in 2007, the DPP decided to include only Green voters in the opinion polling, effectively weighting both stages of the primary process in favor of hard-line candidates. Deep Green radio personalities singled out eleven New Tide-linked legislative hopefuls — including some of the DPP's best-known incumbents — for attack, calling them "traitors" and "bandits" and implying they were lackeys for Beijing. The *United Daily News* captured the effect of the party primary in an editorial: "The DPP has not only abandoned the swing voters but also carried out a ruthless internal purge. All the genes that code for diversity and reform have been removed" (DPP Abandons Swing Voters!).

Yet another complication was the timing of the legislative and presidential elections. Because they were just three months apart, the campaigns overlapped. As a result, the DPP seemed to suffer from split-personality disorder. Frank Hsieh, the presidential candidate, tried to project a moderate image, but he was continually undercut by hard-line statements from legislative candidates and the presidential office. Over the course of 2007, Chen unspooled a long string of Sino-phobic policies, from renaming national institutions to calling for a referendum to seek UN membership under the name "Taiwan".

The hard-line approach was even more pronounced at DPP headquarters, where Yu Si-kun led an effort to toughen the party's official pro-independence stance. When the party adopted a watered-down version of his proposal, Yu resigned, sniping that some in the party cared more about winning elections than protecting Taiwan. His departure opened the way for Chen Shui-bian to take over as party chair. Meanwhile, Frank Hsieh went into seclusion for two weeks, cancelling his campaign events and complaining that the debate had left him sick at heart.

The presidential candidate's two-week disappearance was but one event in a bizarre electoral season. The chaos in the DPP — the strategic wrangling between president and would-be president, the bad-mouthing of electable candidates by the lunatic fringe, the careening from one issue position to another — continued through to its disastrous conclusion. When the dust from the two elections had settled, the DPP was facing a complete collapse of its executive and legislative influence. The KMT wound up with 81 out of 113 seats; its coalition partners captured another four, bringing the Blue Camp to the brink of the three-fourths majority required to amend the constitution. The DPP won just 27 seats, and none of its Green Camp allies won any. As for the presidential election in March, Hsieh was never able to extricate himself from Chen's shadow, and he lost to the KMT's Ma Ying-jeou by a 58–42 percent margin.

Given the challenges it faced, the DPP did remarkably well in holding onto its traditional vote share. Its legislative candidates won more votes than in 2004, and its vote share increased in 18 of the island's 23 municipalities by an average of four percentage points. In a handful of cases, the negative influence of the DPP's pre-election infighting was evident,[3] but the real culprit was the new electoral formula. Under SNTV rules, the DPP would have held its own, but the new rules required the DPP to increase its vote share to a majority, which it was unable to do.

CONCLUSION

The Chen Shui-bian presidency was the best of times and the worst of times for the DPP. It offered the party an opportunity to try its hand at governing, but the Blue majority in the legislature stymied its efforts to translate its ideas into law. His presidency proved to the voters that a DPP-led government could solve problems and guide the nation through difficult times, but it subjected the Democratic Progressives' performance to a level of scrutiny they had never faced.

It thrilled and energized the party's supporters, but it exposed the infeasibility of cherished goals and dreams.

Perhaps the most damaging aspect of the Chen presidency for the DPP was that it cultivated antagonism within the party at the same time that it closed off channels for resolving tensions. The Democratic Progressives have always been fractious, cantankerous, and democratic. Out of power, they shared a common goal: gaining the authority to implement their ideals. The only way to achieve that goal was to cultivate a free market for ideas; to that end, the party institutionalized techniques that allowed debate, but also ensured that unity ultimately would triumph. These techniques included institutionalized factionalism and a democratic process for setting party strategies and programs.

After Chen Shui-bian was elected president, the pressures and opportunities of holding national office overwhelmed the party's structures. Suddenly, DPP officials controlled a vast array of resources — money, positions, appointments, nominations, policy initiatives — without any good way to allocate them. The price the presidential office set for gaining access to those resources was "protecting A-Bian". At first, it was easy enough to rally around the party's highest-ranking elected official, but as Chen's frustration mounted and his actions became more erratic and extreme, defending him against all charges grew harder. In the all-or-nothing political climate after the 2004 election — with KMT legislators launching recall petitions, PRC leaders excoriating Chen, even the U.S. president taking a critical line — even measured criticism from within the DPP was called treason. For a party raised on idealism, the need to close ranks around a clearly flawed leader was profoundly demoralizing.

After the 2008 elections the DPP continued to struggle with these issues. Once he lost the legal immunity of office, Chen Shui-bian was taken into custody and indicted for corruption. His slow-motion trial was a protracted nightmare for his DPP colleagues, who longed to put the Chen years behind them but still were loathe to hand their standard-bearer over to his (and their) enemies. They carried on their dreary debate over cross–strait policy, but without any illusion that it would translate into policy. Their only hope of influencing the direction of Taiwan's cross–strait strategy was to take to the streets to attack President Ma Ying-jeou's ideas.

A year after Ma's inauguration the DPP began to awake from its torpor and show signs of new life. Ideas for reconstructing the party — perhaps as the representative of the groups and individuals in Taiwan for whom cross–strait economic ties promise loss, not gain — began to appear in the press. Chairwoman Tsai Ying-wen confessed that the DPP had not always done a good job of welcoming Taiwanese of all backgrounds and promised to do better. The phrase "out of the shadow of Chen Shui-bian" began appearing with some frequency in media coverage of the DPP. Green-leaning think tanks began publishing essays with titles like "The Inconvenient Truth of China's Rise". Taiwan is a democracy, and its electoral rules encourage (virtually dictate) a two-party system. As the second-largest party, the DPP seems destined to survive, and eventually to rise again. But it is unlikely to return to national power until it learns to balance its ideals — above all its determination to promote a Taiwan that is as independent from China as it can be — with its need to win elections in a skeptical nation.

REFERENCES

Antiseptic becomes carcinogenic: New tide needs to learn some decency (*fangfuji bian zhiaiwu: Xinchaoliu ying zhi jintui*), 18 March 2007. http://enews.tacocity.com.tw/index.php3?action=history&url=/kent123/20070320125855.html.

Central Election Commission documents can be accessed at: www.cec.gov.tw.

Chu, Y-H (1997). The political economy of Taiwan's mainland policy. *Journal of Contemporary China*, 6(15) (July), 229–258 (Accessed on-line).

DPP Abandons Swing Voters! *United Daily News*, 18 May 2007. Translation at: http://www.kmt.org.tw/english/page.aspx?type=article&mnum=113&anum=3131.

Hsu, S-C (2009). *Yong shenlu daiti shenlu: miandui Zhongguo jueqi zheige bufangbian de shishi*. 8 June 2009, *Taiwan Xin Shehui Zhiku* (New Society for Taiwan Think Tank). 15 June 2009: http://www.taiwansig.tw/index.php?option=com_content&task=view&id=1482&Itemid=136.

Kuo, C-L (1998). *Minjindang zhuanxing zhi tong* (The DPP's painful transformation). Taipei: Tianhsia Publishing Company.

Rigger, S (2001). *From Opposition to Power: Taiwan's Democratic Progressive Party.* Boulder: Lynne Rienner Publishers.

Sutter, R (1988). *Taiwan Entering the 21st Century.* Lanham, MD: University Press of America.

ENDNOTES

1. Simulations of the new system that modeled the new rules and assumed no change in voters' party preference from 2004 to 2008 predicted the DPP would win substantially more seats than they did, suggesting that support for the DPP had declined.
2. The DPP swept Tainan City and Tainan County, won a one-seat edge in Pingtung County and tied the KMT in Chiayi County. KMT seats outnumber DPP seats in every other municipality in Taiwan. In 70 percent of Taiwan's municipalities (16 out of 23), the DPP won no seats at all.
3. An analysis of previous election results found 12 districts in which the DPP should have gained a majority, but did not. The DPP nominees in at least four of those districts were caught up in the factional infighting between New Tide and its opponents.

Chapter

4

Trust in Institutions and the Democratic Consolidation in Taiwan[1]

Huo-yan Shyu

INTRODUCTION

Democratic consolidation by definition implies that democracy has taken root; that is, those backbone institutions that sustain a working democracy have gained popular support and have been trusted by the people. Trust in democratic institutions is crucial for the functioning of democracy and the viability of democracy. Popular trust in political institutions is the pivotal component of democratic consolidation as it lends legitimacy to the nascent democratic regime (Diamond, 1999, 2002; Johnson, 2005; Luhiste, 2006; Mishler, and Rose, 1997, 2000). Ironically and paradoxically, a decline of political trust in established and new democracies has been accompanied by the worldwide expansion of democracy in the past two decades (Abramson, 1983; Catterberg and Moreno, 2005; Dogan, 2005; Hibbing and Theiss-Morse, 2001; Newton and Norris, 2000). What then are the origins of political trust in general, and institutional trust, specifically, is the focus concern for both politician and political scientist as well. (Catterberg and Moreno, 2005; Luhiste, 2006; Mishler and Rose, 2000).

Taiwan is a newly democratized society, and by 2008 it had twice experienced peaceful alternations of power: first, in 2000 the opposition party, Democratic Progressive Party (DPP), came in power and replaced the long-ruling party, the nationalist Kuomintang (KMT); then, in 2008 the KMT regained its power. What is the state of citizens' trust in institutions in this period of democratic consolidation? What are the origins of Taiwanese trust in political institutions? This chapter aims to explore these research questions to shed light on Taiwan's democratic consolidation by analyzing Taiwan's two waves of survey data made available by the Asian Barometer Survey (ABS).[2]

THE CONCEPT OF INSTITUTIONAL TRUST AND ITS CORRELATES

Trust is critical to social and public life intuitively and logically. Trust links people to people, people to institutions, and institutions to institutions. In a word, trust is an important socio-psychological concept serving as the base of society, the social virtue, and the social capital, with which social well-being, prosperity, and democracy are realized and enhanced (Bianco, 1994; Cook, 2001; Fukuyama, 1995; Hardin, 2006; Putnam, 1993; Warren, 1999). Trust in general has two main variants: social trust and political trust. Social trust refers to citizens' trust (or confidence) in each other as members of a social community, while political trust refers to citizens' trust in political terms. Political trust can be directed toward the political system and its organizations as well as the individual political incumbents. Political trust has long been studied theoretically (Easton, 1965) and empirically (Aberbach and Walker, 1970; Abramson, 1983; Citrin, 1974; Gamson, 1968; Miller, 1974), and of course it has shown its importance to the function of political systems and, especially, democratic government (Bianco 1994).

Institutional trust or trust in institutions[3] is a subset of political trust, and it refers to the degree of confidence that people have entrusted to the institutions of the country where they live. Therefore, the core objects of citizens' trust or confidence are specific political institutions such as the courts, the parliament, the political parties, the civil service, and other public institutions such as newspaper and television. People's institutional trust in Eastonian terminology is referred to as "specific" rather than "diffused" political trust.

THE ORIGINS OF INDIVIDUAL TRUST IN INSTITUTIONS

As Mishler and Rose (2001, 31), propose two theoretical traditions compete as explanations for the origins of individual trust in institutions. "Cultural theories hypothesize that trust in political institutions is exogenous. Trust in institutions is hypothesized to originate outside the political sphere in long-standing and deeply seeded beliefs about people that are rooted in cultural norms and communicated through early-life socialization". And, "Institutional theories, by contrast, hypothesize that political trust is politically endogenous. Institutional trust is the expected utility of institutions performing satisfactory.... it is a consequence, not a cause, of institutional performance" (Mishler and Rose, 2001, 31). What Mishler and Rose propose above is worthwhile enough to quote fully, and in the following I will take great advantage of their theoretical insights to formulate the hypotheses to be tested and to build a model of Taiwanese institutional trust. I will assess Taiwan's democratic consolidation through an empirical model of Taiwanese trust in institutions built on analyzing the survey data sets.

Working from Mishler and Rose's (2001) point of two competing theoretical traditions for the explanations of trust in institutions as well as empirical findings shown in their analysis of microlevel data collected in postcommunist societies, I thus formulate some hypotheses in the following to be tested with data collected in Taiwan about people's institutional trust. First, as cultural theory emphasizes, individual socialization is important to the formation of a generalized sense of trust or distrust in other people. Although the sources of this generalized interpersonal trust (and of a sense of "political" trust that is projected onto the political world) lie outside the political system, cultural theory clearly assumes that people who trust each other are more likely to cooperate with each other in forming both formal and informal institutions such as social clubs, bowling leagues, or community associations (Putnam, 1993, 2000). Deriving this hypothesis from the cultural origins of institutional trust, I select Taiwanese individuals' age, gender, education, income, and subjective social status as prior socialization variables to see how Taiwanese generalized socio-political characteristics leading to specific institutional trust are determined by these socio-demographic backgrounds. Therefore, I propose that Taiwanese individual origins of institutional trust are impacted by these backgrounds that confine an individual's track of socialization either directly or indirectly.

Second, generalized socio-political characteristics of individuals such as social capital (psychological plus group organizational links), democratic values, partisan orientation, political interest (or psychological involvement in politics), and political efficacy are often widely taken as determinants of deep-seated personal psycho-political traits for those attitudes toward political objects including political institutions in point. I propose and hypothesize that these prior leading generalized socio-political psychological characteristics also function as important predictors of individual institutional trust.

Third, Taiwanese institutional trust directly targets political institutions, and political trust or distrust in institutions is a rational response by individuals to the performance of institutions, as Mishler and Rose have pointed out in institutional theory (Mishler and Rose, 2001; Newton and Norris, 2000; North, 1990). In regards to how to detect the way in which people's institutional trust–distrust is leveled by their rational responses to the institutional performance, I then test how Taiwanese people's perception of both political and economic performance of a regime is related to or causally leads to their trust in institutions. First, a generalized indicator of political performance of the regime is people's satisfaction with democracy in general; and second, a more specific indicator is people's satisfaction with government. Third, the two criteria of the most critical dimensions, Taiwanese evaluation of freedom and equality, of democratization in Taiwan's and in other postauthoritarian societies are of course important for people to evaluate the political performance of the regime in the process of democratic transition and consolidation. As corruption is widely problematic in most transitional societies and heavily damages political stability in general, therefore, Taiwanese perception of corruption is necessarily considered as an important predictor to see how individuals' institutional trust is affected accordingly.

Fourth, people in their daily life are more concerned with their direct economic situations than the remote political world, and economic performance is one important function of the government and its governing institutions. Even if one is not a Marxist, it is quite reasonable to include economic factors in a proper explanatory model of people's trust in institutions. This is especially true in the case of Taiwan, where the peaceful alternation of power has been accompanied by an increasing economic deterioration due to the efforts of the DPP to reduce the economic links with Mainland China and to promote Taiwanese independent status in the world. Building on these economic factors as Taiwanese rational-economic determinants of their institutional trust, I follow the economic voting literature to test the individual's both "sociotropic" and "pocketbook" economic evaluations (e.g., Kieweit, 1983) as indicators of economic performance of the regime to see how these impact people's trust in institutions.

Finally, based on some findings about the origins of individual trust in institutions of Taiwanese, I will argue that Taiwan's democratic consolidation has been, is, and will be running to the point of no return. In so doing, I further show that Taiwan's democratic consolidation, which is embedded in the support for democracy generally and objects to nondemocratic alternatives specifically, is affected less by people's institutional trust and more determined by individual social and psycho-political factors.

THE DATA, MEASUREMENT, AND EXPLANATORY MODEL

The data sets I utilize in the following analysis are obtained from two waves of the ABS in Taiwan collected in 2001 and 2006. I capitalize on those available measurements to build those indicators used in my following analysis. First, socio-demographic variables are intuitively obvious without needing more words to specify. Socio-political characteristics such as social capital, democratic values, partisan orientation, political interest, and political efficacy are commonly used, and their measurements are listed in the Appendix, as are those for political performance and economic performance. Second, those applied as important indicators for democratic consolidation, such as support for democracy and objections to nondemocratic alternatives, are also common to democratization studies (see Appendix).[4]

The model of Taiwanese individual origins of institutional trust and democratization is built on testing how exogenous cultural theory and endogenous institutional theory factors in the explanation of Taiwanese trust in institutions and then links to democratic consolidation. The analytical model to be empirically explored is shown in Fig. 1. The core of the analysis reported in this chapter is twofold. The first step is to take people's individual trust in national, civil, and public institutions (either separately or together) as dependent variables to detect how those leading independent variables shown in Fig. 1 are causally related to people's trust in different kinds of institutions. The second step is to put two indicators of democratic consolidation, people's support for democracy and objection to authoritarian alternatives, as the final dependent variables, following the causal path drawn in Fig. 1, to detect the impact of those independent and intervening variables.

The following interpretation of Taiwanese individual origins of institutional trust unfolds as follows. First, I would like to show there is a decline of Taiwanese institutional trust between 2001 and 2006. Second, I would like to explore the nature of Taiwanese individual trust based on empirical measure items. Third, I shall examine how these different kinds of institutional trust — namely, trust in national institutions, trust in civil institutions, and trust in public institutions — are determined by the socio-demographic backgrounds, learned socio-political characteristics, and politico-economic performances of

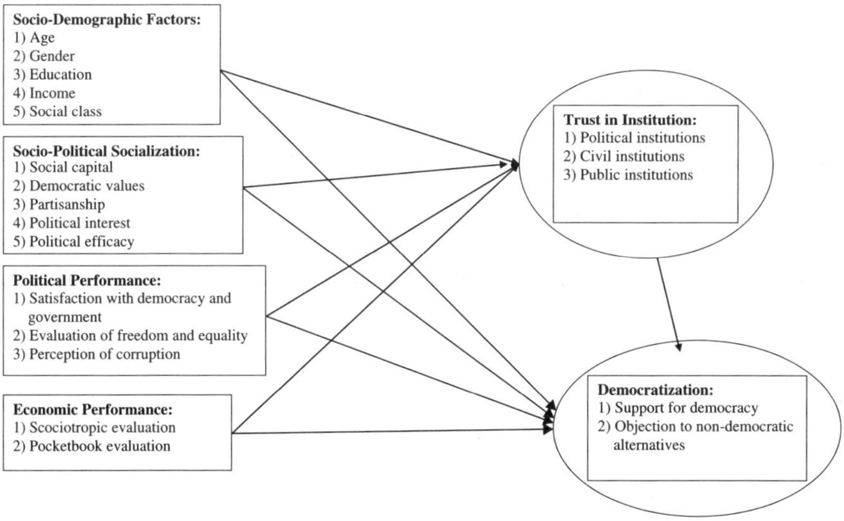

Figure 1: The analytic model of Taiwanese individual origins of institutional trust and democratic consolidation.

the regime. Finally, I hypothesize that all of these factors related to individual origins of institutional trust and those discernable patterns of institutional trust themselves have varied impacts on democratic consolidation in Taiwan.

THE DECLINE OF INSTITUTIONAL TRUST IN TAIWAN

First, let us look at the decline of institutional trust in Taiwan between 2001 and 2006, when the first peaceful power alteration happened, witnessed also in a parallel trend found in most established and other nascent democracies (Catterberg and Moreno, 2005; Dogan, 2005; Hibbing and Theiss-Morse, 2001; Newton and Norris, 2000). Table 1 shows people's trust in institutions as measured by how much they trust the courts, the national government, political parties, the parliament (the "Legislative Yuan" in Taiwan),

Table 1: Percentage of Trusting and Distrusting Institutions.

	2001 ($N = 1415$)			2006 ($N = 1587$)			Change in distrust (%)
Institutions	Trust* (%)	Neutral$ (%)	Distrust# (%)	Trust* (%)	Neutral** (%)	Distrust# (%)	2001–2006
Courts	41.3	17.1	41.6	30.6	11.4	58.0	+16.4
National govt.	39.4	13.4	47.2	34.7	10.1	55.2	+8.0
Political parties	15.8	15.1	69.2	15.4	11.0	73.6	+4.4
Parliament	18.3	13.6	68.1	19.4	9.0	71.6	+3.5
Civil service	52.4	12.2	35.4	52.6	7.4	40.0	+4.6
Military	58.5	15.2	26.3	53.0	11.2	35.8	+9.5
Police	45.3	8.1	46.6	46.6	4.7	48.7	+2.1
Local govt.	48.5	11.3	40.2	52.2	7.4	40.3	+0.1
Newspaper	32.2	13.5	54.3	24.8	11.8	63.3	+9.0
Television	41.2	8.5	50.3	29.4	6.9	63.6	+13.6
Election Commission	47.2	15.5	37.3	50.5	10.3	39.3	+2.0

Source: 2001 and 2006 ABS in Taiwan.

Note: Percentage is based on surveys in response to the following question: "I am going to name a number of institutions. For each one, please tell me how much trust do you have in them? Is it a great deal of trust, quite a lot of trust, not very much trust, or none at all?"

* Including "a great deal of trust" and "quite a lot of trust".

$ Including "not very much trust" and "none at all".

Including "don't understand the question", "can't choose" and "refuse to answer".

the civil service, the military, the police, local government, newspaper, television, and election commission.

First, as shown in Table 1, people's trusts in courts and in television have declined the most compared to that in other institutions between 2001 and 2006. The more stable institutional trust without large increases in distrust in this period is found in local government, police, parliament, and political parties. Second, in 2001, the lowest institutional trust is found in political parties (15.8% trusting and 69.2% distrusting) and parliament (18.3% trusting and 68.1% distrusting). These two institutional trusts remain the lowest in 2006, with 73.6% of people holding distrusting evaluations of political parties (15.4% trusting) and 71% of people showing distrust in parliament (19.4% trusting), though this distrusting trend is fairly stable with little increase in 5 years. Third, it is noteworthy that Taiwanese people lost a great deal of trust in newspaper and television, two nonpolitical institutions, between 2001 and 2006, the period of peaceful power alternation and of increasing open-party competition and more commercialization in such mass media. The increasingly market-oriented and liberalized mass media are experiencing a growing of distrust from their public audience and clients.

In sum, in Taiwanese cases of individual trust in institutions, we find a trend of declining popular trust in institutions similar to that found in other countries in the world. Two institutions — the courts and the television — have lost popular trust in stark magnitude in the process of democratic consolidation. And last but not least, two presumably nonpolitical institutions, newspaper and television, have unexpectedly lost their clients' popular confidence at the time of becoming more open to political parties.

THE NATURE OF TAIWANESE INSTITUTIONAL TRUST

There is a great deal of variation in the percentage of "trusting, neutral, and distrusting" individuals for each institution shown in Table 1. It is worthwhile to explore further the nature of Taiwanese individual trust in institutions. Is Taiwanese trust in different institutions unidimensional or multidimensional? If there are different kinds of institutional trusts in nature, what are they? To answer these research questions, an exploratory factor analysis is applied to analyze the interitem correlations among these measured institutions. As shown in Table 2, there are three patterns of institutional trust for both the 2001 and 2006 data sets. This finding shows that Taiwanese individuals trust in institutions as a whole, as measured by referring to the most important democratic institutions in Taiwan's postauthoritarian era. This shows the stability of mass psycho-political characteristics on one hand, and,

Table 2: Dimensions of Institutional Trust (Rotated Factors).

	2001 ($N = 1415$)			2006 ($N = 1587$)		
Institutions	1st factor	2nd factor	3rd factor	1st factor	2nd factor	3rd factor
National institutions	*				*	
Courts	0.534	0.284	0.036	0.394	0.591	–0.014
National government	0.587	0.369	–0.081	0.505	0.589	–0.098
Political parties	0.713	0.071	0.138	0.122	0.769	0.198
Parliament	0.755	–0.037	0.235	0.076	0.757	0.286
Civil institutions		**		**		
Civil service	0.133	0.684	0.079	0.684	0.150	0.154
Military	0.105	0.709	–0.020	0.715	0.156	0.045
Police	0.416	0.504	0.033	0.685	0.204	0.076
Local government	0.359	0.533	0.129	0.593	0.242	0.242
Election commission	–0.027	0.562	0.318	0.672	0.054	0.076
Public institutions			***			***
Newspaper	0.118	0.085	0.873	0.143	0.133	0.879
Television	0.154	0.137	0.858	0.146	0.153	0.872
Eigenvalue	3.361	1.398	1.097	4.043	1.451	1.038
% of variance	30.55	12.71	9.97	36.75	13.19	9.44
Total of variance		53.24			59.38	

Source: 2001 and 2006 ABS in Taiwan.

on the other hand, it also confirms that there are three discernable patterns of institutional trust as individual Taiwanese put their confidence and trust in different institutions.

According to the different governing institutions as measured items shown in Table 2, these distinguishable patterns of institutions are classified as “national institutions”, “civil institutions”, and “public institutions”. These name-tags are not only convenient for discussion, but they are appropriate also because they fit common understandings of Taiwanese in their daily political life. National institutions include the state government, the political parties, and the parliament (Legislative Yuan). Although there are courts at the local level, Taiwanese political minds cut across the democratic transition period and are more likely to point to an "independent judicial system" of the regime rather than to specific courts in the local level. Therefore, individual trust in "the courts, the national government, the political parties, and the parliament" as a factor is classified as the "trust in national institutions". Second, individual trust in "civil service, military, police, local government, and election commission" as a common factor is called the "trust in civil institutions".[5] In most countries, these institutions are represented by instrumental functionaries, and these positions in Taiwan are filled through an examination system rather than by political appointment. Finally, newspaper and television — whether they are publicly or privately owned — are all presumably functioning to improve or provide the "public" goods in nature. Therefore, individual trust in these mass media are termed "trust in public institutions".

In comparison, these patterns (or factors) of institutional trust are weighted differently with their importance in a global sense of Taiwanese "trust in institutions". Taiwanese trust in "national institutions" in 2001 was the most important dynamic, comprising the first factor of global institutional trust. However, in 2006 Taiwanese' trust in "civil institutions" became the most important component of their institutional trust, evidenced in "eigenvalue" and "total variance explained", reported in Table 2. This finding has implied two substantive meanings of democratic politics in Taiwan. First, in 2001 when an initial peaceful power alternation had just been realized, people's trust in national institutions focused on democratic institutions at the national level. Second, as time elapsed in the new DPP regime, Taiwanese people lost their confidence and sense of trust in all institutions shown in Table 1, and the core component of their general institutional trust was maintained mostly by civil institutions, which have been less politically tinted.

Finally, these three factors of institutional trust are fairly able to explain the individual's general trust in institutions, as Table 2 shows. More than half of the total variance of people's trust in institutions in 2001 (53.24%) and 2006 (59.38%) are well explained by these three factors. In the following, I will explore individual origins of people's trust in three kinds of institutions separately and as a whole.

THE INDIVIDUAL ORIGINS OF INSTITUTIONAL TRUST

As shown in Fig. 1, individual trust in institutions are hypothesized as the function of those leading factors such as socio-demographic backgrounds, socio-political characteristics, and politico-economic performances. These explanatory variables are expected to impact not only on people's general (composite) institutional trust, but also on specific trust in either national institutions, civil institutions, or public institutions.

First, concerning predictors for people's trust in national institutions, the individual's level of education, perception of corruption, and sociotropic evaluation of the national economy are three significant predictors; and their significant impacts on trust in national institutions remain consistent across different times. As reported in the result of ordinal least square (OLS) regression analysis of both 2001 and 2006 data sets in Table 3, people who are more educated are more likely to hold distrusting evaluation toward the national institutions. Those who perceive higher level of corruption of the government tend to have less trust in national institutions, and those whose vision of the national economy is rosier are more likely trust national institutions. In addition, people's trust in national institutions was also determined by their democratic values and evaluation of freedom in 2001; while in 2006, they were also affected by income, social status, partisanship, satisfaction with democracy and government, and their evaluation of equality. These variant causal links between people's socio-demographic backgrounds, socio-political characteristics, perceived politico-economic performances, and their trust in national institutions partially confirm both the cultural theory and the rational–institutional argument. However, if we further compare the magnitude of "bloc R^2 change" in each respective data set, it seems that people's trust in national institutions is predicted more by the factors of economic–institutional performance in 2001 and of politico-institutional evaluation in 2006. Both favor the endogenous view of individual trust in national institutions, predicted by institutional theory, that people's trust and distrust in institutions are

Table 3: OLS Estimations of Trust in National Institutions, Civil Institutions, and Public Institutions.

	National institutions		Civil institutions		Public institutions	
Predictors	2001	2006	2001	2006	2001	2006
Socio-demographical backgrounds						
Actual age (in years)	–0.012	–0.045	0.074*	0.108***	–0.111**	–0.036
Gender (male)	0.005	–0.070*	0.059	0.033	0.044	0.049
Level of education	–0.122**	–0.185***	0.028	0.106**	–0.032	–0.081*
Income quintile	–0.064	–0.065*	0.021	–0.038	–0.019	–0.019
Subjective social status	–0.061	0.057*	–0.045	0.013	0.019	–0.059
Bloc R^2 change	1.1%	3.0%	0.5%	0.9%	0.6%	0.7%
Socio-political characteristics						
Social capital	–0.023	–0.048	0.070*	0.125***	–0.081*	0.013
Democratic values	–0.125***	–0.040	–0.006	–0.047	–0.074*	–0.073*
Partisan orientation (pan-DPP)	0.008	–0.123***	0.022	0.013	–0.123***	–0.211***
Political interest	–0.055	–0.003	0.078*	0.058*	–0.009	0.046
Political efficacy	–0.026	0.009	0.038	–0.008	0.058	–0.034
Bloc R^2 change	1.6%	1.3%	0.8%	1.6%	2.1%	4.2%

(Continued)

Table 3. (*Continued*)

	National institutions		Civil institutions		Public institutions	
Predictors	2001	2006	2001	2006	2001	2006
Political performance						
Satisfaction with democracy/govt.	–0.028	0.195***	0.001	0.239***	0.085*	0.041
Evaluation of freedom	–0.072*	–0.021	0.067*	0.091***	–0.009	–0.036
Evaluation of equality	0.001	0.096**	–0.048	0.112***	–0.005	0.052
Corruption perception index	–0.153***	–0.095***	–0.285***	–0.128***	–0.063	0.034
Bloc R^2 change	2.3%	5.1%	8.0%	10.5%	0.7%	0.01%
Economic performance						
Sociotropic evaluation	0.189***	0.098**	0.069	0.086**	–0.011	–0.049
Pocketbook evaluation	0.054	0.059	–0.019	0.016	–0.008	0.020
Bloc R^2 change	3.9%	1.2%	0.2%	0.6%	–0.2%	–0.01%
Total adjusted R^2	12.9%	16.5%	13.8%	25.3%	3.7%	6.1%
Valid N	887	1,144	887	1,144	887	1,144

Source: 2001 and 2006 ABS in Taiwan.
*$p < 0.05$; **$p < 0.01$; ***$p < 0.001$.

endogenously determined by their assessment of institutional performance. Yet, cultural impacts on individual trust in national institutions are not trivial. Beyond educational effect, democratic values in 2001 and partisan orientation in 2006 are also significant determinants for people's institutional trust at the national level.

Taiwanese people who are more educated, more democratic oriented in 2001, and more partisan in 2006 are more likely to hold "critical" views about national institutions. Thus, these predictor variables are negatively linked to institutional trust at the national level (cf. Batto, 2005). As Norris (1999) points out, people of the winning camp are more likely to have higher institutional confidence in and offer support to the regime; however, our finding on the causal relationship between partisan orientation and institutional trust is totally different. In the DPP's second term in power, Taiwanese who felt more closely aligned with the governing party were more likely to show less trust in national institutions. However, this finding may well be understood if we closely examine the popularity of the DPP president, Chen Shui-Bian, during his second term. Chen's personal political credits were consumed quickly both among his fellow party supporters and among Taiwanese natives, mainly due to his blatant manipulation of institutional functions to serve his political purposes. The resulting declining trust in institutions (especially trust in courts) between 2001 and 2006 worsened as corruption and deterioration of the Taiwanese economic situation deepened under the DPP regime.

Trust in civil institutions is about people's confidence in government instruments or functionaries, so it is not surprising that we find less fluctuation and more stability in these variables in Table 1. Civil institutions such as civil service, military, police, local government, and election commission are less involved in partisan politics; therefore, people's trust in civil institutions may be more related to individual socio-cultural origins. As Table 3 shows, individual trust in institutions in both the 2001 and 2006 data sets are significantly affected by age, social capital, and political interest variables embedded in cultural theories of political trust. More importantly, political performance variables, such as evaluation of freedom and corruption levels in both 2001 and 2006, better predict individuals' trust in civil institutions.

In comparison, additional significant predictors must be added to the model of explaining trust in civil institutions for the 2006 data set, as shown in Table 3. Education, satisfaction with democracy and government, evaluation of equality, and sociotropic economic evaluation are additional explanatory factors for Taiwanese trust in civil institutions in 2006. This finding shows that the level of people's trust in civil institutions, although more stable between 2001 and 2006, has been affected more by political and economic performances that institutional theories assumed to be endogenous origins, such as satisfaction with democracy and government, evaluation of freedom and equality, and sociotropic evaluation. Additionally, looking at bloc R^2 change in Table 3, it is also fair to say that institutional effects — in terms of political performances — have a larger impact than cultural factors on individual trust in civil institutions, same as that in national institutions.

Public institutions are designated as newspaper and television, the two most popular mass media in the world. As Table 3 shows, only two significant predictor variables, democratic values and partisan orientation, have consistent impact on people's trust in mass media. These negative causal relationships point out that Taiwanese who are more democratic oriented and aligned with pan-DPP parties are more skeptical of the public role of mass media. This lack of confidence in public institutions in 2001 is deepened by age, social capital, and dissatisfaction with democracy and government; in 2006, the only additional significant variable is education. In sum, people's trust in mass media or public institutions is mainly affected by people's learned socio-political characteristics, democratic values, and partisan orientation. Reflecting on the Taiwanese political context in the period of democratic transition, these findings are quite understandable. That is, in earlier times the mass media were owned and dominated by the KMT. People's trust in public institutions, such as mass media, are mainly determined by socio-political characteristics, as evidenced by bloc R^2 change reported in Table 3. Cultural theory has more say than institutional theory concerning the origins of individual trust in public institutions, as measured by confidence in newspaper and television.

Finally, it is necessary to look at people's institutional trust as a whole. A composite index (a summation of factor scores) built on three factors of trust in national, civil, and public institutions is taken as a dependent variable to regress on those hypothesized explanatory variables. As shown in Table 4, three major explanatory variables — democratic values, corruption perception, and sociotropic evaluation — are significant determinants of general institutional trust across time. This pattern of relationship is similar to that found in the trust in national institutions. More specifically, Taiwanese general trust in institutions in 2001 was most affected by their perception of corruption and sociotropic evaluation of national economy, followed by democratic values, and finally gender. In 2006, Taiwanese general trust in institutions was determined by satisfaction with democracy and government, partisan orientation, evaluation of equality, perception of corruption, level of education, and sociotropic economic evaluations, income, and political interest in the order of impact magnitude.

As a tentative conclusion, based on either different patterns of institutional trust separately or general institutional trust in a composite index, Taiwanese institutional trust depends more on institutional factors than cultural origins. That is, first, politico-economic performances of the regime are more important and consistent predictors for individual trust in institutions in 2001 and 2006. Second, given the decline of individual trust in institutions between 2001 and 2006, general individual trust in institutions also depends on the regime's political performance factors, such as satisfaction with democracy, evaluation of equality, and perception of corruption. Finally, individual cultural factors, such as level of education, gender and income, and socio-political characteristics including democratic values, partisan orientation, and political interest, are also significant predictors for individual institutional trust in different patterns.

TAIWAN'S DEMOCRATIC CONSOLIDATION IN PERSPECTIVE

To explore Taiwan's democratic consolidation in the past decade, I turn to examine two empirical indicators based on available measured items (listed in the Appendix) in the 2001 and 2006

Table 4: OLS Estimations of Trust in Institutions (Composite).

	Institutions (composite)	
Predictors	2001	2006
Socio-demographical backgrounds		
Actual age (in years)	–0.030	0.018
Gender (male)	0.064*	0.009
Level of education	–0.072	–0.089**
Income quintile	–0.036	–0.071*
Subjective social status	–0.049	0.006
Bloc R^2 change	0.4%	1.1%
Socio-political characteristics		
Social capital	–0.020	0.055*
Democratic values	–0.119***	–0.094***
Partisan orientation (pan-DPP)	–0.057	–0.186***
Political interest	0.010	0.060*
Political efficacy	0.043	–0.020
Bloc R^2 change	1.2%	4.1%
Political performance		
Satisfaction with democracy/govt.	0.036	0.277***
Evaluation of freedom	–0.007	0.022
Evaluation of equality	–0.032	0.152***
Corruption perception index	–0.292***	–0.110***
Bloc R^2 change	8.1%	11.2%
Economic performance		
Sociotropic evaluation	0.141***	0.078*
Pocketbook evaluation	0.015	0.054
Bloc R^2 change	1.8%	0.9%
Total adjusted R^2	14.5%	26.1%
Valid *N*	887	1,144

Source: 2001 and 2006 ABS in Taiwan.
$^*p < 0.05$; $^{**}p < 0.01$; $^{***}p < 0.001$.

surveys. The first indicator is "support for democracy", and the second is "objection to nondemocratic alternatives". It is a truism that popular support for democracy and objection to nondemocratic alternatives are two important components for continuing democratization

(Rose *et al.*, 1998). Moreover, these two empirical indicators measure theoretically distinct underlying attitudes. Support for democracy refers to people's evaluation of democracy as a political system in terms of preference, capability, and priority, while objection to nondemocratic alternatives is designed to tap into people's attitudes toward possible nondemocratic options in resolving the problems. The former is positive and forward looking, and the latter is negative and backward calculation. These two visions of democracy reflect a long-term democratic culture on one hand and a short-term patience for the defects of democratic rule on the other.

First, as shown in Table 1, individual trust in institutions dropped sharply between 2001 and 2006. This begs the questions, is there a similar pattern for people's support for democracy and objection to nondemocratic alternatives in Taiwan? As reported in Table 5, the mean scores of people's support for democracy and objection to nondemocratic alternatives rose from 2001 to 2006. And the difference between the popular support for democracy in two survey years is statistically significant. This finding implies that, although popular trust declined in various aspects, there is no paralleled decline in individuals' democratic support and objection to nondemocratic alternatives. If popular support for democracy and objection to nondemocratic alternatives are conceived as solid signs for further democratization, Taiwan's democratization has definitely already passed the point of no return, though it has experienced political turmoil and economic downturn in the 2000s.

Second, as reported in Table 6, Taiwanese support for democracy is causally related to the level of education, democratic values, partisan orientation, political interest, sociotropic economic evaluation, and institutional trust at the national level for 2001 data. And in 2006, people's support for democracy is significantly predicted by variables such as level of education, democratic values, political efficacy, and satisfaction with democracy and government. Two explanatory variables clustered as cultural and socialization factors — level of education and democratic values — have a consistent impact on popular support for democracy between 2001 and 2006. It is conceivable that support for democracy is embedded more in cultural

Table 5: Mean Score of Indexes of Democratic Consolidation, 2001–2006.

Dataset		Support for democracy	Objection to nondemocratic alternatives
2001 data	Mean	5.4693	7.8148
	N	1,415	1,415
	Std. D	1.71036	1.53955
2006 data	Mean	5.6371	7.8633
	N	1,587	1,587
	Std. D	1.78599	1.49807
Total	Mean	5.5580	7.8404
	N	3,002	3,002
	Std. D	1.75246	1.51770
Eta coefficient		0.048	0.016
Significance		$p < 0.01$	n.s.

Source: 2001 and 2006 ABS in Taiwan.

values and the long-term socio-political socialization process. Therefore, individual trust in institutions has little impact on this generalized democratic support, except for the trust in "national institutions" found in the 2001 survey data. As shown in bloc R^2 changes in Tables 6 and 7, people's institutional trust (either treated in separate factors or in a combined index) has little impact on their support for democracy.

Third, Taiwanese objections to non-democratic alternatives has been consistently affected by individual level of education, democratic values, and political interest, as shown in Tables 6 and 7. In Taiwan, those people who are more educated, democratic-oriented, and more psychologically involved in politics are more likely to reject nondemocratic alternatives. Individuals' evaluation of freedom and perception of corruption are two additional predictors for Taiwanese antiauthoritarian tendencies in 2001, while age, income, social capital, evaluation of equality, and trust in national institutions are add-on predictors for Taiwanese rejection of nondemocratic alternatives in

Table 6: OLS Estimations of Support for Democracy and Objection to Nondemocratic Alternatives.

	Support for democracy		Nondemocratic alternatives	
Predictors	2001	2006	2001	2006
Socio-demographical backgrounds				
Actual age (in years)	0.036	0.042	–0.042	–0.072*
Gender (male)	0.055	–0.010	0.002	0.038
Level of education	0.088*	0.162***	0.094*	0.084*
Income quintile	0.030	0.025	0.036	0.090**
Subjective social status	–0.032	0.035	0.002	0.005
Socio-political characteristics				
Social capital	–0.037	0.020	0.050	0.057*
Democratic values	0.075*	0.122***	0.240***	0.283***
Partisan orientation (pan-DPP)	0.075*	–0.003	0.019	–0.009
Political interest	0.094**	0.047	0.115***	0.061*
Political efficacy	–0.022	0.061*	–0.012	0.033
Political performance				
Satisfaction with democracy/govt.	0.003	0.185***	0.033	0.046
Evaluation of freedom	0.045	0.059	0.080*	0.023
Evaluation of equality	–0.051	0.059	–0.047	–0.066*
Corruption perception index	–0.029	–0.020	–0.089**	–0.037
Economic performance				
Sociotropic evaluation	0.086*	0.062	–0.031	–0.017
Pocketbook evaluation	–0.031	0.003	0.053	–0.013
Trust in institutions				
National institutions	0.093**	0.029	–0.044	–0.084**
Civil institutions	0.022	0.022	–0.013	–0.016
Public institutions	0.004	0.021	0.017	–0.013
Bloc R^2 change	0.5%	–0.1%	0.001%	0.4%
Total adjusted R^2	5.1%	12.3%	15.7%	20.2%
Valid *N*	887	1,144	887	1,144

Source: 2001 and 2006 ABS in Taiwan.
$^{*}p < 0.05$; $^{**}p < 0.01$; $^{***}p < 0.001$.

Table 7: OLS Estimations of Support for Democracy and Objection to Nondemocratic Alternatives.

	Support for democracy		Nondemocratic alternatives	
Predictors	2001	2006	2001	2006
Socio-demographical backgrounds				
Actual age (in years)	0.038	0.042	−0.045	−0.069*
Gender (male)	0.053	−0.011	0.003	0.044
Level of education	0.081	0.161***	0.097*	0.094**
Income quintile	0.027	0.025	0.037	0.092**
Subjective social status	−0.036	0.036	0.004	0.001
Socio-political characteristics				
Social capital	−0.037	0.019	0.048	0.062*
Democratic values	0.070*	0.122***	0.242***	0.282***
Partisan orientation (pan-DPP)	0.080*	−0.003	0.015	−0.007
Political interest	0.090**	0.047	0.116***	0.064*
Political efficacy	−0.026	0.062*	−0.009	0.031
Political performance				
Satisfaction with democracy/govt.	−0.002	0.186***	0.036	0.041
Evaluation of freedom	0.041	0.059	0.082**	0.025
Evaluation of equality	−0.051	0.059	−0.047	−0.068*
Corruption perception index	−0.032	−0.020	−0.085*	−0.033
Economic performance				
Sociotropic evaluation	0.097*	0.062	−0.038	−0.021
Pocketbook evaluation	−0.027	0.003	0.051	−0.015
Trust in institutions (composite)	0.061	0.040	−0.018	−0.058
Bloc R^2 change	0.2%	0.1%	0.0%	0.2%
Total adjusted R^2	4.8%	12.5%	15.7%	20.0%
Valid N	887	1,144	887	1,144

Source: 2001 and 2006 ABS in Taiwan.
$^*p < 0.05$; $^{**}p < 0.01$; $^{***}p < 0.001$.

2006. It is noteworthy to point out two contrary findings in the 2006 data: first, people who evaluate the governmental treatment as more egalitarian are more likely to accept nondemocratic alternatives; and second, those who have more trust in national institutions tend to object significantly less to nondemocratic alternatives, as their causal relationships are in the negative direction.[6] Either in separate factors in Table 6 or in a composite indicator in Table 7, the magnitude of impact of people's trust in institutions on their attitudes toward objection to nondemocratic alternatives is statistically insignificant. In sum, Taiwanese antiauthoritarian orientations between 2001 and 2006 were mostly determined by their socio-demographic backgrounds and socio-political characteristics.

People's support for democracy and objection to nondemocratic alternatives are causally determined more by individuals' cultural and socialization factors and less by endogenous institutional factors. The least significant factor is people's trust in institutions. As shown, psychological dimensions of democratic consolidation — as measured by popular support for democracy and objection to authoritarian alternatives — are long-term learned or socialized politico-cultural values. These democratic supports would surely be positively reinforced by politico-economic performances of the regime. Second, institutional trust in Taiwan's democratization declined in the past decade; however, people's support for democracy and objection to authoritarian alternatives have been little affected by their institutional trust (Batto, 2005).

DISCUSSION AND CONCLUSION

Most established and nascent democracies have experienced a decline of political trust generally and institutional trust specifically. Taiwan is not exceptional, as it also witnessed an erosion of popular trust in institutions between 2001 and 2006. During this period, the people of Taiwan had just experienced its first peaceful power alternation and were under the governance of the self-proclaimed "native party", the DPP. Among the different institutional objects of trust — newspaper and television — two nonpolitical public institutions have experienced relatively larger declines in public confidence. It is noted that the marketization and liberalization of mass media during the democratization process have been accompanied by a loss of public confidence. That is, in a rapid opening of political and public space, the mass media, both public-owned and private-run, competed for business for clients from political parties. With no consensus for the public regulation of the media or the adoption of any ethical code that the media might use to discipline themselves the partisan stances taken to survive in the unforgiving marketplace have cost the mass media a significant degree of public confidence.

Taiwanese trust in institutions can be categorized empirically in three patterns, namely, national, civil, and public. We found different origins of people's institutional trust for each pattern. Taiwanese trust in national institutions is found to be more determined by institutional factors indexed by politico-economic performances than by socio-cultural characteristics. However, people's trust in public institutions is most affected by individuals' socio-political characteristics, including democratic values and partisan orientation. Institutional theory has stronger predictive power than cultural theory in explaining the individual differences in either institutional trust of different patterns or trust in institutions in general.

Two empirical indicators for democratic consolidation, "support for democracy" and "objection to nondemocratic alternative", are found to have increased from 2001 to 2006 as part of the tendency favoring the continuing democratization. Moreover, the increase in popular support for democracy is statistically significant. These findings show that Taiwan's democratization has reached the point of no return as popular support for democracy and objection to authoritarian alternatives have become integral parts of a growing democratic culture. The democratic culture, as political culture theory posits, is the solid basis of a viable working democracy.

Democratic consolidation, of course, is a complex political task for nascent democracies; as Diamond (1999) puts it, it involves necessarily the politico-economic performances of regime. Indeed, the causal relationship between regime performances and support for democracy or objection to nondemocratic alternatives is significant, although in different ways, in the different years of 2001 and 2006.

Finally, although we argue that the causal relationship between people's trust in institutions and indicators of democratic consolidation measured by support for democracy and objection to nondemocratic alternatives is not significant, it is not to imply that trust in institutions is not important at all to democratic consolidation. Rather, we point to the emerging worldwide ungovernable issue facing the established as well as nascent democracies. This is what the "critical citizen" thesis (Norris, 1999) tries to tackle in the postmodern society characterized by rapid communication through the Internet and a trend of globalization. As citizens have become more cognitively mobilized and critical, it is harder than ever to please them politically.

REFERENCES

Aberbach, JD and J Walker (1970). Political trust and racial ideology. *American Political Science Review*, 64(4), 1199–1219.

Abramson, PR (1983). *Political Attitudes in America: Formation and Change.* San Francisco: W. H. Freeman and Company.

Batto, NF (2005). *The Adverse Consequences of Trust in Government.* Annual Meeting of the Midwest Political Science Association, Chicago, April 7–10, 2005.

Bianco, WT (1994). *Trust: Representatives and Constituents.* Ann Arbor: University of Michigan Press.

Blind, PK (2006). Building trust in government in the twenty-first century: Review of literature and emerging issues. 7th Global Forum on Reinventing Government Building Trust in Government, June 26–29, 2007, Vienna, Austria.

Catterberg, G and A Moreno (2005). The individual bases of political trust: Trends in new and established democracies. *International Journal of Public Opinion Research*, 18(1), 31–48.

Citrin, J (1974). The political relevance of trust in government. *American Political Science Review*, 68, 973–988.

Cook, KS (ed.) (2001). *Trust in Society.* New York: Russell Sage Foundation.

Dalton, RJ (1999). Political support in advanced industrial democracies. In *Critical Citizens: Global Support for Democratic Government*, Norris, P (ed.), pp. 57–77. US: Oxford University Press.

Diamond, L (1999). *Developing Democracy: Toward Consolidation.* Baltimore: The Johns Hopkins University Press.

Diamond, L (2002). Consolidating democracies. In *Comparing Democracies 2: New Challenges in the Study of Elections and Voting,* LeDuc, L, RG Niemi and P Norris (eds.), pp. 210–227. Thousand Oaks: Sage Publications.

Dogan, M (2005). *Political Mistrust and the Discrediting of Politicians.* Leiden: Brill.

Easton, D (1965). *A System Analysis of Political Life.* New York: Wiley.

Fukuyama, F (1995). *Trust: The Social Virtues and the Creation of Prosperity.* New York: Free Press.

Gamson, WA (1968). *Power and Discontent.* Homewood, IL: The Dorsey Press.

Hardin, R (2006). *Trust.* Cambridge: Polity Press.

Hibbing, JR and E Theiss-Morse (2001). *What Is It About Government That Americans Dislike?* Cambridge: Cambridge University Press.

Johnson, I (2005) Political trust in societies under transformation: A comparative analysis of Poland and Ukraine. *International Journal of Sociology,* 35(2), 63–84.

Kiewiet, DR (1983). *Macro-Economics and Micro-Politics: The Electoral Effects of Economic Issues.* Chicago: The University Press.

Luhiste, K (2006). Explaining trust in political institutions: Some illustrations form Baltic States. *Communist and Post-Communist Studies,* 39, 475–496.

Miller, AH (1974). Political issues and trust in government: 1964–1970. *American Political Science Review,* 68, 951–72.

Mishler, W and R Rose (1997). Trust, distrust and skepticism: Popular evaluation of civil and political institutions in post-communist societies. *Journal of Politics,* 59(2), 418–451.

Mishler, W and R Rose (2000). What are the origins of political trust? Testing institutional and cultural theories in post-communist societies. *Comparative Political Studies,* 34(1), 30–62.

Newton, K and P Norris (2000). Confidence in public institutions: Faith, culture, or performance? In *Disaffected Democracies: What's Troubling the Trilateral Countries?* Pharr, SJ and RD Putnam (eds.), pp. 52–73. Princeton, NJ: Princeton University Press.

North, DC (1990). *Institutions, Institutional Change, and Economic Performance.* New York: Cambridge University Press.

Putnam, RD (1993). *Making Democracy Work: Civic Traditions in Modern Italy.* Princeton, NJ: Princeton University Press.

Putnam, RD (2000). *Bowling Alone: The Collapse and Revival of American Community.* New York: A Touchstone Book, Published by Simon & Schuster.

Rose, R, W Mishler and C Haerpfer (1998) *Democracy and Its Alternatives: Understanding Post-Communist Societies.* Baltimore: The Johns Hopkins University Press.

Warren, ME (ed.) (1999). *Democracy and Trust.* Cambridge: Cambridge University Press.

APPENDIX

Measures and Coding of Variables and Indicators.

Variables/Indicators	Measures/Coding
Age	Age in years
Gender	1 = male; 0 = female
Level of education	10-point scale: 1 = no formal education; 2 = incomplete elementary school; 3 = complete elementary school; 4 = incomplete middle school; 5 = complete middle school; 6 = incomplete high school; 7 = complete high school; 8 = some university education; 9 = university education completed; 10 = post-graduate degree.
Income quintile	5-point scale of monthly household income: 1 = lowest quintile and 5 = highest quintile.
Subjective social status	10-point numerical scale (form 1 = lowest status to 10 = highest status)
Social capital	Composite index build on following two measures: (1) *General speaking, would you say most people can be trusted or that you must be very careful?* (1 = you must be very careful in dealing with people; 3 = most people can be trusted; 2 = other response) (2) *Are you a member of any organization or formal group?* (1 = less or equal one; 2 = two; 3 = three)
Democratic values	Summated scale of the 5-point "agree-disagree" measure items: (1) *People with little or no education should have as much say in politics as highly educated people* (5 = strongly agree; 1 = strongly disagree). (2) *Government leaders are like the head of a family; we should all follow their decisions* (1 = strongly agree; 5 = strongly disagree). (3) *The government should decide whether certain ideas should be allowed to be discussed in society.* (4) *Harmony of the community will be disrupted if people organize lots of groups.* (5) *When judges decide important cases, they should accept the view of the executive branch.* (6) *If the government is constantly checked by the legislature, it cannot possibly accomplish great things.*

(*Continued*)

(*Continued*)

Variables/Indicators	Measures/Coding
	(7) *If we have political leaders who are morally upright, we can let them decide everything.* (8) *If people have too many different ways of thinking, society will be chaotic.*
Partisan orientation (pan-DPP)	Constructed index based on two measure items: (1) *Which party if any do you feel closest to?* (2) *How close do you feel to the party?* (5 = very close to DPP or TSU; 4 = moderate close to DPP or TSU; 3 = non-partisan; 2 = moderate close to KMT, PFP, or NP; 1 = very close to KMT, PFP, or NP)
Political interest	A summated index based on two 4-point scale measure items: (1) *How interested would you say you are in politics?* (2) *How often do you follow news about politics and government?* (1 = not very interested/often; 4 = very interested/often)
Political efficacy	A summated index based on two 5-point scale measure items: (1) *I think I have the ability to participate in politics* (5 = strongly agree; …1 = strongly disagree) (2) *Sometimes politics and government seems so complicated that a person like me cannot really understand what is going on.* (1 = strongly agree; ... 5 = strongly disagree)
Satisfaction with democracy/govt.	A summated index based on two 5-point scale measure items: (1) *On the whole, how satisfied or dissatisfied are you with the way democracy works in Taiwan.* (2) *How satisfied or dissatisfied are you with the [name of present] government?* (1 = very dissatisfied; … 5 = very satisfied)

(*Continued*)

(*Continued*)

Variables/Indicators	Measures/Coding
Evaluation of freedom	A summated index built on two measure items: (1) *People are free to speak what they think without fear.* (2) *People can join any organization they like without fear.* (5 = strongly agree; ...1 = strong disagree)
Evaluation of equality	Measured item: *Everyone is treated equally by the government.* (5 = strongly agree; ...1 = strong disagree)
Corruption perception index	A summated index based on two 4-point scale measures: (1) *How widespread do you think corruption and bribe-taking are in your local/municipal government?* (2) *How widespread do you think corruption and bribe-taking are in the national government?* (1 = hardly anyone is involved; 2 = not a lot of officials are corrupt; 3 = most officials are corrupt; 4 = almost everyone is corrupt)
Sociotropic economic evaluation	A composite index based on three 5-point scale measures: (1) *How would you rate the overall economic condition of our country today?* (1 = very bad; 2 = bad; 3 = so and so; 4 = good; 5 = very good) (2) *How would you describe the change in the economic condition of our country over the last years?* (3) *What do you think will be the state of our country's economic condition a few years from now?* (1 = much worse; 2 = a little worse; 3 = about the same; 4 = a little better; 5 = much better)
Pocketbook economic evaluation	A composite index based on three 5-point scale measures: (1) *As for your own family, how do you rate your economic situation today?* (1 = very bad; 2 = bad; 3 = so and so; 4 = good; 5 = very good) (2) *How would you compare the current economic condition of your family with what it was a few years ago?*

(*Continued*)

(*Continued*)

Variables/Indicators	Measures/Coding
	(3) *What do you think the economic situation of your family will be a few years from now?* (1 = much worse; 2 = a little worse; 3 = about the same; 4 = a little better; 5 = much better)
Trust in institutions	*How much trust do you have in the following institutions:*
	(1) the courts; (2) the national government; (3) political parties; (4) parliament; (5) civil service; (6) the military; (7) the police; (8) local government; (9) newspapers; (10) television; (11) the election commission. (1 = none at all; 2 = not very much trust; 3 = quite a lot of trust; 4 = a great deal of trust)
Support for democracy	A composite index built on three measure items:
	(1) *Which of the following statements comes closest to your own opinion?* — *Democracy is always preferable to any other kind of government* (=3). — *Under some circumstances, an authoritarian government can be preferable to a democratic one* (=1). — *For people like me, it does not matter whether we have a democratic or a nondemocratic regime* (=2).
	(2) *Which of the following statements comes closer to your own view?* — *Democracy cannot solve our society's problems* (=1). — *Democracy is capable of solving the problems of our society* (=3) (*other* = 2).
	(3) *If you had to choose between democracy and economic development, which would you say is more important?* (1 = economic development is definitely more important or economic development is somewhat more important; 3 = Democracy is somewhat more important or democracy, is definitely more important; 2 = they are both equally important)

(*Continued*)

(*Continued*)

Variables/Indicators	Measures/Coding
Objection to non-democratic alternatives	A summated index based on two 5-point scale measure items: (1) *We should get rid of parliament and elections and have a strong leader decide things;* (1 = strongly agree; ....5 = strongly disagree) (2) *The army should come in to govern the country.* (1 = strongly approve; ...5 = strongly disapprove)

ENDNOTES

1. Originally, this is a conference paper read at the 2008 Annual Meeting of the American Political Science Association, Boston, Massachusetts, August 28–31, 2008. I thank my discussant Professor Tung-Jen Cheng for a helpful comment and also extend my gratitude to anonymous referees, who gave me some very useful ideas for revising.
2. The ABS represents the region's first collaborative initiative to develop a regional network of democracy studies based on surveying ordinary citizens. Between June 2001 and February 2003, the ABS implemented its first-wave comparative survey in eight Asian countries and territories, namely, Japan, South Korea, Mongolia, Taiwan, the Philippines, Thailand, Hong Kong, and China. The ABS launched its second-wave survey in October 2005 and its geographical scope was enlarged to cover five more countries in the region. By June 2008 the fieldwork in Japan, Hong Kong, South Korean Mongolia, Taiwan, the Philippines, Thailand, Indonesia, Singapore, Vietnam, and Malaysia was completed. All ABS data were collected through face-to-face interviews of randomly selected eligible voters in each participating country. Interested readers are welcome to browse the project's Web site (www.asianbarometer.org) for methodological details.
3. In the following, I use "institutional trust", "trust in institutions", and "confidence in institutions" interchangeably, because they are literally conveying the same meanings.
4. If readers are interested in "measures and coding of variables and indicators" of this study, please contact the author at (hyshyu@gate.sinica.edu.tw) for further details.
5. It is kind of awkward to name it here as "trust in civil institutions" to include "military" as one of its component. However, as people's trusting or distrusting

orientation toward "civil institutions" are highly correlated and concurred with that toward "military". Essentially, it should be more a shortened name to tag a factor of people's trust in "civil–military" institutions.

6. Batto (2005) also showed this relationship in his paper analyzing the survey data from five new democracies in East Asia, including Korea, Mongolia, the Philippines, Taiwan, and Thailand and argues that a higher level of trust indicates a greater willingness to delegate the power without imposing the controls on that power.

Part II

Political Economy

Chapter

5

Taiwan Enters the 21st Century: A Rude Awakening to the Costs of Success

Cal Clark and Alexander C. Tan

From the vantage point of the mid-1990s, Taiwan appeared to represent a pronounced, if not spectacular, international success story. As early as the late 1970s, Taiwan's rapid industrialization and record of "growth with equity" had been widely termed an "economic miracle" (Chan and Clark, 1992; Galenson, 1979; Gold, 1986; Wade, 1990). In the political realm, while development had been clearly retarded by the authoritarian Kuomintang (KMT) regime, Taiwan went through a remarkably smooth and consensual democratic transition between the mid-1980s and mid-1990s (Chao and Myers, 1998; Cheng and Haggard, 1992; Chu, 1992; Copper, 1997; Rigger, 1999; Tien, 1989, 1996). Yet, the country was soon to "enter troubled waters" marked by growing conflict with and threat from the People's Republic of China (PRC), fears about the "hollowing out" of its previously vaunted economy, and vicious polarization and gridlock in its domestic politics (Clark, 2006). This chapter argues that the challenges facing Taiwan in the early 21st century derive from unanticipated and unintended costs of its previous successes. The first part provides a summary conceptualization of the country's very successful development; the second presents a model of how several central characteristics of this development pattern created problems for the future development of Taiwan; and the third discusses several political and economic controversies in more detail.

TAIWAN'S DEVELOPMENTAL SUCCESS

Given the difficulties in achieving structural transformations from one type of economy and society to another, perhaps the most impressive facet of Taiwan's development has been that the country has successfully negotiated several sharp structural transformations with what, in retrospect, appears to be surprisingly few problems. In particular, five periods of major structural transformation can be discerned. The first four encompassed Taiwan's successful industrialization and democratization, while the last is more open-ended as several "costs of success" have emerged in the country's political economy.

During the first stage in the 1950s, Taiwan developed beyond a basically agricultural economy. A dramatic land reform and a decade of import-substitution enhanced the ROC's productive capabilities in agriculture and light industry; mass education created human capital; and the government substantially increased its economic leadership capability by bringing skilled technocrats into the top levels of the regime (Galenson, 1979; Lin, 1973). Despite the initial success of this transformation, import-substitution soon reached its inevitable high point with the local market saturation of light industrial goods, setting off a new challenge for Taiwan. The resources accumulated during this first stage then formed the foundation for a new transformation to exporting light industrial products in the 1960s. The technocrats conceived and implemented major policy changes which made this transformation possible, while its success rested on the human capital that had been developed in the work force and business community (Chan and Clark, 1992; Galenson, 1979; Gold, 1986;

Wade, 1990). Hence, strangely, advocates of both neoclassical economics (Linder, 1986) and state-led development (Amsden, 1985; Wade, 1990) could point to the Taiwan case during this era for evidence confirming their clashing models.

Just as with import-substitution, the success of Taiwan's export-led strategy contained the seeds of its own destruction in the sense that the island's rising prosperity and wages began to price it out of the world economy niche of low-cost manufactured products. Economically, the country responded to this new challenge with two somewhat disparate transformations: first, a state-led push into heavy industry (e.g., steel and petrochemicals); second, the small-scale business sector began to upgrade its production techniques (Fields, 1995; Kuo, 1995; Noble, 1998; Wade, 1990). Also, considerable change occurred in the political and social realms as well with the emergence of a strong middle class (Cheng, 1990; Hsiao, 1991) and a growing role for electoral politicians (Clark, 1989; Copper, 1988, 1997; Tien, 1989).

The next structural transformation commenced in the mid-1980s and was completed about a decade later. Economically, Taiwan emerged as a major player in the global high tech industry (e.g., ranking third in the semiconductor production as the new millennium opened) and saw a correspondingly massive movement to offshore production, primarily to the PRC, in its traditional labor-intensive industries as the increasingly prosperous nation priced itself out of this niche in the global economy (Leng, 1996; Wang, 1992; Wu, 1995). Unlike earlier eras, though, economic change was probably dwarfed by the transformation of the polity, as Taiwan went through a very successful democratic transition that was pushed both by reformers within the KMT government and by the opposition Democratic Progressive Party (DPP), which was founded in 1986 (Chao and Myers, 1998; Cheng, 1989; Cheng and Haggard, 1992; Chu, 1992; Copper, 1997; Hood, 1997; Moody, 1992; Rigger, 1999; Tien, 1989, 1996; Wu, 1995a).

Unfortunately for Taiwan, economic and political change did not end in the mid-1990s. Its basic industries, even high-tech ones, continued to be squeezed by new competitors, such as China.

Consequently, the nation is being forced into a new transformation to a much more information-focused economy with a growing emphasis on innovation and competition with the most advanced economies in the world, where the competitiveness of its political economy is much more problematic (Wong, 2010). Politically, Taiwan's democracy has certainly become consolidated, but it is now marked by vicious partisan polarization (see the section on "The Rise of Identity Politics" below) which certainly inhibits effective response to the challenges presented by the new economic transformation.

This discussion suggests the following pattern or model of successful structural transformation in Taiwan. At each stage, significant economic, social, and political change occurred which resulted in the creation of significant new societal resources. These resources, in turn, formed the basis for the upgrading of the island's political economy in the next stage. The observance of such a recurring pattern, however, should not be taken to mean that Taiwan has followed an explicit grand design since the early 1950s. Rather, Taiwan's development appears to have been much more open-ended with the resources created at one stage permitting more sophisticated responses when subsequent economic challenges have arisen.

INSTITUTIONAL LEGACIES AND THE COSTS OF SUCCESS FOR TAIWAN

Institutionalist theory argues that fairly permanent economic structures and policy-making arrangements create "institutions" which shape future policy-making and economic performance to a considerable extent (March and Olsen, 1989; North, 1990). This perspective suggests that it might be valuable to look for economic and political institutions that evolved during Taiwan's development which may have inhibited the county's adaptability after the mid-1990s. Two such institutions stand out, one in the polity and one in the economy. Taiwan's government had long been dominated by strong authoritarian leaders, such as Chiang Kai-shek and his son Chiang Ching-kuo. While the move to an electoral democracy in the late 1980s and early 1990s went smoothly (Rigger, 1999; Tien, 1996), the give-and-take of normal democratic policy-making had not been established; indeed, the institutional legacies from the past seemed to push the nation toward a fairly dysfunctional politics. Economically, the export boom at the center of Taiwan's rapid industrial transformation had been dominated by small and medium enterprises (SMEs), which from the 1960s through the 1980s had proven to be extremely entrepreneurial, flexible, and efficient (Lam and Clark, 1994). Yet, by the mid-1990s, these firms were finally beginning to hit economic barriers that undercut their economic dynamism and competitiveness.

Figure 1 sketches the dynamics by which these two institutional legacies set off dynamics that brought very considerable challenges to Taiwan. The authoritarian tradition blurred governmental lines of authority and helped stimulate very personalistic politics. These factors, in turn, had several deleterious consequences for policy-making in Taiwan, as indicated in the top part of Fig. 1: (1) never-ending conflict and gridlock; (2) corruption and the politicization of supposedly technical policy realms, like financial regulation; and (3) the eruption of divisive cultural and identity politics as the centerpiece of party competition. In the economic sphere, limitations on the further

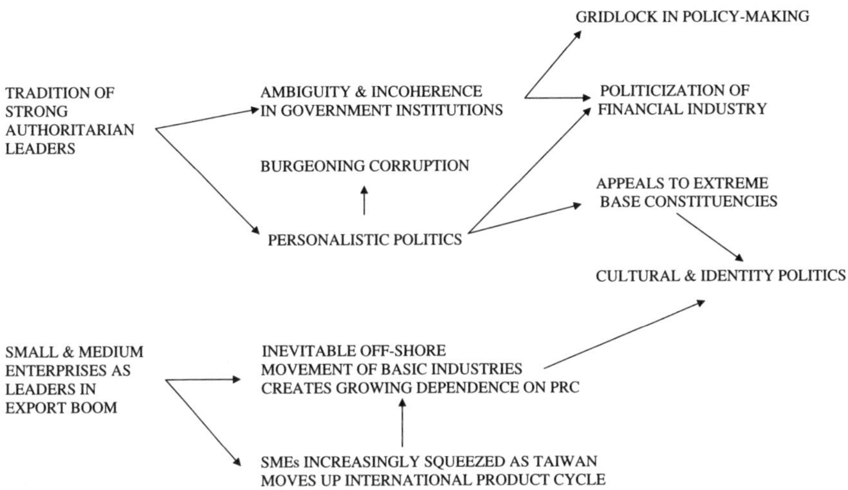

Figure 1: How the institutional legacies of Taiwan's development created "costs of success".

development of most SMEs inhibited their ability to upgrade as Taiwan became an increasingly post-industrial society. As outlined in the bottom of Fig. 1, this probably helped to accelerate the movement of Taiwan industry to China, creating an integrated cross–strait economy that increased Taiwan's dependence on its implacable political rival. Moreover, the growing importance of the PRC for Taiwan's domestic economy raised fears about the "China threat" that exacerbated identity politics at home, thereby linking the economic and political processes summarized in the diagram.

Taiwan's government was structured by the 1946 Constitution of the Republic of China, which reflected Sun Yat-sen's advocacy of political institutions with five basic branches, which made the government somewhat more complex, if not more convoluted, than most democratic regimes. While the Constitution itself promised a democratic polity, in fact the authoritarian party-state of the Nationalist or KMT Party headed by a strong autocratic leader implemented the constitution. Consequently, for most of its postwar history, the government of Taiwan functioned much more by informal authoritarian rule than by rule-bound democratic processes. In addition, the actual lines of authority and responsibility among major leaders and institutions, such as the President, the Premier, and the Legislative Yuan, remained somewhat ambiguous and undefined (Clark, 1989; Copper, 2009). With the growth of more competitive party politics in the late 1990s, this institutional ambiguity and incoherence made policy-making more difficult and undoubtedly contributed to the political gridlock that has marked Taiwan for the last decade.

Another consequence of the authoritarian era, with its contempt for democratic norms and rules, has been a highly personalistic politics in which informal connections or *guanxi* predominate and politicians become fairly independent entrepreneurs. As sketched in the middle of Fig. 1, this has set off several untoward chains of consequences. First, the surge in corruption, such as the black and gold politics of the Lee Teng-hui era (Cheng and Chang, 2003; Lu, 2002) and the scandals that engulfed Chen Shui-bian at the end of his presidency (Chu, 2007; Gold, 2009), clearly reflect personalistic politics and a lack of political institutionalization. Second, several seemingly technical policy realms, such as the country's financial system, have become politicized during the last two decades with rather questionable and mixed results for good administration (see the case study in the next section). The third and probably most momentous impact of personalistic politics has been the growing tendency of politicians to appeal to fairly radical "base constituencies" (e.g., the "deep Greens" and the "deep Blues"), especially during campaigns (Clark, 2006). This has also been at least partially stimulated by the legislative election system in which candidates run in multi-member districts where citizens can only cast one vote, so that only fairly small minorities are required for victory (Rigger, 1999). As described in a case study in the next section, this has fueled the explosion of cultural and identity politics this decade, which has led to a hostile and polarized party system.

The political effects in this model are somewhat perverse and debilitating for Taiwan. The economic dynamics, while mixed, appear to be less challenging, at least before the global economic crisis that erupted in 2008. As detailed in a case study in the next section, Taiwanese SMEs are increasingly challenged. Still, they performed extremely well even in the early high tech period and clearly were the backbone of Taiwan's "economic miracle" (Greenhalgh, 1988; Kuo, 1995, 1998; Lam and Clark, 1994; Skoggard, 1996). The balance sheet for the "Mainland revolution" in Taiwan's economic relations is also hard to calculate. The loss of many basic industries is simply a part of successfully climbing the international product cycle. A clear division of labor has emerged between Taiwan and China that has integrated their economies (Clark, 2007; Naughton, 1997; Wu, 1995b). Though such growing dependence on a political rival is certainly worrisome, the actual economic effects have yet to be clearly harmful to Taiwan. What is clear, however, is that cross–strait economic ties are perceived in an extremely polarized manner, with deep Blues seeing such issues as the 2008 opening of the "three direct links" as Taiwan's salvation, while deep Greens see them as a major step toward Taiwan's destruction by China (Gold, 2009).

THREE CASE STUDIES OF CHALLENGES TO TAIWAN

Our model of Taiwan's "costs of success" has of necessity been fairly abstract and summary. In this section, hence, we present three case studies of challenges facing the country that were included in Fig. 1 above. The first concerns the rise of identity politics as the central cleavage in Taiwan; the second describes how the financial system became politicized; and the third discusses the growing problems of SMEs.

THE RISE OF IDENTITY POLITICS

The current contribution of the rise of identity politics to the vicious polarization in Taiwan reflects a "cost of success" of Taiwan's delayed democratization. Over the 1970s and 1980s, political opposition advocated the end of the KMT's authoritarian rule. At one level there was an appeal to universal norms of democracy, while at a more implicit level (because of authoritarian repression of freedom of speech) there was an appeal for ethnic justice (Gold, 1986; Wachman, 1994). With the achievement of democracy, democratization per se ceased to be an important issue. In addition, economic development policy never became a central cleavage in Taiwan's politics, presumably because of the country's very successful industrialization; and partisan divisions over social welfare policy were fairly muted as well, leaving national identity as the central cleavage dividing the two major parties (Clark, 2002).

Since the evacuation of the Chiang Kai-shek regime to Taiwan in 1949 at the end of the Chinese Civil War, the island has suffered from a clear ethnic cleavage between the Mainlanders who came with Chiang (about 15 percent of the population) and the long-time residents of Taiwan, or Islanders who were almost all ethnically Han Chinese. The Mainlanders dominated the government and imposed a harsh and repressive rule termed the "White Terror". However, Islanders dominated the economy (Brown, 2004; Gold, 1986; Phillips, 2006; Wachman, 1994). The advent of democracy raised the serious possibility that Taiwan's polity could be split by the ethnic cleavage between the Islander majority and the old ruling Mainlander minority on two interlinked but distinct issues regarding the country's national identity: (1) rejection of the Mainlander-dominated political regime; and (2) growing hostility toward and the absolute rejection of China's claim to sovereignty over Taiwan, which was at least tacitly supported by the KMT's policy of "Mainland Recovery". Ironically perhaps, this split did not occur when democratization ended the repression of discussing these issues in the early 1990s. Rather, ethnic polarization became much more pronounced only after the turn of the century.

As the 1990s opened, both the DPP and KMT seemingly placed opposing bets on how the citizens of Taiwan, who were being increasingly empowered by the country's democratization, would respond. The DPP bet that the end of authoritarian controls would permit Islander resentments to be expressed, winning over voters to the DPP as the champion of Taiwanese nationalism. For example, the DPP added support for Taiwan Independence to its Charter in 1991. Conversely, the KMT bet that the satisfaction of the general population with the prosperity created by Taiwan's "economic miracle" would make them supportive of the political status quo both domestically and in cross–strait relations with China. Thus, the KMT continued to adhere to their version of the "One China" principle that Taiwan represented as the legitimate government of all China. A little thought, though, would have suggested that neither of these bets were particularly well placed. On the one hand, the KMT's strong performance at the polls in the late 1980s and early 1990s demonstrated the dubiousness of the DPP's assumption that it could ride to power on a wave of Taiwanese nationalism. On the other hand, the KMT both ignored signs of the large majority's growing resentment against the treatment of Taiwanese culture and language as second class and failed to realize that democratization would make the maintenance of official myths unsustainable (Clark, 2006).

Therefore, in such a situation of two less than desirable alternatives, the potential opened up for a creative policy entrepreneur to transcend the existing policy debate. President Lee Teng-hui responded to this opportunity with what appeared to be inspired statesmanship as he managed to straddle the national identity issue quite astutely, implicitly portraying himself as a moderate between the pro-Independence DPP and the pro-Unification "old" KMT. He also ended the Mainlander monopoly on power at the top levels of the party and effectively "localized" the KMT as a political organization (Lin and Tedards, 2003). For its part, the DPP began to moderate its position on Taiwan Independence in the mid-1990s as well, in part because a radical image on this issue seemed to be limiting its popularity. Additionally, the moderation reflected the realization after the Taiwan Strait crisis of 1995–1996 that China would never allow Taiwan to proclaim *de jure* Independence. Consequently, some (but far from all) DPP leaders began to argue that Taiwan was already an independent nation, making a Declaration of Independence immaterial (Rigger, 2001; Wang, 2000). This moderation and even convergence of positions reached its peak in the 2000 presidential elections when the three primary candidates (Chen Shui-bian of the DPP, Lien Chan of the KMT, and James Soong who ran as an Independent after not being picked for the KMT ticket) took surprisingly similar positions on cross–strait relations, as all claimed that they would protect and promote Taiwan's sovereignty while not needlessly provoking the PRC by, for instance, declaring Independence (Clark, 2000).

An increasing emphasis on national identity in Taiwan's politics followed the election of Chen Shui-bian, but the process by which this occurred was not exactly straightforward. Initially, Chen took a moderate position toward the PRC, a moderation which the Chinese refused to reciprocate. Then, in the summer of 2002, Chen radically changed positions when he advocated the concept of one country on each side of the Taiwan Strait, which infuriated Beijing and clearly strained relations with Washington (Rigger, 2003). Chen's motivation was somewhat unclear, though. Had he become frustrated by Chinese intransigence? Did he feel freer to express his long-cherished beliefs as he gained a stronger grip on power? Or, had he become something of a prisoner to the "base constituency" of the DPP which saw national identity and ethnic justice as the overriding issues in Taiwan?

In the somewhat less visible sphere of domestic politics, Chen had already begun to implement policies in line with Taiwanese nationalism. The administration used its executive power to promote what it called a "Taiwanese subjectivity" that certainly was aimed at its base constituency. Lee (2004), for example, has argued that Chen promoted a "cultural revolution" (with intentional reference to Mao's Cultural Revolution) that included such initiatives as changing the name of many agencies and organizations to stress "Taiwan", promoting Taiwanese in language policy, revising the official policy toward the mass media to reverse the previous KMT domination of outlets (including the encouragement of underground radio stations), and changing the educational policy focus from Chinese to Taiwanese history. Lynch (2004) has termed this a "self-conscious nation-building project", indicating that Chen and the pan-green bloc were trying to create a new nation rooted in Taiwanese history and culture.

Changes in Taiwan's party system following the 2000 presidential elections also promoted the polarization in identity politics, in particular the partial break-up of the KMT. Hostility between Soong supporters and KMT loyalists led Soong to create a new party in 2000, the People First Party (PFP). Moreover, Lien Chan pushed out Lee Teng-hui, his former patron, as KMT Chairman to take responsibility for the election loss. Lee was soon at war with the KMT establishment and became the "godfather" of another new party, the Taiwan Solidarity Union (TSU), underscoring his transformation to a champion of Taiwanese nationalism toward the end of his presidency. Taiwan's party system then quickly transitioned to one based on two competing blocs or coalitions of parties. The DPP and TSU became allied in the pan-green coalition (named for the primary color in the DPP's flag), while the KMT, PFP, and the minor New Party formed the pan-blue bloc (named for one of colors associated with the KMT and its symbols). This restructuring of the party system promoted identity politics in several ways. First, the smaller parties (the TSU, PFP, and New Party) had more extreme public images, thereby pressuring the DPP and KMT to move away from the center because of the previously noted peculiar nature of Taiwan's electoral system at that time. Second, Lee's departure from the KMT reinforced the position of "deep Blues" within that party (Wu, 2001).

Identity politics clearly became the central issue in Taiwan following Chen's switch to a more aggressive policy toward the PRC, though two separate stages can be discerned. From 2002 through 2006, Chen stressed Taiwanese nationalism during election campaigns, for example by advocating referenda that Beijing and even Washington saw as mechanisms for achieving Taiwan Independence. Then Chen moved in a more moderate direction after the votes were counted, such as his short-lived "consensus" with James Soong on cross–strait relations in early 2005. On the pan-blue side of the spectrum, the massive demonstrations after Chen's narrow re-election victory in 2004 and the recurring criticism of the KMT's rising star Ma Ying-jeou for being too conciliatory toward the Greens showed that the growing polarization in Taiwan was decidedly two-way (Clark, 2006). The major corruption charges against Chen Shui-bian and his family that surfaced in the summer of 2006 and culminated in his arrest after leaving office in 2008 re-enforced identity politics, creating a second stage of heightened polarization. Chen became almost entirely dependent upon the "deep Greens" for his remaining support and, consequently, encouraged their taking over the DPP after he left office to retain political support as he faced criminal charges. Subsequently the DPP stridently opposed the agreement that the new KMT President Ma reached with China in the Fall of 2008 about opening direct economic links across the Strait. This opposition demonstrated the fundamental disagreement over Taiwan's basic national identity between significant minorities who felt, respectively (but certainly not respectfully toward each other), that Taiwan's future would be increasingly tied to China or that economic ties with China would destroy Taiwan as a separate society and polity (Chu, 2007; Gold, 2009). Obviously, such a situation makes policy-making in Taiwan quite challenging.

THE POLITICIZATION OF THE FINANCIAL INDUSTRY

The growing politicization of the financial industry represents a "cost of success" that is associated both with Taiwan's rapid industrialization and with its democratization. The strong contribution of financial chaos and collapse to the KMT's loss in the Chinese Civil War in the late 1940s led the regime both to control the industry after moving to Taiwan and to mandate fairly conservative financial practices. For several decades, this system worked fairly well as the formal financial system funded primarily large-scale investments (both public and private), while the informal "curb-market" proved sufficient for small enterprises. However, Taiwan's success in industrial upgrading generated significant pressures for liberalizing and opening its financial institutions both domestically — from firms that wanted more access to it — and internationally — from advanced industrial nations that wanted greater participation in East Asia's globalization (Clark, 1997; Fields, 1995; Tan, 2001). While financial reform remained fairly limited through the 1990s, which was given credit for Taiwan's escape from the Asian Financial Crisis of 1997–1998 with relatively little damage (Tan, 2001), the country's financial institutions did become significantly more open; and the democratization of the 1990s increasingly brought political pressures to bear on the system (Tan, 2008).

The global economic crisis that began in 2008 has strongly highlighted the importance of the financial industry in economic growth and development. As a service industry, the financial sector plays the role of facilitator to other sectors of the economy. By making credit available, banks and financial institutions act as the "oil that greases the wheels of industry". In Taiwan's 50-year economic development into an industrialized economy, the role of its financial institutions cannot be overstated. Haunted by the financial crisis and economic collapse before 1949 when it was governing in mainland China, the KMT established a financial system that would ensure that what happened in China would not occur in Taiwan and undermine its control of the state.

Scholars, historians, and political elites have all pointed to the failure of the KMT government to manage the economy as well as to control hyper-inflation as a culprit for why the KMT lost power in 1949 and was exiled to Taiwan. For elites in the early days of KMT Taiwan, the key was to make sure that the government strongly influenced the financial industry to serve the regime's overall economic development plan. The KMT government's desire coincided with the realities that financial capital was scarce and that the government was the only institution that could act as a credible financier for the economy. Consequently, Taiwan's financial and banking industry was dominated by a variety of government-owned, government-controlled, or party-owned banks.

Oversight of the banking and finance sector was assigned to the Ministry of Finance (MOF) as well as the Central Bank (CBC). As the key players in Taiwan's financial sector, both the MOF and the CBC used a heavy regulatory hand to ensure that the financial industry served the government's development priorities. Before the liberalization of the financial industry in 1991, Taiwan's financial sector played a supporting role to SMEs by facilitating credit and trade finance. Clearly, the government's industrial policy placed greater emphasis on the development and the strengthening of Taiwan's manufacturing base to generate export revenues, as well as to create employment in the island. While Taiwan's manufacturing base and production capability were being expanded, Taiwan's financial industry remained relatively underdeveloped and continued to be heavily controlled and regulated by the government through the CBC and the MOF.

The preference for a more decentralized industrial structure, as evidenced by the dominance of the SMEs, has been balanced by the presence of government-owned corporations, especially in the heavy industries, as well as in finance and banking. By decentralizing the industrial structure, the KMT government was able to inhibit the rise of concentrated interest groups in key industries and, at the same time, cultivate a diffuse base of social support by aiding the development of SMEs (Tan, 2008). Indeed it is appropriate to describe Taiwan's interest groups as either "weak, concentrated interest groups or performance-based, dispersed interest groups" (Tan, 2001, 171). Consequently, the dispersed nature of Taiwan's interest groups sheltered the economic technocracy from rent-seeking pressures, thereby creating a relatively autonomous decision-making environment for it (Tan, 2008). As Taiwan continued to develop in the late 1980s, the financial industry began expanding to cater to cash-rich corporations and high net-worth individuals. With the onset of political liberalization (later democratization) and the election of President Lee Teng-hui as Taiwan's first Islander president in 1996, the government began to set in motion plans to liberalize the financial industry by allowing private commercial banks.

In 1991, Taiwan opened up the banking industry to allow for private commercial banks. Many of Taiwan's major business groups decided to invest in private banks as either full owners or part owners of these new start-ups. The resulting increase in the number of banks in Taiwan created an environment where competition for customers and business was very intense. In July 1998, the government passed a new law — the Trust Enterprise Law — with the aim of diversifying the banking and trust industry. The beneficiaries of this new law have been the private commercial banks that are members or part of large business groups. Consequently, close to one-third of Taiwan's largest 100 business groups have financial institutions among their holdings. These include institutions like insurance companies, stock brokerage firms, bill finance companies, trust companies, and commercial banks.

By November 2000, the government passed the Amendments to the Banking Law that further liberalized the financial industry by trying to increase the competitiveness of the industry. In less than a month, the Legislative Yuan passed another law — the Financial Institutions Merger Law — this time to promote mergers and acquisitions. By the time these bills were signed into law, Taiwan's financial liberalization was already beginning to exhibit serious signs of perversity. In October 2000, Wheatley (2000) writing for *Business Asia* called Taiwan's banking woes a "time bomb" as the industry was sitting on a large proportion of non-performing loans and was overbanked. The increasing percentage of non-performing loans not only in the commercial banking sector but also in grassroots financial institutions so threatened to undermine Taiwan's economic growth that in an article published in November 2000 the *Economist* (2000) dubbed it a mini-financial crisis. In an attempt to avert a full-blown financial crisis on the island and address the issue of overbanking, the government passed a Finance Restructuring Fund Law to halt the operations of mismanaged finance companies and then promulgated the Finance Holding Company Law in July 2001. The effect of these two laws was to promote the conglomeration of the banking and financial industry. Interestingly, in contrast to the initial intent to increase competition and efficiency in 1990, banks that are part of large business groups have come to dominate Taiwan's financial industry.

The Finance Holding Company Law resulted in the rapid conglomeration of Taiwan's banking industry as well as the privatization of government-controlled financial institutions. Analysts have suggested that consolidation of the banking sector is needed to address the problem of overbanking in Taiwan (Cavey, 2002). Indeed, the government's rationale for passing the Finance Holding Company Law was to address overbanking and to permit mergers and diversification within the industry to help banks' profit margins. In 2003, the government established a new Executive Yuan commission to oversee the financial industry and supposedly resolve overlapping authorities of finance-related agencies. The Financial Supervisory Commission (FSC) was established and essentially peeled away some of the regulatory and supervisory functions of the Ministry of Finance, the Bureau of Monetary Affairs, the Department of Insurance, and the Securities and Futures Commission. The FSC is headed by commissioners who are appointed by the President; and the membership is apportioned according to the political parties represented in the Legislative Yuan.

Unfortunately, means-to-end perfect organizational rationality is not a strong characteristic of bureaucratic decision-making. As Tan (2008, 161) argues, "up until the introduction of political liberalization that culminated in the 1996 direct presidential election and the relative weakening of the KMT, Taiwan's economic decision-making was the purview of the economic technocracy, which is largely autonomous of society. The political democratization process has also forced the democratization of the economic decision-making process. The opening of the economic decision-making sector empowered interest groups and other relevant social actors. Consequently, the increase in the number of actors has led to the reduction in the policy choice set of the government".

The decrease in the government's set of viable policy choices has been aided in part by a competitive policy-making environment where powerful social actors are able to influence and affect policy-making and pull decisions toward their preferred position. In addition, the ambiguity and incoherence of governmental institutions, due in part to the half-baked transition and reform has led to multiple entry points for interest groups to influence governmental decision-making. It is therefore safe to infer that the creation of the FSC signals the penetration of party politics into Taiwan's bureaucratic autonomy.

The strength of the developmental state has been weakened over time as the political institutions that were effective in sheltering the technocracy and allowing for relatively autonomous decision-making were not reformed and strengthened but instead became porous, allowing strong and influential interest groups to influence and even control policy-making. Coupled with a tradition of strong leaders and personalistic politics, the multiple entry points and the ambiguity and incoherence of government institutions have provided influential interest groups as well as entrepreneurial politicians considerable power to shape governmental policy.

In the case of the financial industry, the financial reforms that were initiated by the Financial Holdings Law have led to a marked increase in the number of mergers and acquisitions of the huge financial holdings companies. Interestingly, most of these financial mergers and acquisitions have featured private financial holdings companies acquiring larger public financial holdings companies or banks. For example, the Fubon Financial Holdings Company acquired the then

Taipei City Bank, a public bank with large shareholdings by the Taipei City Government. In 2006, a high profile attempt to acquire significant shares (15.5 percent) of the Mega Financial Holding Company by the Chinatrust Group raised eyebrows among the media and observers. The Mega Financial Holding Company had been established by the amalgamation of two large public commercial banks — the Bank of Communications (BOC) and the International Commercial Bank of China (ICBC). Both of these two banks had long histories as very successful and profitable commercial banks. When BOC and ICBC merged and formed Mega Financial Holding to become Taiwan's second largest financial holdings company, it immediately became a competitive and formidable presence in financial markets. The media and public attention following the stock acquisition of Mega Financial Holdings by Chinatrust Financial Holdings was due to the fact that the smaller and less profitable Chinatrust (Taiwan's fourth largest financial holdings company) acquired a significant share of the larger and more profitable Mega Finance Holding Company. Instead of large competitive and profitable banks acquiring smaller financial companies, the financial reform has resulted in a paradoxical situation of "a small fish eating up a big fish". One common denominator among many of these acquisitions is that they have involved a smaller private finance holding entity acquiring a larger public holdings company. Since the inauguration of President Ma Ying-jeou's administration in May 2008, the corruption and money laundering investigation of the former President Chen Shui-bian, his family, and their associates has uncovered improprieties relating to the financial reforms, in particular to mergers and acquisitions in the financial industry (*Asian Banking and Finance Magazine*, 2006; Gold, 2009).

THE CURRENT PROBLEMS OF THE SMEs

SMEs provided the dynamism for Taiwan's export boom from the 1960s through the 1980s. Their flexibility and entrepreneurship allowed them to take advantage of changing market conditions, and they proved to be surprisingly capable of upgrading to the production of advanced electronics goods (Greenhalgh, 1988; Lam and Clark, 1994; Wu and Huang, 2003). They then were able to take advantage of the growing integration across the Taiwan Strait during the 1990s by moving production to China (Naughton, 1997). However, over the last two decades they have become increasingly squeezed between low-cost producers from developing nations and much larger and more sophisticated corporations in the developed world (Wu and Huang, 2003). Moreover, because they are small and dispersed, their political influence in Taiwan is fairly limited, making it hard for them to get aid from the government. Consequently, Taiwan's historical reliance on this sector as an engine for growth has created a "cost of success", in that the country's rapid industrialization now limits the contribution that it can make to the nation's continued economic upgrading.

To state that Taiwan's "economic miracle" was made possible by the major contribution of Taiwan's SMEs is certainly not an understatement. Taiwan's export dynamo economy relied less on the large conglomerates (like the *chaebol* in South Korea) than on the economic performance and contributions of SMEs. Taiwan's SMEs comprised 99.60 percent of all types of Taiwanese companies in 1961; and by 1997 SMEs still comprised a very high 97.81 percent of all companies and enterprises (Wu and Huang, 2003). In terms of employment, SMEs employed 61 percent of all Taiwanese workers in 1976, and this figure increased to 78.43 percent in 1997 (Wu and Huang, 2003). As far as share of exports is concerned, in 1981 SMEs accounted for 68.10 percent of all exports, though this figure dropped to a still high proportion of 48.77 percent in 1997 (Wu and Huang, 2003). Clearly evident in these statistics are the critical role and significance of the SMEs to Taiwan's march toward economic development and industrialization.

Interestingly, these agile and nimble SMEs were both a unique feature of Taiwan's rapid industrialization and a consequence of Taiwan's political history. By default or by design, the KMT's fear of any challenge to its political dominance had given preference to an industrial structure that was relatively decentralized so as to inhibit the emergence of large, strong, and concentrated interest groups (Chu, 1999; Tan, 2001). By co-opting local Taiwanese elites, effecting land reform, and later creating state-owned enterprises that dominated finance and heavy industry, the KMT encouraged the development of SMEs and was thereby able to develop social support for the regime (Chu, 1999). A relatively stable social support-base was also a consequence of the decline in the unemployment rate, increasing household incomes, and the rapid decline in income inequality — which were all unintended gains resulting from the proliferation of SMEs.

By the early 1980s, the SMEs were already beginning to be challenged in global markets. While South Korea during the same period developed brand names like Samsung, Hyundai, and LG, Taiwan's SMEs relied on original equipment manufacturing (OEM) (i.e., producing products for other brand names under contract or subcontract) to be able to produce high volume and high demand export products. This particular mode of operation has continued to the present with OEM revenues accounting for a large proportion of total revenues even in large Taiwanese information technology and computer firms like Acer, Asus, and Foxcomm. From a high of a 69.68 percent share of total exports in 1982, SME's share of Taiwan's total exports has continued to decline *vis-à-vis* the large corporations to a respectable proportion of 48.77 percent in 1997 (Wu and Huang, 2003) to a much lower level of 28.24 percent by 2006 (SMEA, 2008). As Taiwan's production costs increased (through the tightening of the labor market and increasing labor costs), SMEs were pushed by the international product cycle to produce increasingly capital-intensive manufactures.

As manufacturers from developing countries in Southeast Asia and especially China entered the global market, Taiwan's SMEs began to face stiffer challenges to be competitive and remain profitable. In the midst of the 1997 Asian Financial Crisis, the KMT government adopted measures to help the SMEs through the very tough export and economic environment by such measures as providing export guarantees, tax incentives, and assistance in financing. As the challenges of industrial restructuring continued beyond the late 1990s, the government became more cognizant of the challenges faced by SMEs and, in fact, incorporated an SME Protection Clause into the nation's constitution (SMEA, 2008).

At the same time, as public investment and tax incentives for research and development were being implemented, the government encouraged SMEs to upgrade and transform into knowledge-intensive industries.

While many SMEs have been able to adjust structurally, the nature of Taiwan's position in the international product cycle as well as the problem of economies of scale are now seriously undermining their viability. Taiwan's industrial development has priced its companies out of labor-intensive production to more sophisticated knowledge-intensive production, such as information technology, computers, and software. At this stage of the product cycle, Taiwan's SMEs are increasingly squeezed between the developing countries that can provide cheap manufacturing and the developed countries that produce technologically advanced products. With their limited resources and inability to capitalize on economies of scale, Taiwan's SMEs are forced to move offshore to China (and to a lesser extent Southeast Asia), creating a growing and dangerous dependence on the PRC. Yet, since SMEs are the largest employers in Taiwan and have to a certain extent contributed to the increase in household incomes as well as the equitable income distribution on the island, the offshore movement of this bedrock of Taiwan's industrial structure is not only creating an industrial vacuuming effect on Taiwan, but also resulting in stagnant incomes, relatively higher unemployment, and an increasing inequality of income distribution.

Despite the recognition of the importance of SMEs and their historical contribution to Taiwan's economic growth and development, there are several factors that hamstring the SMEs' ability to maintain their role and share in Taiwan's economy. First, the very nature and structure of the SME limits its ability to easily transform itself. Since the inauguration of Chen Shui-bian in 2000, Taiwan's economy has entered a rather challenging period in its path to economic development. From the year 2000 onwards, Taiwan has been pushed to a phase in the international product cycle that requires massive investment, innovation, and research and development in knowledge-based industries, such as information technology. Though the financial liquidity of SMEs, in general, remains at very healthy levels, the amount of investment in infrastructure, research and development, and human resources required in this new form of a knowledge-based economy presents a difficult challenge to existing SMEs in Taiwan. As the *2008 White Paper on SMEs in Taiwan* written by the Ministry of Economic Affairs' Small and Medium Enterprises Administration (SMEA) reported, "because of their small size and limited resources, coupled with the mindset created by a long-standing focus on standardized, large-volume manufacturing, Taiwan's SMEs are often reluctant to invest in R&D, and lack experience in this area. As a result, Taiwan's SMEs have become less competitive compared with those of China and India" (SMEA, 2008, xiv). From this report, we can infer that the structure of the SMEs has become a constraint making it difficult for them to meet the challenge of transforming themselves into knowledge-based industries.

Second, the changing nature of Taiwan's political economy has also hamstrung the SMEs since 2000. As noted earlier, the historical importance of the SMEs in Taiwan's economic miracle cannot be over-emphasized. From a political standpoint, in the past the KMT has encouraged the development of SMEs as a way to limit challenges to its power and claim political legitimacy not through a democratic regime but through its adept economic management. For a significant number of decades after the KMT's exile to Taiwan, the regime's economic management (through the proliferation of SMEs) allowed it to cultivate broad social support. However, with Taiwan's democratization and the accompanying transition of power as well as executive-legislative gridlock during 2000–2008, the SMEs have become one of many equally powerful groups vital in party competition. That is, political parties have more groups to which they can appeal, while groups have to vie for the attention of politicians.

Consequently, SMEs are now forced to compete in a more plural and competitive interest group environment to obtain preferred government policies. Because the SMEs are organizationally dispersed and politically weak, it is hard for them to be very influential. Indeed, the very rationale for encouraging the development of

SMEs and the creation of large state-owned enterprises during the authoritarian era was to prevent business from becoming a counterweight to KMT rule. The democratization of the 1990s, however, has created a more plural and competitive policymaking environment in which larger, more organized, and more concentrated interest groups such as business groups can thrive.

The relative weakening of SMEs in Taiwan's political economy can be evidenced from the government's plan to promote an "innovation-oriented industrial policy" in the areas of high-tech, biotechnology, information technology, and software (SMEA, 2008). While the official government position is to assist the SMEs toward these high-value-added industries, the reality is that SMEs (by their structure and resources) are simply not equipped to take advantage of these plans. The liberalization of the political decision-making environment both presents new opportunities for powerful interest groups to influence policy decisions and gives party politicians new avenues to cultivate political and social support. These new avenues and opportunities, while favorable to some, are not particularly helpful for dispersed and weaker interest groups such as SMEs.

TAIWAN'S SUCCESS DESPITE THE COSTS OF SUCCESS

This chapter has developed a model demonstrating how Taiwan's very impressive economic and, later, political development during the postwar era brought with it some very significant costs of success as the country entered the new century. Yet, the ongoing challenges that Taiwan faces should not obscure the nation's major accomplishments. Its hard-won democracy can now be considered consolidated and legitimate, certainly no mean accomplishment. For example, election results and power transitions are widely accepted, and the political repression and abuses of the authoritarian era are now unthinkable. In the economic realm (at least before the current global crisis), Taiwan had become a fairly prosperous society; decent levels of growth were maintained; and China had not been able to gain much leverage from the growing economic integration across the Taiwan Strait. Overall, therefore, it would be hard not to foresee a continuing Taiwan success.

REFERENCES

Amsden, AH (1985). The state and Taiwan's economic development. In *Bringing the State Back In*, Evans PB, D Rueschemeyer and T Skocpol (eds.), pp. 78–104. New York: Cambridge University Press.

Asian Banking and Finance Magazine (2006). November 23rd Issue.

Brown, MJ (2004). *Is Taiwan Chinese? The Impact of Culture, Power, and Migration on Changing Identities.* Berkeley: University of California Press.

Cavey, P (2002). Banking blues? December 1, 2002. *Taiwan Review.* [16 March 20] <http://taiwanreview.nat.gov.tw/site/Tr/fr.asp?xItem=792&CtNode-128>.

Chan, S and C Clark (1992). *Flexibility, Foresight, and Fortuna in Taiwan's Development: Navigating Between Scylla and Charybdis.* London: Routledge.

Chao, L and RH Myers (1998). *The First Chinese Democracy: Political Life in the Republic of China.* Baltimore: John's Hopkins University Press.

Cheng, TJ (1989). Democratizing the Quasi–Leninist regime in Taiwan. *World Politics*, 41, 471–499.

Cheng, TJ (1990). Is the dog barking? The middle class and democratic movements in the East Asian NICs. *International Studies Notes*, 15, 10–16.

Cheng, TJ and PPC Chang (2003). Limits of statecraft: Taiwan's political economy under Lee Teng-hui. In *Sayonara to the Lee Teng-hui Era: Politics in Taiwan, 1988–2000*, Lee WC and TY Wang (eds.), 113–148. Lanham, MD: University Press of America.

Cheng, TJ and S Haggard (eds.) (1992). *Political Change in Taiwan.* Boulder, CO: Lynne Rienner.

Chu, YH (1992). *Crafting Democracy in Taiwan.* Taipei: Institute for International Policy Research.

Chu, YH (1999). Surviving the East Asian financial storm: The political foundations of Taiwan's economic resilience. In *Politics of the Asian Economic Crisis*, Pempel TJ (ed.), pp. 184–202. Ithaca, New York: Cornell University Press.

Chu, YH (2007). Taiwan in 2006: A year of political turmoil. *Asian Survey*, 47, 44–51.

Clark, C (1989). *Taiwan's Development: Implications for Contending Political Economy Paradigms.* Westport, CT: Greenwood.

Clark, C (1997). Taiwan's financial system: Prosperity from countervailing perversities? In *Global Perspectives on Economic Development: Government and Business Finance*, Bingham RD and EW Hill (eds.), 116–165. New Brunswick, NJ: Center for Urban Policy Research, Rutgers University.

Clark, C (2000). *Asia Update: The 2000 Presidential Elections.* New York: The Asia Society.

Clark, C (2002). Democratization and the evolving nature of parties, issues, and constituencies in the ROC. In *Taiwan's Modernization in Global Perspective*, Chow PCY (ed.), 135–159. Westport, CT: Praeger.

Clark, C (2006). Taiwan enters troubled waters: The elective presidencies of Lee Teng-hui and Chen Shui-bian. In *Taiwan: A New History*, Rubinstein M (ed.), 496–535. Revised edition Armonk, NY: M.E. Sharpe.

Clark, C (2007). Economic integration between China and Taiwan: No spillover into the identity and security realms. In *Identity and Change in East Asian Conflicts: The Cases of China, Taiwan, and the Koreas*, Horowitz S, U Heo and AC Tan (eds.), 71–90. New York: Palgrave Macmillan.

Copper, JF (1988). A *Quiet Revolution: Political Development in the Republic of China*. Washington, DC: Ethics and Public Policy Center.

Copper, JF (1997). *The Taiwan Political Miracle: Essays on Political Development, Elections and Foreign Relations*. New York: University Press of America.

Copper, JF (2009). *Taiwan: Nation-State or Province?* 5th edn. Boulder, CO: Westview.

Economist (2000). Heavily indebted Taiwan. November 9th Issue.

Fields, KJ (1995). *Enterprise and the State in South Korea and Taiwan*. Ithaca: Cornell University Press.

Galenson, W (ed.) (1979). *Economic Growth and Structural Change in Taiwan: The Postwar Experience of the Republic of China*. Ithaca: Cornell University Press.

Gold, TB (1986). *State and Society in the Taiwan Miracle*. Armonk, NY: M.E. Sharpe.

Gold, TB (2009). Taiwan in 2008: My Kingdom for a horse. *Asian Survey*, 49, 88–97.

Greenhalgh, S (1988). Families and networks in Taiwan's economic development. In *Contending Approaches to the Political Economy of Taiwan*, Winckler EA and S Greenhalgh (eds.), 224–245. Armonk, NY: M.E. Sharpe.

Hood, SJ (1997). *The Kuomintang and the Democratization of Taiwan*. Boulder, CO: Westview.

Hsiao, HHM (1991). The changing state–society relations in the ROC: Economic change, the transformation of class structure, and the rise of social movements. In *Two Societies in Opposition: The Republic of China and the People's Republic of China After Forty Years*, Myers RH (ed.), 127–140. Stanford: Hoover Institution Press.

Kuo, CT (1995). *Global Competitiveness and Industrial Growth in Taiwan and the Philippines*. Pittsburgh: University of Pittsburgh Press.

Kuo, CT (1998). Private governance in Taiwan. In *Beyond the Developmental State: East Asia's Political Economies Reconsidered*, Chan S, C Clark and D Lam (eds.), 84–95. London: Macmillan.

Lam, D and C Clark (1994). Beyond the developmental state: The cultural roots of 'Guerrilla Capitalism' in Taiwan. *Governance*, 7, 412–430.

Lee, WC (2004). Taiwan's 'cultural revolution:' Identity politics and collective action since 2000. Annual Meeting of the American Political Science Association. Chicago.

Leng, TK (1996). *The Taiwan-China Connection: Democracy and Development Across the Taiwan Straits.* Boulder, CO: Westview.

Lin, CY (1973). *Industrialization in Taiwan, 1946–1972: Trade and Import Substitution Policies for Developing Countries.* New York: Praeger.

Lin, CL and B Tedards (2003). Lee Teng-Hui: Transformational Leadership in Taiwan's Transition. In *Sayonara to the Lee Teng-hui Era: Politics in Taiwan, 1988–2000*, Lee WC and TY Wang (eds.), 25–62. Lanham, MD: University Press of America.

Linder, SB (1986). *The Pacific Century: Economic and Political Consequences of Asian-Pacific Dynamism.* Stanford: Stanford University Press.

Lu, YL (2002). Lee Tenghui's role in Taiwan's democratization: A preliminary assessment. In *Assessing the Lee Teng-hui Legacy in Taiwan's Politics: Democratic Consolidation and External Relations*, Dickson BJ and CM Chao (eds.), pp. 53–72. Armonk: NY: M.E. Sharpe.

Lynch, DC (2004). Taiwan's self-conscious nation-building project. *Asian Survey*, 44, 513–533.

March, JG and J Olsen (1989). *Rediscovering Institutions: The Organizational Basis of Politics.* New York: Free Press.

Moody, PR (1992). *Political Change on Taiwan: A Study of Ruling Party Adaptability.* New York: Praeger.

Naughton, B (ed.) (1997). *The China Circle: Economics and Electronics in the PRC, Taiwan, and Hong Kong.* Washington, DC: Brookings.

Noble, GW (1998). *Collective Action in East Asia: How Ruling Parties Shape Industrial Policy.* Ithaca: Cornell University Press.

North, DC (1990). *Institutions, Institutional Change, and Economic Performance.* Cambridge: Cambridge University Press.

Phillips, S (2006). Between assimilation and independence: Taiwanese political aspirations under nationalist Chinese rule. In *Taiwan: A New History*, Rubinstein M (ed.), 275–319. Revised edition. Armonk: NY: M.E. Sharpe.

Rigger, S (1999). *Politics in Taiwan: Voting for Democracy.* London: Routledge.

Rigger, S (2001). *From Opposition to Power: Taiwan's Democratic Progressive Party.* Boulder, CO: Lynne Rienner.

Rigger, S (2003). Taiwan in 2002: Another year of political droughts and typhoons. *Asian Survey*, 43, 41–48.

Skoggard, IA (1996). *The Indigenous Dynamic in Taiwan's Postwar Development: The Religious and Historical Roots of Entrepreneurship.* Armonk, NY: M.E. Sharpe.

Small and Medium Enterprises Administration, Ministry of Economic Affairs (SMEA). (2008). *2008 White Paper on SMEs in Taiwan.* Taipei: Ministry of Economic Affairs.

Tan, AC (2001). Taiwan: Sustained state autonomy and a step back from liberalization. In *The Political Economy of International Financial Crises: Interest Groups, Ideologies, and Institutions*, Horowitz S and U Heo (eds.), 165–176. Lanham, MD: Rowman and Littlefield.

Tan, AC (2008). From state entrepreneurs to political entrepreneurs: Democratization and the politics of financial liberalization in Taiwan. In *Democratization in Taiwan: Challenges in Transformation*, Paolino P and J Meernik (eds.), 153–166. Burlington, VT: Ashgate.

Tien, HM (1989). *The Great Transformation: Political and Social Change in the Republic of China*. Stanford: Hoover Institution Press.

Tien, HM (ed.) (1996). *Taiwan's Electoral Politics and Democratic Transition: Riding the Third Wave*. Armonk, NY: M.E. Sharpe.

Wachman, AM (1994). *Taiwan: National Identity and Democratization*. Armonk, NY: M.E. Sharpe.

Wade, R (1990). *Governing the Market: Economic Theory and the Role of Government in East Asian Industrialization*. Princeton: Princeton University Press.

Wang, NT (ed.) (1992). *Taiwan's Enterprises in Global Perspective*. Armonk, NY: M.E. Sharpe.

Wang, TY (2000). One China, one Taiwan: An analysis of the democratic progressive party's China policy. In *Taiwan in Perspective*, Lee WC (ed.), 159–182. Leiden: Brill.

Wheatley, A (2000). Taiwan's bank timebomb — Debt Crisis — Brief Article. October 2000. *Business Asia*. 16 March 2009. <http://findarticles.com/p/articles/mi_m0BJT/is_14_8/ai_67148964>.

Wong, J (2010). From imitator to innovator: The political economy of industrial upgrading in the 21st century. In *Taiwan's Politics in the 21st Century: Changes and Challenges*, Lee W-C (ed.). London: World Scientific Press.

Wu, JJ (1995a). *Taiwan's Democratization: Forces Behind the New Momentum*. Hong Kong: Oxford University Press.

Wu, RI and CC Huang (2003). Entrepreneurship in Taiwan: Turning point to restart. US-Japan Dialogue on Entrepreneurship in Asia. Tokyo.

Wu, YS (1995b). Economic reform, cross–straits relations, and the politics of issue linkage. In *Inherited Rivalry: Conflict Across the Taiwan Straits*, Cheng TJ, C Huang and SSG Wu (eds.), 111–133. Boulder, CO: Lynne Rienner.

Wu, YS (2001). Taiwan in 2000: Managing the aftershocks from power transfer. *Asian Survey*, 41, 40–48.

Chapter 6

From Imitator to Innovator: The Political Economy of Industrial Upgrading in the 21st Century

Joseph Wong

The story of Taiwan's postwar economic miracle is well known. Having been a relatively backward economy during the immediate postwar period, Taiwan has since become an unequivocal economic dynamo. Taiwan's is an economy that is thoroughly industrialized, and one in which a growing proportion of the labor market is engaged in technology and tertiary sectors of the economy — in other words, those parts of the economy which earn higher value-added returns. Indeed, the crux of the island-state's development throughout the postwar period has been predicated on Taiwan's ability to continually industrially upgrade. This is not an economy that settled on one or two export sectors. Rather, Taiwan's industrial economy has been industrially diversified over time. As one of the region's paradigmatic developmental state models, Taiwan's economy has been steered in ways which have continually "created" new comparative and competitive advantages. From light manufacturing to electronics to advances in information and communication technologies, Taiwanese firms have climbed the commercial value chain.

Despite efforts to maintain this upgrading trajectory in Taiwan — to stay ahead of the competition, as it were — Taiwan began to face severe competition from other countries in Southeast Asia and China in the 1990s. As a net exporter of manufacturing goods and higher-end technology products, Taiwan's competitive advantage was based essentially on price competition; local firms could produce high quality goods at competitive prices to global buyers. With the rise of China, the continued sophistication of Southeast Asian economies, and relatively lower wages inside these competitors, Taiwan's price advantage began to erode beginning in the 1990s. Indeed, Taiwanese firms began moving parts of their manufacturing operations offshore. Fears surrounding the "hollowing out" of Taiwan came to a head during the mid 2000s, when the Taiwan Semiconductor Manufacturing Corporation (TSMC) moved a significant portion of the firm's lower-end manufacturing to China, primarily because of cost concerns. The current global economic crisis, in which consumer markets for Taiwan's export goods have begun to dry up and price competition has become even more acute, further underscores the imperative for Taiwan to move further and higher up the technology value chain.

In the face of such competitive pressures during the 1990s, Taiwan's economic planners and industry stakeholders recognized yet again the imperative of further industrial upgrading. Only this time, upgrading meant transitioning from a political economy of able technology assimilation and imitation to one of cutting-edge technological innovation. It was believed that if Taiwan were to maintain its growth trajectory, it would need to become a creator of new knowledge, a beneficiary of what economists refer to as "first mover advantages". It also meant that Taiwan could no longer compete on price with other late developers, but instead it would need to compete head-on with industrial innovative leaders of the West and to some extent Japan.

This chapter examines this ongoing transformative process in Taiwan. More specifically, this chapter identifies the ways in which the political economy of industrial upgrading in Taiwan today is vastly different than the processes of industrial development during the postwar period. Taiwan's current efforts to enter into science-based industries such as nanotechnology, new materials, advanced information and communication technologies, and biotechnology mark a new political economic paradigm, which is characterized by its *extreme uncertainty*. The main argument in this chapter is that Taiwan's future economic prospects rest on its ability to manage such technological, economic, regulatory, and political uncertainties.

A NEW POLITICAL ECONOMY OF INDUSTRIAL UPGRADING

Eugene Wong of Taiwan's National Science Council and Academia Sinica remarked that "[o]ur high-tech industry has tended to adapt technologies rather than create new ones. We look up to the leaders of these companies because they are perceived to be innovators, when in fact, they haven't created anything new" (cited in Tsai, 2008). Wong's comments illuminate one of Taiwan's critical economic realities: despite having been a key player in global high-tech sectors, especially in advanced electronics and information and communication technologies (ICT), Taiwan has been nonetheless primarily an importer of technologies as opposed to a creator of technological innovation. Until recent decades, Taiwan, along with the other Asian NICs, was a relative laggard in science and technology (S&T). As such, the state and industry have expended tremendous effort to "backfill" as rapidly as possible and thus compensate for Taiwan's prevailing S&T deficit.

Developing Science and Technology

In 1980, total spending allocated to R&D in Taiwan, comprising both public and private sources, amounted to just over half of one percent (0.55 percent) of GNP. Other advanced industrial nations at the time were spending well over 2 percent of national product on R&D (Arnold, 1988). Putting in place various science and technology development plans and institutes during the late 1970s hastened the growth of Taiwan's S&T capacities. However, the vast majority (70 percent in 1978) of R&D spending was contributed by the state, rather than industry, the latter being the norm among most advanced industrial countries at the time.

Moving forward to the 2000s, the picture of Taiwan's S&T development could not present a starker contrast. In 2006, total R&D spending in Taiwan equaled 2.58 percent of GNP, an approximately 500 percent increase from two-and-a-half decades earlier. Industry's share of R&D spending had also been reversed (compared with the late 1970s), accounting for 67 percent of total spending in 2005 (NSC, 2007). The proportion of research scientists and engineers (to the total labor market) was 89 per 10,000 during the mid-2000s, putting Taiwan ahead of Korea and Singapore and in-line with most advanced industrial countries. Taiwan ranked among the top twenty countries in the world with respect to science (17th) and engineering (11th) publications. Also, Taiwan's inventors ranked fourth globally in US patents approved (NSC, 2007). The marked growth of S&T inputs has translated into impressive outputs. In short, it would be inaccurate to say that Taiwan has remained an S&T laggard.

Growth in Taiwan's S&T capabilities has not been reflected merely in the billions of dollars that government and industry have invested in R&D and personnel. The state has also made significant efforts to create a sophisticated R&D infrastructure. Universities have been transformed from primarily training institutions to R&D-intensive knowledge producers. In addition to the Academia Sinica, the Taiwan government has created new public R&D centers over the past several decades, including technology-specific research facilities in nanotech, biotechnology, ICT, optics, and environmental technology, among others. These have been modeled after Hsinchu's Industrial Technology Research Institute (ITRI), which was established in 1973 as the birthplace of Taiwan's semiconductor industry. Moreover, the enhancement of R&D facilities has been accompanied by efforts to translate upstream and midstream research into commercializable outputs. The Hsinchu Science Industry Park, for instance, was formed in 1980 to foster collaboration between firms and the ITRI labs. Since then both the Park and ITRI have grown in tandem. Investment in firms located inside the Hsinchu Park increased from U.S. $332 million in 1987 to around U.S. $26 billion in 2002, an over 50 fold increase in just 15 years (HSIP, 2005). Publicly funded R&D labs are expected to supply technologies to Taiwan's high-tech industries. To that end, ministerial resources allocated for R&D have, by and large, been earmarked for applied research and downstream technology development.

Government policies have been formulated and refined to promote technology transfer and R&D collaboration among public labs and private firms (Wong, 2006). Taiwan's intellectual property rights protection regime has been strengthened considerably in recent years to encourage innovative research. Incentives have been put into place to encourage technology commercialization, such as tax rebates, credits for personnel training, and subsidies for equipment. Technology clusters have been encouraged, where public resources have been used to bring firms and labs together both to collaborate in R&D and to share common resources. In terms of investment, the government has created new incentives to encourage venture capital (VC) investment and seed financing for early-stage technology start-ups. Public funds have been used to capitalize VC funds. Additionally, the state has relaxed many regulations that had previously constrained the ability of large institutional investors (such as banks and insurance companies) to finance venture firms. Finally, the government has reformed the stock exchange and listing rules to facilitate more "exit" options for early stage investors (i.e., VCs and angel investors). Indeed, industry observes note that Taiwan has the financial capital to seed the growth of new technology sectors; the task for the government thus far, however, has been to encourage or compel would-be investors to take on what are much riskier and uncertain commercial propositions.

The prevailing challenges of encouraging investors and stakeholders to "take on what are much riskier and uncertain commercial propositions" in new science-based industrial sectors precisely get at the heart of the issue for Taiwan's economic planners. For it is this *appetite for myriad uncertainties* which compels a new strategic mindset necessitated by the imperatives of first-order technological innovation and science-based industrialization. The remainder of this section elaborates on this new "mindset" in Taiwan as it looks to transition from being a capable technology importer and creative imitator into a full-fledged industrial innovator.

From Risk to Uncertainty

To understand the "new" we must first examine the "old", from where Taiwan's political economy of industrial upgrading is transitioning. The story of Taiwan's entry into the global semiconductor sector is instructive. The formation of the ITRI in 1973 was intended to promote a "license-in, license-out" technology development strategy. Foreign technologies, usually second-generation technologies, were licensed-in to ITRI, further developed and refined, and then licensed-out or transferred to industry. ITRI's midstream development role was therefore intended to deliver nearer-to-market technologies for Taiwan's otherwise risk averse industrial sector during the 1970s. United Microelectronics (UMC), Taiwan's first efforts in semiconductor manufacturing, was created through this strategy. The state brokered an in-licensing agreement with the American firm, RCA, for its then obsolete integrated circuit (IC) technology. The ITRI's labs, specifically the Electronics Research Service Organization (ERSO), reverse-engineered the IC technology. With considerable public investment, ITRI spun out UMC during the late 1970s. The creation of the TSMC and its pureplay foundry model mirrored the UMC story. During the 1980s, the government again played an instrumental role in licensing-in foreign DRAM chip technology from U.S. sources, in reverse-engineering the technology in its ITRI labs, and in heavily financing the eventual TSMC spin-off (see Matthews and Cho, 2000; Breznitz, 2007; Fuller *et al.*, 2003).[1] Both UMC and TSMC quickly captured a significant share of the global IC market.

Taiwan's entry into the IC and semiconductor market during the 1970s and 1980s was a high risk endeavor, to be sure. It was unknown at the time if Taiwanese firms would be able to ramp-up production quickly enough in order to gain global market share. The economic risks of these endeavors were magnified by the fact that Taiwan's firms were entering into what was already a relatively crowded industry. It was also unknown at the time if other Taiwanese firms would form lasting forwards and backwards linkages to ensure a dense IC sector in Taiwan. There were, in the words of Amsden and Chu (2003), "economic unknowns".

Industrial upgrading was a risky proposition. However, certain things that Taiwan's economic planners and stakeholders did know helped decision-makers mitigate such risk. First, as Wang (1994/1995) and others (Amsden and Chu, 2003) point out, Taiwan's entry into the IC market during the 1970s and 1980s built upon a pre-existing knowledge base in electronics. Gaining entry into the higher value-added IC manufacturing reflected an existing "pathway of learning" in Taiwan, which in effect lowered the transaction costs of learning an entirely new field. Second, by importing technologies that had been developed elsewhere (i.e., the United States), Taiwanese imitators were *a priori* assured the technology and related applications worked, thus reducing technological uncertainty. Third, reverse-engineering and re-exporting existing technologies meant that local firms were confident that markets for such goods existed. When UMC and TSMC entered into the IC sector, for instance, global demand was virtually guaranteed. They did not need to create demand, a risk–reward proposition that is absorbed by first-, and not second-, movers in any technology field. Japanese electronics exports were essentially priced out of the global (and especially the United States) market when it was forced during the mid-1980s to revalue the yen and to correct its trade imbalance with the United States. This assured late entrants from Taiwan that they could quickly gain market share. Indeed, both the UMC and TSMC earned commercial returns soon after they were created, quickly moving Taiwan's industries further upstream.

Industrial upgrading during the postwar developmental state was, on the one hand, a high risk endeavor. However, state economic policymakers did, on the other hand, have the information (i.e., a pathway of learning, assurances of technological certainty, and market share) with which to prospect the probability of industrial success. Industrial upgrading was risky, but at least policymakers knew the type (and severity) of technological and commercial risks they were taking. They could therefore choose potential winners. Furthermore, and critical to the developmental state experience in East Asia, the state intervened in ways which mitigated the risks. The state allocated large amounts of public resources to "buy" foreign technologies, to establish and fund R&D facilities, to set up a facilitative policy infrastructure, to seed capacity building in science and technology development, and to invest directly into firms. In other words, the state expended public resources to minimize the risks of entry for firms — and for Taiwan's industrial economy more generally — into higher risk and higher value-added technology industries. By mitigating risk through the allocation of public resources, the developmentally oriented Taiwanese state *both strategically picked and made winners.* The developmental state made industrial bets relatively surer bets.

Economists make an important conceptual distinction between risk scenarios and uncertainty. Risk is defined as a calculable probability distribution. There are unknowns, which make risk scenarios and outcomes uncertain (evidenced by Taiwan's failed efforts to mitigate risk in the auto sector, for instance). However, as I have argued above, risk scenarios are ones in which decision-makers do know some things for certain. Risk scenarios can be more or less risky; in some cases, the probability of a preferred outcome is higher, or in the case of industrial upgrading in Taiwan, the probability of success can be *made even higher* through strategic state intervention. Meanwhile, uncertainty, according to economists, characterizes those situations in which decision-makers are without any certainties or "knowns" at all. Knight (1921) refers to such situations as instances of "primary uncertainty", or as Pisano (2006, 7, 8) of Harvard Business School puts it, "unknown unknowns", or "*everything you did not even know you did not know*". Primary uncertainty, the hallmark of innovation, precludes the calculation of risk. Truly innovative outcomes are unprecedented. They are, by definition, unpredictable. Thus, while a risk scenario can be expressed as a probability distribution, the odds of a preferred outcome under truly uncertain circumstances are unknown and cannot be known.

Cutting-edge technology innovation in science-based industries such as biotech, nanotech, advanced ICT, new materials, and environmental technology among others, is characterized by primary uncertainty. Technological uncertainty — will it work? — is at the core of innovation. As we know, truly path-breaking discoveries are rare; most "hunches" in the lab do not work out. The data shows us that the ability of researchers to translate upstream research into industrial products or services is uncertain. Upstream knowledge is often too raw, too unrefined, and far-from-market to predict commercial applications. This sort of technological uncertainty is even further magnified in places such as Taiwan, where science and technology regimes have only recently been institutionalized and where upstream R&D capacity in science-based industries remains vastly undeveloped. The uncertainties of the innovation process are equally problematic in terms of economic uncertainty — does the knowledge have any economic value? In risk scenarios, such as when TSMC introduced its pureplay foundry to meet market demand in the IT sector, firms know with some (though never complete) confidence that markets do in fact exist and that their products have economic value. Economically valuating truly innovative breakthroughs and upstream basic research, however, is inherently uncertain and particularly susceptible to the uncertainties of market failures. Breakthroughs are too distant from the market. They are unprecedented, that is, no market referents exist with which to confidently calculate value (Arrow, 1962; Berman, 1990; Faulkner *et al.*, 1995). A truly innovative idea, as a concept in the lab or a product pitch in the boardroom, may or may not bear economic value further downstream.

It is precisely these sources of uncertainty in innovation which undermine the postwar developmental state model in Taiwan and more specifically the strategies it once used to pick and make winners. Industrial upgrading in the postwar period relied on strategies of technology imitation, where state intervention could help mitigate the risks of climbing the technology value chain. However, when technological innovation is uncertain, both in terms of technological output and the eventual realization of commercial value, then the state is without the interventionist tools that would allow it to effectively pick and make winners. *The state cannot choose what it does not know, and it cannot make winners it is unable to choose.* The state cannot, therefore, mitigate uncertainty as it mitigated the risks of industrial upgrading in the past. Rather, all the developmentally oriented state and its stakeholders can do is, at best, to cope with uncertainty. Herein lies the key challenge for Taiwan as it looks to transform into an industrial innovator at technology's cutting-edge: coping with uncertainty. The remainder of this paper explores biotechnology industry development in Taiwan to illuminate the challenges of coping with uncertainty in an important, expensive, and high profile science-based industry.

BIOTECHNOLOGY IN TAIWAN

The global biotechnology revolution began during the 1970s, when scientists discovered that the biological "heuristic" rather than conventional synthetic chemistry allowed researchers potentially to better understand the bio-mechanisms of disease. This was a new "technological paradigm" (Dosi, 1982) which could facilitate the discovery of new diagnostic tools, innovative drug development processes, and an entirely new class of therapies ("smart" drugs). Health care industry was expected to be revolutionized, both technologically and economically. It was anticipated that biotechnology innovation would create new spin-off industries and revenue streams for advanced industrial economies willing to bet on biotech. Though Taiwan was a relatively late entrant into the life sciences sector, it nonetheless wanted to gain entry into the biotech race. Feeling the imperatives of industrial upgrading, the state identified biotechnology as a future pillar and star industry during the 1990s.

The Taiwan government has invested tremendous amounts of resources into the life sciences sector. Public sector funding of biotech R&D grew manifold during the 1990s and 2000s. In 2006, the government allocated $21.5 billion NT (approximately U.S.

$620 million) to biotechnology R&D, which accounted for nearly one-third (31 percent) of total public R&D spending, double the proportion of the resources allocated by the Korean state (15.3 percent) and about fifteen times that of the U.K. government (1.6 percent) (STPI, 2007; van Beuzekom and Arundel, 2006). New policies and incentive programs have been implemented to jumpstart public and private sector activity in biotechnology. Various government ministries have entered into the policy mix, each vying for and allocating public resources and designing biotechnology promotion strategies. Also the government has created new or revitalized older biotech-dedicated research institutes, such as the Biomedical Engineering Center in ITRI, the National Health Research Institute (NHRI), and the Development Center for Biotechnology (DCB), as well as several biotech industry clusters in all areas of Taiwan. Most recently the government initiated a new commercial endeavor, TaiMed, which is intended to be a semi-private "super-incubator" of new drug leads for eventual commercialization or clinical R&D.

Industry activity has, not surprisingly, grown quite considerably in Taiwan. Observers estimate that there are between 200–300 biotechnology firms in Taiwan, of which most were created recently in the past decade or so. And though the ratio of biotech sales to R&D spending has remained quite low, general sales of health technology goods and services have grown significantly since the biotech drive began during the 1990s (NSC, 2002). The government expects biotechnology industries, broadly defined, will eventually be a multi-billion dollar sector for Taiwan.

Despite great effort on the part of the government and industry to upgrade into the biotechnology sector, the prospects of success in biotech remain extremely uncertain in Taiwan. To be sure, the performance of the *global* biotechnology sector has been less than stellar and much poorer than expected, even among bio-industrial pioneers such as the United States. According to a recent report by Hopkins *et al.* (2007), the notion of a biotech revolution is "misplaced", and the prevailing "expectations about the impact of biotechnology are over-optimistic". Biotech techniques in R&D have not, for instance, resulted in more efficient and effective drug development. The growth of bio-pharmaceuticals has been very slow. Despite the rapid growth in the number of biotechnology start-ups, the rate of economic returns has been much lower than the rate of investment. The sector has lost money as a whole. Only a handful of firms are in positive cash-flow situations, and just two American firms account for nearly half the cash in the entire sector. Profitability among US biotech firms has been miniscule across the board. As of 2003, there were close to 1,500 biotech firms in the United States, though fewer than 200 biotech products had actually been commercialized in the market. Simply put, the future of global biotech industry innovation remains terribly uncertain.

It is quite clear that the prospects of cutting-edge innovation in biotechnology suffer from the same sort of technological and economic uncertainty which I describe above in reference to science-based industries. *Technological uncertainty* is rooted in the fact that biotechnology innovation is dependent upon myriad applications of knowledge, including various scientific fields, biology, and engineering, as well as expertise in legal issues, intellectual property (IP) management, and technology transfer to industry. Biotech's multidisciplinary nature means that knowledge bases are highly specialized, disintegrated as well as institutionally disparate. Furthermore, the promise of biotech remains very distant from market, too raw and unrefined to know with any certainty whether a particular discovery or technological breakthrough has commercial potential, the basis of *economic uncertainty*. The long distance to market, combined with uniquely rigorous (and highly variable) regulatory gatekeepers, frustrates economic efforts to valuate biotechnology innovation. Economists teach us that, as with all science-based industries, it is difficult to predict market demand, identify niches, and forecast market potential for new knowledge.

And finally, economic and technological uncertainty contributes to *temporal uncertainty*. We know, for instance, that technological innovation is an inherently long-term process. Science-based industries such as biotechnology thus demand both tremendous patience among stakeholders and an appetite for unpredictable results. In this respect, the relatively slow pace of biotechnology innovation and bio-industrial growth in Taiwan are to be expected. How long Taiwan can sustain its appetite for such uncertainty, a reflection of *political uncertainty*, remains unknown, however. Each of these sources of uncertainty will be discussed in turn in the remainder of this chapter.

ECONOMIC AND TECHNOLOGICAL UNCERTAINTY

The challenge for biotechnology stakeholders in Taiwan, in government or industry, is deciding where to allocate scarce resources strategically in order to grow a domestic biotechnology sector. In the postwar period, when the government chose to bet on its ability to make winners in the IC sector, the state essentially played a game of risk; there were unknowns, but they had enough information to know roughly the odds (good or bad) of their gamble. In biotech, as I have described, stakeholders have little sense of the odds of success, and in the case of latecomers, such as Taiwan, with little experience in the life sciences sectors, stakeholders have no sense of where their comparative and competitive advantages lie. In fact, given how new biotechnology is in Taiwan, it would be fair to assert that stakeholders have little sense of even where their competencies are.

The allocation of resources dedicated to biotech innovation within and outside the state illuminates how stakeholders in Taiwan have tried to manage biotechnology's myriad of uncertainties. When the government initiated its biotechnology development program during the 1990s, the number of ministerial stakeholders was quite large, including the National Science Council, the Council on Agriculture, the Ministry of Economic Affairs, the Department of Health, and the Ministry of Education, among others. Each of these ministerial stakeholders were able to claim specialized expertise in the biotechnology innovation process, from evaluating S&T research projects to industry investment to education policy to health regulation. Power and authority, unlike during the postwar rendition of the developmental state, have thus been devolved and decentralized. And this horizontal shift in power and authority has been carried out in the absence of any overarching coordinating mechanism.

Though the government has attempted to establish various "steering" committees and agencies, the multi-disciplinary nature of biotech has eluded the authority of generalist decision-making bodies. No single state actor, unlike the Council for Economic Planning and Development (CEPD) or the Industrial Development Bureau (IDB) of the earlier postwar period (see Wade, 1990), has been able to legitimately coordinate the biotech sector from the top-down. As a result, decentralized authority on the bases of varied claims of specialized expertise has also flattened the allocation of R&D budgets dedicated to life sciences and biotech innovation. Between the late 1990s and mid 2000s, the share of resources allotted to the National Science Council (NSC) decreased as did the share of public funds slated for the Ministry of Economic Affairs (MOEA). Meanwhile, resources for explicitly multi-ministerial R&D and for the Council on Agriculture have increased.

Flattening the state allocation of R&D resources is not merely a functionalist reflection of the decentralization of expertise in biotech innovation. Rather, the strategic rationale has been to focus R&D activities of each of these ministerial stakeholders toward *downstream* technology development. Compared with regional competitors, Taiwan is an interesting outlier in that the share of public funding for upstream basic research has remained virtually unchanged since the 1990s; basic research funding has increased considerably in Korea and nearly doubled in Singapore over the last decade. The majority of publicly funded R&D resources (upwards of 70 percent) in Taiwan have been allocated to applied development or commercialization. This has been the case even in nominally upstream research organizations such as the National Science Council. Mirroring this downstream-oriented strategy, various state ministries have funded either the creation or revitalization of dedicated life sciences midstream technology R&D institutes. In essence, they have looked to institutionally reproduce institutionally the ITRI model of technology development, where publicly funded researchers deliver inherently uncertain biotechnologies closer to industry and the market. The ITRI, which is funded by the MOEA, created the Biomedical Engineering Center, and the Department of Health established the

National Health Research Institutes during the 1990s. The Academia Sinica and universities have strengthened their technology transfer operations in the life sciences. Meanwhile, the MOEA has revitalized the once moribund Development Center for Biotechnology.

Taiwan's strategy for managing biotechnology's uncertainties has not been anarchic, however. The absence of institutional coordination has not meant that there are no coordinative principles at work in the re-organization of the innovation-driven state apparatus. The strategy for managing biotechnology's uncertainty in Taiwan reflects a "hit-and-miss" strategic logic. With very little idea of where Taiwan's R&D strengths actually lie (technological uncertainty) in the life sciences field or where its commercial and industrial advantages can be realized (economic uncertainty), the allocation of resources within the state is intended to discover, through trial and error as well as over time, where Taiwan ought to focus in biotechnology. A flattened R&D budget has thus ensured the different bases of specialized knowledge have had an adequate, if not a preponderant, amount of resources to develop potential R&D niches in biotech. Spreading rather than concentrating state resources across different ministerial stakeholders has diversified the potential sources of commercial success. It has also diffused the costs of expected failures. Spreading rather than concentrating the allocation of resources is therefore intended to increase the probabilities of discovering potential areas of bio-industrial success over time (Wong, 2006). In other words, the state is no longer interested in "picking" winners from the top-down, but rather discovering potential winners by hedging their bets *as broadly* as their scarce resources will allow.

To the extent that there has been any overarching coordinative institutions directing the development of biotechnology in Taiwan, the NSC's Science and Technology Advisory Group (STAG) and its Strategic Review Board have indirectly shaped this hit-and-miss strategy when they imposed "soft" performance benchmarks on all publicly-funded research centers during the mid 2000s. Each research center (i.e., the ITRI, the NHRI, the DCB, etc.) is expected to spin-off a specified number of biotech firms (defined as "success cases") by 2010; the specific number of firms is proportional to the amount of funding the center has received from public sources. While the STAG's initiative was met initially with considerable skepticism by stakeholders, the benchmarking exercise has deepened expectations that research centers' performance is to be measured in terms of commercial output, which has further reinforced the downstream orientation of publicly-funded R&D. And while the STAG (and the NSC more generally) has recognized that it is without the resource leverage to enforce its commercial targets, its implications nonetheless have deepened a sense of competition among the varied ministerial stakeholders. Such competition is intended to hasten the process of identifying potential niches (author interview).

In sum, due to biotechnology's technological and economic uncertainties, which have been exacerbated by the fact that Taiwan is a recent entrant into the life sciences field, the state and related stakeholders are neither able nor willing to gamble on picking winners. Unlike earlier risk scenarios, where economic and industrial policy decision-makers were able to mitigate the risks of entry into higher tech sectors, Taiwan has had to rely on a hit-and-miss strategy of identifying niches, a process of broad-based and relatively uncoordinated experimentation. The expectation, however, is that once viable niches and areas of specialized competence have been identified, then state and private sector resources will flow more forcefully, and in a more targeted way, to these specific niches. But until such niches have been identified, the state has retreated from the past practice of picking and making winners.

Regulatory Uncertainty

Biotechnology, unlike other industrial sectors, is highly regulated — and for good reason. Because biotechnology involves the health of patients, as well as the use of human subjects during pre-market R&D, regulatory regimes need to be effective, transparent, and in-line with international regulatory standards. In this respect, regulation is a comparative advantage. Recent regulatory scandals in the United States (i.e., the case of Vioxx) and China (i.e., tainted foods) affirm the importance of regulatory stringency in commercializing new health technologies; the absence of such stringency can be disastrous not only for patients and human subjects in clinical R&D, but also for the credibility of regulatory bodies and firms. As a recent Ernst and Young report (2008, 92) succinctly noted, regulation is a "competitive differentiator" among national economies. Regulatory *certainty* (i.e., transparency, enforceability, policy clarity), in this respect, is an important factor in shaping the growth and development of the bio-industry.

Taiwan's regulators have been keenly aware of the need for strengthening local regulations to support domestic biotechnology industry innovation. Led by the Department of Health, Taiwan was among the first Asian economies to put into place safety-related regulations beginning in the 1970s. In 1996, around the time that Taiwan looked to enter into the life sciences sector, the government, again led by health policymakers, implemented national guidelines for good clinical practices (GCP). These were internationally harmonized shortly thereafter. During the 1990s and 2000s, health regulators adopted the institutional review board (IRB) model from other advanced industrial nations to govern the peer review of all clinical R&D protocols. Attached to public research facilities, IRBs have ensured that all clinical research conducted in Taiwan adheres to international norms and regulations concerning ethical procedures and research best practices. IRBs were also intended to assure that all sanctioned clinical R&D projects were of high quality and research integrity (see Chern *et al.*, 1998). Furthermore, to increase regulatory efficiency, in 1998 the government created the Center for Drug Evaluation (CDE) to review and pre-screen all clinical R&D protocols submitted to the Department of Health's Bureau of Pharmaceutical Affairs (BPA). This organizational reform lightened the workload of the increasingly stretched BPA. Approval times for clinical trial protocols were significantly reduced, from an average of 90 days to just 30–45 days (Jao *et al.*, 2003).

Regulators will explain, however, that regulation is not an exact or absolute science (author interview). The most thorough regulatory regimes, for instance, cannot eliminate the risk of threats to patient safety, and from the industry perspective, getting past regulatory hurdles does not guarantee that commercialized products will gain significant market share. In addition, regulatory regimes, as I have described, can be market-supporting institutions, yet they can also be market-constraining mechanisms. Regulation thus illuminates the tension between industry promotion on one hand, and industry constraint on the other hand. Regulators will explain that the art of regulation is in maintaining balance, ensuring that the "pendulum" swings neither too far towards lax regulation, which may benefit industry, nor too far toward over-regulation, in which the safety of patients is the paramount concern. Indeed, the tension between industry promotion and patient protection is difficult to resolve and is a source of great uncertainty for bio-industry stakeholders. The state plays dual — sometimes conflicting — roles, and comparative experiences tell us that reconciling these roles is not easy (Jacobzone, 2000; Ceccoli, 2003; Ernst and Young, 2008).

Examples of regulatory uncertainty, and specifically the tensions inherent in the state's dual roles of promoting and protecting, have emerged in Taiwan precisely at a time when government and industry efforts have accelerated to grow domestic biotechnology (and health technology more generally) industries. For example, the Center for Drug Evaluation (CDE) was established during the late 1990s to make the regulatory approvals of clinical R&D (i.e., clinical trials, product registration) effective and more efficient. The Department of Health's BPA worried, however, that the regulatory pendulum had begun to swing towards efficiency at the expense of regulatory effectiveness, and that the role of the CDE would compromise the BPA's very strong regulatory thresholds. For the BPA, patient safety is the regulator's paramount concern, even if over-regulation might constrain the growth of local biotechnology and health technology industry. The CDE, meanwhile, increasingly felt that the BPA's efforts to ensure patient safety had been unnecessarily strict. Under pressure from the economic ministry, which oversees the growth of local biotechnology industry in Taiwan, some of the BPA leadership was dismissed during the mid 2000s. This particular episode emphasizes the ongoing, and as yet unresolved, tensions within the state apparatus, specifically among those whose interests are to promote industry and those whose objectives are to protect patients (author interview).

Regulatory uncertainty has also played out in seemingly irreconcilable ways in pricing policies for health care goods and services. Similar to many other cases, the state in Taiwan plays an important role in "constructing" health care markets. As the administrator of the national medical insurance program, the state, and specifically the Bureau of National Health Insurance (BNHI), is the de facto monopsonistic purchaser of all health care goods and services. As the sole buyer of health care through the nationalized medical insurance scheme, the state has tremendous power in determining the price of health care interventions. From the industry perspective (especially innovation-driven firms such as novel pharmaceutical companies), competitive market pricing is optimal as it best ensures a reasonable rate of return on the sale of products and services. However, in Taiwan the state-controlled price (paid by the BNHI) of novel or R&D-intensive drugs has been estimated to be between 15 and 30 percent below competitive international prices (APBN, 1998). Indeed, for state regulators and health policymakers, lower rather than inflated prices serve their core interests in maintaining health care accessibility. Crude price controls imposed by the state have also been an important policy instrument with which to contain total health care spending (see Ernst and Young, 2008, 5–7). Given that nearly one-quarter of Taiwan's health care bill is accounted for by prescribed drugs, centrally regulating prices has been an effective way to keep spiraling health care costs in check. Between 2000 and 2002, the BNHI cut prices on almost 20,000 items on the national medical insurance reimbursable list (Cheng, 2003).

It is important to point out that regulatory uncertainty and the dual, often conflicting roles played by the state are not unique to Taiwan. The tension between promoting industry and protecting patients is prevalent in all advanced industrial countries looking to grow their health technology industries while maintaining a commitment to ensuring their citizens' safety. Nonetheless, it is important to emphasize that achieving regulatory clarity (as opposed to uncertainty) is critical to both of the state's aforementioned objectives. And while Taiwan is not unique in continuing to grapple with such challenges, the core of intra-state conflict has remained far from being resolved.

Political Uncertainty

The analysis thus far has centered on questions of the administrative role of the state in managing biotechnology's uncertainties. Additionally, much of the analysis has been informed by the insights of economists, technologists, and theories of technological innovation. But what about politics? Most Taiwanese bio-industry observers and stakeholders hedge at articulating any role that politics might play in shaping biotechnology innovation and industrial upgrading. After all, the imperatives to move into cutting-edge science-based industries appear to be unequivocally clear, and thus above politics. Science is purportedly apolitical. Experimenting with a hit-and-miss strategy is, they claim, really a question of public administration, not politics. Still, it would not be unreasonable to offer some speculative takes on how political developments in Taiwan have influenced, or might come to influence, the course of biotechnology innovation and bio-industry development.

First, the politics of cross–strait relations have shaped Taiwan's strategy towards building-up its domestic biotechnology industry and life sciences R&D capacity. Though China has lagged far behind Taiwan in terms of S&T development and the prospects of technological innovation throughout the postwar period, it has been catching up very rapidly in recent years. Furthermore, China's scale advantages are not insignificant, particularly as multinational R&D-intensive firms have begun to seriously examine the China market and to consider moving some of their R&D operations directly to the mainland. Many strategic policymakers in Taiwan see that China presents an excellent opportunity for Taiwan. Indeed, Taiwan's policy toward China with respect to the biotechnology sector has been to position Taiwan as a "spring board" (or *tiao ban*) into China. Leveraging its relatively stronger IPR regime and R&D facilities,

Taiwan has attempted both to market itself as the R&D base for foreign firms and to facilitate greater cross–strait R&D collaboration. Taiwan's economic policymakers have also looked to utilize its financial markets as the ideal entry point into the Chinese market.

Such efforts, however, have encountered some political resistance at home. During the early 2000s, legislators from the Taiwan Solidarity Union (TSU) proposed to restrict the movement of Taiwan-based scientists to China, reasoning that lost R&D opportunities needed to be traded-off in order to maintain Taiwan's autonomy. Though the TSU's policy did not gain traction within either the legislature or the executive branch, hard core nationalists have continued to express fears about the eventual deterioration of Taiwan's autonomy, the deepening of Taiwan's economic dependence on China, and the likelihood that Taiwan's technological advances (i.e., intellectual property) will be subsumed by China. These domestic political pressures have constrained the scope of policy options as policymakers deal with critical questions of Taiwan's political–economic relationship with the rapidly rising China. Many observers note that the window of opportunity for Taiwanese researchers and firms to gain a strong foothold in China is quickly closing and that soon China's own domestic R&D capacities will have either caught up to or exceeded those of Taiwan's.

Second, managing the political uncertainties of cross–strait relations and the prospects of greater collaboration between Taiwan and China reflect an even larger debate which has gained political resonance in Taiwan, and that is the tension between technonationalist aspirations and technoglobalist realities (Ostry and Nelson, 1995). Political pressures, and in particular democratic political pressures, have shaped the policy discourse about technological innovation in highly nationalistic terms. Taiwan's democratic politicians have staked their political legitimacy not only on the growth of biotechnology industries (and other science-based industries), but also on the assertion that such growth occur *in Taiwan*. Drawing on the economic nationalist myths of the postwar period, industrial upgrading has remained a uniquely national project. However, as we know, the realities of cutting-edge technological innovation increasingly rest on transnational collaboration; proponents of the technoglobalist perspective contend that nationalist aspirations bear less meaning in the context of global technological innovation. Part of this global shift has been attributed to the increasing complexity of science-based innovation, and part of it can be explained by the greater ease with which researchers, firms, and technology can cross borders (Archibugi and Iammarino, 1999). As a result, the politics of "credit-taking" in this globalized political economy of innovation, where the attribution of credit has become increasingly difficult to discern, offers much less political capital to local politicians. Which perspective — technonationalist or technoglobalist — will eventually win out politically, or how the two perspectives will be politically accommodated, remains to be seen. Either way, the persistence of this high-stakes political debate inside Taiwan betrays a deep sense of political uncertainty regarding the future direction of Taiwan's economic policies.

Third, the politics of credit-taking in democracies is a necessarily short-term political strategy. Thus, it was not at all surprising when former President Chen Shui-Bian, in an effort to legitimate his government's investments into the biotechnology sector during the early 2000s, said, "if we don't do this today, we will regret it tomorrow" (cited in Boyce, 2002). Chen's assertion, one which has been echoed by policymakers and politicians over the past decade in Taiwan, reveals the political logic of credit-taking in competitive democracies: Taiwan must not only develop its own biotech industry, it must do so sooner rather than later. Success in the near-term translates into political capital, particularly in political systems which are dictated by rhythms of a regular and competitive electoral cycle. However, we also know that cutting edge innovations, such as biotechnology development and science-based industrial growth, take a long time to emerge and even longer to commercialize. Moreover, innovation's temporal uncertainty precludes strategic planning. As I argued earlier in this chapter, innovation by definition is random and unpredictable, where probabilities are incalculable in the first place. In these respects, technological innovation does not fit well with short-term political calculations. There have been fears, therefore, that Taiwan's political appetite for biotechnology's long-term uncertainties has been determined by short-term political considerations. Continual administrative turnover, the hallmark of democracy in Taiwan, has thus diminished the state's resolve to sustain an appetite for biotechnology innovation over the much, much longer term (Wong, 2005).

CONCLUSION

Taiwan's economy is in the midst of a significant transition. Facing price competition from other export-led economies in East and Southeast Asia, Taiwan has had to climb the technology value chain. More specifically, Taiwan has looked to transform itself from an able creative imitator of technology to a world-class technology innovator. This transformation, which began during the 1990s, has not been easy. Nor should we expect it to be. The main thrust of this chapter has been to consider the challenges of a new political economy of industrial upgrading.

To best illuminate this "new" political economy, this chapter began by revisiting the postwar developmental state model, and in particular its strategies for industrial upgrading. The core of my argument is that both by having imitated technologies developed elsewhere and by having allocated significant amounts of public resources to help deliver that technology to domestic industry, the developmental state was able to mitigate the risks of industrial upgrading. By understanding the political economy of copying (as opposed to creating) technology, I have also asserted that the state was able to pick and make eventual winners more effectively. My point was not that the state always picked correctly — the failed auto sector in Taiwan demonstrates bad choices — but rather that the state had been able to turn long-shot bets into surer bets through strategic state intervention.

In the new political economy of technology innovation, I have argued that the imperatives of creating something novel and hence unprecedented and unpredictable have revealed situations of primary uncertainty as opposed to calculable risk scenarios. Technological and economic uncertainty (will it work? does the knowledge have any value?) has therefore eluded efforts by the state to pick and make winners effectively. In short, under conditions of uncertainty, the state has little idea what to pick and what to make. And in science-based sectors such as biotechnology, stakeholders in late entrants such as Taiwan barely have a sense of their own competencies. As before, the state has continued to allocate tremendous amounts of resources to science-based industrialization; however, decision-makers have had little to go on in deciding how best to allocate such resources.

To demonstrate the political economy of dealing with such uncertainty, I have focused on Taiwan's aspirations to becoming a global player in biotechnology, a sector in which Taiwan had little existing expertise. In so doing, I have highlighted different sources of uncertainty in the biotechnology industry which have posed significant challenges to the developmentally oriented state. More specifically, I have elaborated on how economic planners have had to rely on a hit-and-miss strategy of identifying potentially viable niches; how the built-in tensions about promoting and regulating industry within the state have contributed to a lack of regulatory clarity; and the ways in which domestic political pressures have shaped how strategic planners have had to accommodate differing perspectives on cross–straits relations, the tensions between nationalist and globalist approaches to technology development, and the conflict between short-term political calculations and the long-term political economy of innovation. My point is not to say that these sources of uncertainty are intractable or unresolvable, but rather to demonstrate how the presence of such uncertainties belies the strategic best practices of the postwar developmental state. The postwar rendition of state-led model has become less relevant in the new political economy of industrial upgrading. In short, the transition from imitator to innovator has required a deep transformation of the developmentally oriented state and its past strategies of mitigating risk to a new political economic mindset that can, at best, merely cope with uncertainty.

REFERENCES

Amsden, A and W-W Chu (2003). *Beyond Late Development: Taiwan's Upgrading Policies*. Cambridge, MA: MIT Press.

Archibugi, D and S Iammarino (1999). The policy implications of the globalization of innovation. *Research Policy*, 28(3), 317–336.

Arnold, W (1988). Science and technology development in Taiwan and South Korea. *Asian Survey*, 28(4), 437–450.

Arrow, K (1962). Economic welfare and the allocation of resources for inventions. In *The Rate and Direction of Inventive Activity: Economic and Social Factors*, Nelson R (ed.), pp. 609–626. Princeton: Princeton University Press.

Asia-Pacific Biotech News (APBN) (1998). Taiwan asked to revised pharmaceutical pricing policy. *APBN Newletter*, 1(30), June 2003. (www.asiabiotech.com).

Berman, E (1990). The economic impact of industry-funded university R&D. *Research Policy*, 19(4), 349–355.

Boyce, J (2002). Taiwan's biotech clock is ticking. *Topics*, 32(2), March. (www.amcham.com.tw/content/blogcategory/74/292/).

Breznitz, D (2007). *Innovation and the State: Political Choice and Strategies for Growth in Israel, Taiwan and Ireland*. New Haven: Yale University Press.

Ceccoli, S (2003). *Pill Politics: Drugs and the FDA*. Boulder CO: Lynne Rienner.

Cheng, T-M (2003). Taiwan's new national health insurance program: Genesis and experience so far. *Health Affairs*, 22(3), 61–76.

Chern, H-D *et al.* (1998). The joint institutional review board in Taiwan. *Drug Information Journal*, 32 (Oct.–Dec.), 1275S–1277S.

Dosi, G (1982). Technological paradigms and technological trajectories. *Research Policy*, 11(3), 147–162.

Ernst and Young (2008). *Beyond Borders: Global Biotechnology Report 2008*, July 2009. (www.ey.com/beyondborders)

Faulkner, W and J Senker (1995). *Knowledge Frontiers: Public Sector Research and Industrial Innovation in Biotechnology, Engineering Ceramics and Parallel Computing*. Oxford: Clarendon Press.

Fuller, D, A Akinwande and C Sodini (2003). Leading, following or cooked goose? Explaining innovation successes and failures in Taiwan's electronics industry. In *Global Taiwan: Building Competitive Strengths in a New International Economy*, Berger S and R Lester (eds.), 76–96. Armonk, NY: M.E. Sharpe.

Hopkins, M *et al.* (2007). The myth of the biotech revolution: An assessment of technological, clinical and organizational change. *Research Policy*, 36(4), 566–589.

HSIP (Hsinchu Science Industry Park) (2005). *Quarterly Statistics*, September.

Jacobzone, S (2000). Pharmaceutical policies in OECD countries: Reconciling social and industrial goals. *Labour Market and Social Policy Occasional Papers*, No. 40.

Jao, SH-L, H-D Chern and M-L Chu (2003). Reinventing drug regulation in the Asia pacific region: Taiwan's experience and a vision for the region. *Drug Information Journal*, 37(Suppl. 23), 41S–48S.

Knight, F (1921). *Risk, Uncertainty and Profit.* Boston, MA: Houghton Mifflin.

Matthews, J and D-S Cho (2000). *Tiger Technology: The Creation of a Semiconductor Industry in East Asia.* Cambridge: Cambridge University Press.

NSC (National Science Council) (2007). *Indicators of Science and Technology 2007.* Taipei: National Science Council.

——— (2002). *Indicators of Science and Technology 2002.* Taipei: NSC.

Ostry, S and R Nelson (1995). *Techno-Nationalism and Techno-Globalism: Conflict and Cooperation.* Washington DC: Brookings.

Pisano, G (2006). *Science Business: The Promise, The Reality and the Future of Biotech.* Cambridge MA: Harvard Business School Press.

STPI (Science and Technology Policy Research and Information Center) (2007). *Yearbook of Science and Technology, Taiwan, 2007.* STPI.

Tsai, J (2008). Science council acts to sustain GDP growth. *Taiwan Journal*, 25, 27.

Van Beuzekom, B and A Arundel (2006). *OECD Biotechnology Statistics — 2006.* OECD.

Wade, R (1990). *Governing the Market.* Princeton: Princeton University Press.

Wang, V (1994/1995). Developing the information industry in Taiwan: Entrepreneurial state, guerilla capitalists and accommodative technologists. *Pacific Affairs*, 68(4), 551–576.

Wong, J (2006). Technovation in Taiwan: Implications for industrial governance. *Governance*, 19(4), 651–672.

——— (2005). Re-making the developmental state in Taiwan: The challenges of biotechnology. *International Political Science Review*, 26(2), 169–191.

ENDNOTE

1. The state accounted for 49 percent and 48 percent of equity investment in UMC and TSMC, respectively.

Part III

Taiwan–US–China Relations

Chapter

7

Symbolic Politics, Self-Interests, and Threat Perceptions[1]: An Analysis of Taiwan Citizens' Views on Cross–Strait Economic Exchanges

T. Y. Wang, Lu-huei Chen, and Shu Keng

Determinants of citizens' positions on policy issues in democratic polities have been a subject of scholarly debate. Theorists of rational choice maintain that individuals' stands on various issues are primarily governed by the perceived costs and benefits of possible policy outcomes. As individuals tend to minimize the associated costs and maximize related benefits, "self-interest" is thought to be a major determinant of citizens' attitudes on various policies (Downs, 1957; Riker and Ordeshook, 1973). An alternative perspective on the determinants of policy preferences comes from "symbolic politics" analysis which maintains that individuals acquire stable affective preferences through a socialization process. As individuals develop various personal attachments in the form of party identification, ideological orientations, and ethnic or national identity, they respond to issues according to these attachments on the basis of cognitive consistency (Sears *et al.*, 1979, 1980). A third perspective contends that individuals adopt positions on issues that have implications for national security in large part on the basis of their perceptions of threat. When imposed dangers are felt by citizens of democratic polities, they are likely to believe that they are engaging in zero-sum political battles. Different policy outcomes thus may be perceived as having a life or death consequence (Gordon and Arian, 2001; Schafer, 1999; Wang, 2005; Wang and Chang, 2006).

The analysis of Taiwan residents' preferences on cross–strait economic exchanges provides an ideal opportunity to test these three competing explanations for the formation of policy positions. Indeed, trades and investments between Taiwan and China have expanded dramatically during the past two decades even though Beijing constantly threatens the island with military force for its cause of unifying Taiwan with the "motherland". The rapid democratization on the island in recent years has also brought changes to the island citizens' identifications as Chinese or Taiwanese, changes which have serious implications to their preferences over Taiwan's future relations with China, commonly known as the issue of "unification vs. independence". While repeatedly emphasizing that the future of Taiwan "be determined by peaceful means" (Taiwan Relations Act (or TRA), Section 2 (b)), the United States has also indicated that its role as Taiwan's protector is not unconditional. That is, it would not give Taipei a blank check resulting in the declaration of Taiwan *de jure* independence. With these developments, some citizens on the island feel that cross–strait economic exchanges have expanded too fast and worry that Taiwanese economy that is over-dependent on the Chinese market may harm the island's national security. They demand that Taipei adopt policies of restricting cross–strait trades and investments. Others, however, see the rapid development on the Chinese mainland as an economic opportunity that may enrich individuals as well as the Taiwanese society. Thus, they argue that the government should take on measures facilitating the growth of cross–strait economic interactions. As Taiwan citizens' political attitudes are determined in an environment where identity, self-interests, and threat perceptions interact, the findings of this study will provide significant insights to the three competing theoretical explanations for individuals' policy preferences. Specifically, does Taiwan citizens' support for their corresponding positions on cross–strait economic exchanges originate from their identities? Or, are their policy preferences mainly based on the consideration of self-interest? As Beijing constantly waves their military might against Taiwan, to what extent do the islanders' threat perceptions affect their policy preferences?

In addition to theoretical significance, the findings of this study also have important policy implications for Taipei's Nationalist (Kuomintang or KMT) government under the newly elected President Ma Ying-jeou. Unlike former President Chen Shui-bian of the Democratic Progressive Party (DPP) who implemented a series of policies to distance Taiwan from China, Ma has vowed to improve cross–strait relations (Ma, 2007, 2009). After proclaiming that his administration would pursue a 3-no policy of "no unification, no independence, and no use of military force", aiming to maintain the cross–strait political status quo, the government relaxed restrictions on Taiwanese investment in the mainland economy and reached agreements with Beijing that realized "three links": direct flights, direct shipping, and direct postal mail between Taiwan and the Chinese mainland. The Ma administration further proposed negotiating a Comprehensive Economic Cooperation Agreement (CECA) (later renamed the "Economic Cooperation Framework Agreement" (ECFA)) with Beijing. This set of policies pursuing rapprochement with China has generated substantial controversy on the island.

The policies of Ma's and Chen's administrations thus represent two divergent strategies of approaching cross–strait economic interactions. While Ma can claim legitimacy of his policy of rapprochement on the landslide victory in the 2008 presidential election, it is important to know that his policies could falter without strong public support. As Taiwan has become a full-fledged democracy, any political leader on the island must now pursue policies that will win the majority's support.

This study utilizes a survey conducted through telephone interview by the Election Study Center of the National Chengchi University, Taipei, Taiwan in September, 2007, with a total sample size of 1,069. Treating the island citizens aged 20 and above as the population, the sample was identified through the equiprobability sampling method. Telephone numbers were first selected through systematic sampling of the telephone directory and weighted by county and city population. The last two or four digits of the telephone numbers were then modified randomly to avoid selection biases. A further enumeration and random selection process was used to identify the desired respondent from among members of the household. Only one eligible respondent was selected to be interviewed from every household. Data were weighted to ensure that the demographic characteristics of the sample resemble those of the population.

DETERMINANTS OF POLICY CHOICE

In the discussion of the determinants of individuals' policy positions, three theories have been offered in the previous literature: the theory of symbolic politics, the theory of self-interest, and the theory of threat. All three theories will be employed to construct the theoretical framework for the current analysis.

The theory of symbolic politics maintains that individuals form values early in their lives. These predispositions may be crystallized later in the forms of left/right ideology, party identification, racial prejudice, and political or ethnic identity. When individuals encounter issues that resemble targets from which their predispositions originate, the pressure of cognitive consistency may lead them to respond in a similar fashion. Following this logic, individuals' policy positions are not based on rational calculation of some tangible gains or losses. Rather, because "personal 'stake' in the issue is an emotional, symbolic one" (Sears *et al.*, 1979, 371), party identification, political identity, and ethnic identity will affect individuals' policy attitudes. The key to understanding individuals' positions lies in "the similarity of symbols posed by the policy issue to those of long-standing predispositions"

(Sears *et al.*, 1980, 671). In its analysis of Taiwan citizens' policy preferences, a previous study has found that elements of affective identity play a far more important role than other factors in determining public opinion on cross–strait issues (Keng *et al.*, 2006).

While the theory of symbolic politics maintains that individuals' policy positions are shaped by their long-standing values, rational choice theory suggests that they can also be influenced by individuals' perceived costs and benefits. Scholars of this theoretical tradition attribute human beings' political decisions to a calculation of personal utilities. That is, individuals' stands on a particular issue are based on what they expect to gain or to lose from the outcome. Since each outcome has different costs and benefits, individuals will choose positions that maximize gains and minimize losses (Downs, 1957). Precisely due to this desire of maximizing utilities, the perceived costs and benefits of a given policy outcome are thus likely to affect individuals' policy preferences. Chief among these utilities are economic benefits, such as personal economic interests or the overall economic well-being of society. Other perceived utilities include personal safety or national security.

In this context, the literature of threat perception can also be added to the theoretical underpinning of our analysis of individuals' policy positions. Previous studies show that the perceptions of threats have a causal effect on individuals' decision-making. While identity does affect human behaviors, Schafer's study (1999) indicates that an increased sense of security corresponds to more cooperative decisions. Gordon and Arian (2001) find that the more threatened people feel, the more their policy choice tends to maintain or intensify the conflict. The lower the perceived threat level, the more peaceful their policy choice will be. Using survey data collected in Taiwan, Wang (2005) concludes that the islanders' policy choices on the issue of unification vs. independence are the results of rational responses to the perceived threat. In general, the higher the threat perception is, the less likely an individual supports either independence or unification. How does threat perception affect citizens' positions on economic issues? The structural realist perspective of international relations argues that national security is the primary concern in an inherently anarchical international system. All sources of power, military or economic, are not readily usable and have to be subsumed to the issue of national security. As economy can be used as sources of power, economic dependence may easily be a threat to the safety of a nation if trade and investment become hostages to political conflict. Thus, when individuals sense high threat from a given country, they tend to be more cautious about economic dependence on that country.

The above theoretical arguments thus provide a framework for the analysis of the island residents' policy preferences regarding Taiwan's economic relations with China. As will be detailed below, cross–strait relations since 1949 have involved both political confrontations and economic interactions. Therefore, the analysis of Taiwan citizens' policy preferences on the island's economic exchanges with China requires an understanding of the environment in which policy choices are made.

CROSS–STRAIT RELATIONS

Modern cross–strait relations started at the end of World War II when the sovereignty of Taiwan was returned to the KMT government led by Chiang Kai-shek. After being defeated by Communist troops in 1949, Chiang and his two million mainland followers retreated to the island. To maintain their claim that they were still the sole legitimate rulers of the mainland, KMT leaders preached "recovering the Chinese mainland" as the sacred mission. Although any form of communication between the two sides of the Taiwan Strait was strictly prohibited, the unification of Taiwan and China was taken as a given. To make local residents accept the view that both Taiwan and the Chinese mainland were parts of China and that China was their motherland, the Chiang regime took a series of discriminatory measure to "re-Sinicize" local residents in order to foster a Chinese identity. Activities that might arouse local identities and promote Taiwan independence were censored and suppressed.

As the Chiang regime was building Taiwan into a base for recovering the mainland, Communist leaders in Beijing vowed to unify

Taiwan with the "motherland". Several major battles were fought over Taiwan's off-shore islands in the 1950s and 1960s. Although the 1970s saw a shift of China's strategy from a reliance on "military liberation" to an emphasis on "peaceful initiatives", its unification plan, known as "one country, two systems", have considered Taiwan only as a local government under Beijing's command (Taiwan Affairs Office, 1993). To force Taipei to accept its unification plan, the Chinese government has isolated the island diplomatically and has threatened Taiwan with its military might constantly. While Beijing's coercive strategies have successfully prevented Taipei from declaring *de jure* independence, they have only alienated the island's citizens and invited resentments.

Meanwhile, the rapid democratization in Taiwan during the 1990s has affected the island citizens' identity. As martial law was lifted, so were bans on organizing political parties and restrictions on public assembly and freedom of speech. School curricula shifted from the China-centered programs to lessons that focused on Taiwan's history and culture. Exiled advocates of Taiwanese independence were also allowed to return to the island and openly espouse an independent Taiwan. The ensuing constitutional changes in the 1990s further diluted the heritage and sense of mission brought by the Chiang family from the Chinese mainland. The 2000s saw an increased pace of "Taiwanization" as Chen Shui-bian was elected to the office of the president. Chen has strong pro-independence credentials, and his affiliated DPP is the only major political party on the island that has adopted a plank in support of the pursuit of Taiwan's *de jure* independence. With the backing of Pan-Green supporters, the Chen administration successfully overcame the opposition of Pan-Blue alliance and implemented a series of significant policies to arouse Taiwanese consciousness.[2] These policies included adding the words "Issued in Taiwan" to the island country's green passport cover, launching "the rectification movement" by replacing "China" with "Taiwan" in the names of all relevant government and state-run agencies, and holding a referendum for UN membership in the name of "Taiwan" in the 2008 presidential elections (*New York Times*, 2002; Enav, 2007; Lu, 2008). These political developments have affected the island citizens' identification as Chinese or Taiwanese and have also impacted their preferences over Taiwan's future relations with China. Unlike the era of the authoritarian rule by the KMT, during which cross–strait unification was treated as a given, unification is now no longer taken for granted.

For their part, Beijing leaders worry about the Taipei DPP government's attempts to arouse Taiwanese identity on the island as manifesting a desire to change the island's international status gradually toward *de jure* independence. To demonstrate its determination to protect the country's territorial integrity, Beijing has deployed hundreds of short-range missiles on the coast facing Taiwan and has repeatedly threatened the island with the use of military force should Taipei declare itself independent. In 2000, a second white paper was issued by China's State Council declaring three conditions, known as "the three-ifs", under which Beijing would launch military attacks against the island (Taiwan Affairs Office, 2000). The Chinese government also passed a tough "Anti-Secession Law" in 2005 that effectively pre-authorized military action should Taiwan take concrete steps toward formal independence (*Xinhuanet*, 2005; Su, 2005).

While Beijing's military threats constantly cast a cloud over Taiwan citizens' minds, such threats have been mediated by U.S. involvement in cross–strait relations. Through carefully crafted diplomatic languages, America's Taiwan policy is crystallized in the Taiwan Relations Act (TRA) and the three Sino-America Communiqués: the Shanghai Communiqué of 1972, the Normalization Communiqué of 1978, and the Joint Communiqué of 1982. The essence of the U.S. policy is that the U.S. upholds a "one China" policy and recognizes Beijing as the sole legal government of China while maintaining unofficial relations with the people of Taiwan. With an ambiguous military posture, Washington's policy of "strategic ambiguity" comprises both credible threats and convincing reassurances, and it constitutes a web of incentives and disincentives (Christensen, 2002; Ross, 2002; Schelling, 1966). That is, to deter Beijing from taking aggressive actions against Taiwan, Washington has repeatedly shown its resolve that "any effort to determine the future of Taiwan by other than peaceful means, including boycotts or embargoes" would be of "grave concern" to the United States (TRA, Section 2 (b)).[3] Washington has also made it clear that its role as the protector of Taiwan is not unconditional. To discourage Taipei from taking any move that could be deemed provocative by Beijing, the US has refused to spell out exactly what would trigger an American military response on behalf of Taiwan. Thus, in addition to Beijing's constant military intimidation, Washington's uncertain security commitment has become another source of threat perception for Taiwan citizens.

Interestingly, contrary to mercantilist thinking that the level of economic contacts between two countries declines as their political relations become more hostile, cross–strait economic exchanges have flourished during the past two decades. What started as a policy with the modest aim of allowing Taiwan residents to visit their mainland relatives in 1987 has later expanded into a flood of contacts across the Taiwan Strait. As Table 1 demonstrates, cross–strait trade has increased from \$3.9 billion in 1989 to \$31.2 billion in 2000, and further to \$102.3 billion in 2007. About two-thirds of Taiwan's trade with China consists of the island's exports, indicating Taiwan's heavy economic dependence on the mainland market. While Taiwanese direct investment in the Chinese mainland was restricted by the government, approved indirect investment, as Table 2 shows, has increased from \$421 million in 1991–1992 to \$2.6 billion in 2000 and to about \$10 billion in 2007. According to the data from the Beijing government, the realized Taiwanese investment in China during the past 15 years has reached a total of \$45 billion. Along with these investments, an estimated one million Taiwanese investors have now relocated to the Chinese mainland, many of whom have high-tech and managerial skills. Meanwhile, cross–strait exchanges are not limited to economic relations. Data in Table 3 show that the interactions between residents of both sides of the Taiwan Strait have increased rapidly during the past 15 years, and the number of visits by Taiwan residents traveling to China also has surged dramatically from less than one-half million in 1988 to three million in 2000, and further to 4.6 million in 2007.

Table 1: Indirect Trade Between Taiwan and China.

Year	Total indirect trade between Taiwan and China (in U.S.$ millions)	Taiwan's exports to China (in U.S.$ millions)	Percent of Taiwan's exports on total indirect trade to China
1989	3,918.8	3,331.9	85.0
1990	5,160.0	4,394.6	85.2
1991	7,786.7	7,493.5	96.2
1992	11,294.7	10,547.6	93.4
1993	15,008.6	13,993.1	93.2
1994	17,881.2	16,022.5	89.6
1995	22,525.2	19,433.8	86.3
1996	23,787.1	20,727.3	87.1
1997	26,370.6	22,455.2	85.2
1998	23,954.8	19,840.9	82.8
1999	25,841.4	21,312.5	82.5
2000	31,239.2	25,009.9	80.1
2001	31,510.4	25,607.4	81.3
2002	39,497.4	31,528.8	79.8
2003	49,310.6	38,292.7	77.7
2004	65,722.7	48,930.4	74.4
2005	76,365.2	56,271.5	73.7
2006	88,115.5	63,332.4	71.9
2007	102,260.9	74,245.9	72.6

Source: Mainland Affairs Council (2009). *Liang-An Jing-gi Tong-gi Yue-bao* (Monthly Report on Cross–Straits Economy) No. 191 <*http://www.mac.gov.tw/*>.

As interactions between Taiwan and China have expanded at a dizzying speed, the Taipei government has been keeping a watchful eye on the increasing economic ties between the two sides of the Taiwan Strait. In order to avoid economic over-dependence on the mainland market, the Taipei government under the leadership of former President Lee Teng-hui instituted the "no haste, be patient" (*jie-ji yong-ren*) policy in the 1990s to reduce the overheated "mainland fever".[4] The succeeding Chen administration further tightened the control of trades and investments between Taiwan and China with the "proactive management and effective liberalization" (*ji-ji guang-li you-xiao kai-fang*) policy (Chen, 2006). For Chen and his

Table 2: Taiwan Indirect Investment in China (in U.S.$ Millions).

Year	Amount approved by the ministry of economic affairs, Taiwan	Taiwanese investment compiled by Chinese government sources
1991–1992	421.5	1,894
1993	3,168.4	3,138.6
1994	962.2	3,391.0
1995	1,092.7	3,161.6
1996	1,229.2	3,474.9
1997	4,334.3	3,289.4
1998	2,034.6	2,915.2
1999	1,252.8	2,598.7
2000	2,607.1	2,296.3
2001	2,784.1	2,979.9
2002	6,723.1	3,970.6
2003	7,698.8	3,377.2
2004	6,940.7	3,117.5
2005	6,007.0	2,151.2
2006	7,642.3	2,135.8
2007	9,970.6	1,774.4
Total 1991–2007	64,869.1	45,666.9

Source: Mainland Affairs Council (2009). *Liang-An Jing-gi Tong-gi Yue-bao* (Monthly Report on Cross–Straits Economy) No. 191, <*http://www.mac.gov.tw/*>.

supporters, the concern was that increased cross–strait exchanges are likely to result in increased economic integration, which in turn would both promote political integration between Taiwan and China and hurt the cause of independence. Others, like the newly elected President Ma, think it unwise to distance Taiwan from China because cross–strait exchanges can provide economic as well as political benefits to Taiwan. For them, Chen's policies placed obstacles between the island's investors and one of the largest markets in the world, which deprived Taiwanese investors of a huge business opportunity. The distancing approach is also deemed ineffective judging from the flourishing interactions between two sides of the Taiwan Strait. Most importantly, sensing Beijing's threat and Washington's uncertain

Table 3: Contacts Between Taiwan and China.

Year	Letter delivery	Calls to Taiwan	Calls to China	Number of Taiwanese tourists to China (Persons)
1988	N/A	N/A	N/A	437,700
1989	10,810,693	N/A	N/A	541,000
1990	13,249,545	N/A	N/A	948,000
1991	15,170,127	8,025,958	8,719,209	946,632
1992	18,222,614	14,305,592	16,204,107	1,317,770
1993	17,402,487	21,168,576	26,790,107	1,526,969
1994	19,111,657	26,973,808	34,191,993	1,390,215
1995	17,658,398	36,286,354	41,519,318	1,532,309
1996	18,042,925	42,956,178	53,541,006	1,733,897
1997	16,301,746	56,652,934	69,077,688	2,117,576
1998	14,681,935	69,187,986	79,951,814	2,174,206
1999	13,523,907	82,295,197	96,033,222	2,584,648
2000	13,987,115	95,048,691	111,604,024	3,108,650
2001	12,630,660	114,970,716	154,668,202	3,441,961
2002	16,270,458	169,332,270	213,866,226	3,660,565
2003	16,836,146	185,782,187	250,073,756	2,731,897
2004	16,187,030	228,595,500	289,035,219	3,685,250
2005	16,168,114	298,044,463	318,610,184	4,109,187
2006	12,486,723	358,902,498	350,297,538	4,413,470
2007	11,595,145	282,248,004	352,274,657	4,627,881

Source: Mainland Affairs Council (2002). *Liang-an Jing-ji Tong-ji Yue-bao* (*Cross–Straits Economic Statistics Monthly*) No. 124 (December, 2002), pp. 33–35; Mainland Affairs Council (2009). *Liang-An Jing-gi Tong-gi Yue-bao* (Monthly Report on Cross–Straits Economy) No. 191, <*http://www.mac.gov.tw/*>.

security commitment, Ma and his supporters expect that expanded cross–strait economic interactions would reduce the political tension between Taiwan and China as a result of Chen's distancing approach (Ma, 2007, 2009).

Thus, Ma's and Chen's policies represent two divergent strategies toward cross–strait economic interactions, and each has its own supporters. Since Taiwan citizens' positions on the issue are made in an environment in which self-interests, changing identities, and perception of threats interact, the following analysis will examine the three competing hypotheses utilizing recently collected survey data in Taiwan.

POSITIONS ON CROSS–STRAIT ECONOMIC EXCHANGES

To assess Taiwan citizens' policy preferences on cross–strait economic exchanges, the survey asked respondents the following question:

> Do you think the government should enhance cross–strait economic exchanges or restrict cross–strait economic exchanges?

Table 4 shows that about 37 percent of the respondents took a more cautious attitude toward cross–strait economic interactions. They would like to see the Taipei government tighten its restrictions on Taiwanese trades and investments on the Chinese mainland. Close to 42 percent of the island citizens, however, wanted to loosen such restrictions, while one fifth express no opinions on the issue. Because the proportional differences between the two positions are merely five percentage points, it shows that the island citizens' positions on cross–strait economic exchanges are rather divided.

As previously indicated, three competing hypotheses based on "symbolic politics", "self-interest", and "threat perceptions" have

Table 4: Taiwan Citizens' Positions on Cross–Strait Exchanges (N = 1,069).

The government should restrict cross–strait economic exchanges	36.9 (395)
The government should enhance cross–strait economic exchanges	41.6 (445)
No response/don't know	21.5 (229)

Note: Column percentages on top are followed by corresponding frequencies in parentheses.

Table 5: Taiwan Citizens' Identities and Positions on Cross–Strait Exchanges.

	The government should restrict cross–strait economic exchanges	The government should enhance cross–strait economic exchanges
Taiwanese identifiers	66.47	33.53
	(224)	(113)
Dual identifiers	26.27	73.73
	(124)	(348)
Chinese identifiers	16.98	83.02
	(9)	(44)
$X^2 = 144.84$, $p < 0.01$		
Pan-blue identifiers	22.16	77.84
	(76)	(267)
Pan-green identifiers	78.26	21.74
	(162)	(45)
No partisan affiliation	39.33	60.67
	(129)	(199)
$X^2 = 168.34$, $p < 0.01$		

Note: Row percentages on top are followed by corresponding frequencies in parentheses.

been proposed to explain citizens' policy preferences in democratic polities. Tables 5–7 show that all three explanations appear valid as Taiwan citizens' assessment of costs and benefits of policy outcomes, ethnic identities, and party identifications, and perceptions of threats do seem to affect their positions on cross–strait interactions. Specifically, Table 5 shows that citizens with either a Chinese identity or an affiliation with the Pan-Blue alliance tend to support policies that enhance cross–strait economic exchanges, whereas respondents with either a Taiwanese identity or an affiliation with the Pan-Green alliance are more likely to oppose an unrestricted economic policy toward China. This should not be a surprising finding because Taiwanese identifiers and Pan-Green backers are generally more supportive of the island's *de jure* independence. They worry that expanded cross–strait exchanges may increase Taiwan's economic dependence on China and promote political integration between two sides of the Taiwan Strait. What is interesting is that respondents with

Table 6: Taiwan Citizens' Perceived Self-Interest and Positions on Cross–Strait Exchanges.

	The government should restrict cross–strait economic exchanges	The government should enhance cross–strait economic exchanges
An unrestricted policy will make my economic conditions better or the same	26.18 (161)	73.82 (454)
An unrestricted policy will make my economic conditions worse	87.44 (181)	12.56 (26)
$X^2 = 239.23$, $p < 0.01$		
An unrestricted policy will make Taiwanese society better or the same	21.35 (120)	78.65 (442)
An unrestricted policy will make Taiwanese society worse	83.97 (220)	16.03 (42)
$X^2 = 289.09$, $p < 0.01$		

Note: Row percentages on top are followed by corresponding frequencies in parentheses.

no partisan affiliations or with a dual identity — considering themselves to be both Chinese and Taiwanese — also support a relaxed economic policy toward China. Because Pan-Blue supporters and dual identifiers constitute one-third to half of the electorate, their policy preferences will play an important role in Taipei's cross–strait policies. On the effects of elements of self-interest, Table 6 shows that when respondents believe an unrestricted policy on cross–strait economic exchanges would hurt personal or social economic benefits at personal or societal level, they are likely to oppose such a policy. If they feel that such a policy would bring benefits to themselves and to the Taiwanese society, they tend to support it.

While the effects of self-interest and symbolic politics are generally consistent with the hypothesis, threat perceptions seem to affect Taiwan citizens' positions differently. Following the structural realist perspective, one would expect that individuals with a higher level of threat perception are more likely to be cautious of cross–strait trades and investment for fear of economic dependence on the Chinese

Table 7: Taiwan Citizens' Threat Perceptions and Positions on Cross–Strait Exchanges.

	The government should restrict cross–strait economic exchanges	The government should enhance cross–strait economic exchanges
If Taiwan declares formal independence, Beijing will attack (high threat)	30.4 (114)	69.6 (261)
If Taiwan declares formal independence, Beijing will not attack (low threat)	53.36 (230)	46.64 (201)
$X^2 = 43.23$, $p < 0.01$		
If Beijing attacks, the United States will not intervene militarily on Taiwan's behalf (high threat)	28.57 (116)	71.43 (290)
If Beijing attacks, the United States will intervene militarily on Taiwan's behalf (low threat)	54.3 (202)	45.7 (170)
$X^2 = 53.18$, $p < 0.01$		

Note: Row percentages on top are followed by corresponding frequencies in parentheses.

market. However, the findings in Table 7 show that citizens in Taiwan are actually more supportive of an unrestricted policy toward cross–strait economic exchange when they sense Beijing's military threat and Washington's uncertain security commitment. Apparently, citizens with a high sense of threat want to use economic exchanges as a means of alleviating cross–strait hostility.

To ensure that the relationship between Taiwan citizens' threat perceptions and their policy positions are not spurious, a multivariate analysis is in order. The dependent variable, respondents' *policy positions*, is coded dichotomously using responses listed in Table 4, with 1 indicating support for a relaxed policy on cross–strait economic exchanges and 0 otherwise. Based on hypotheses of symbolic politics, self-interest, and threat perceptions, several independent variables are included in the analysis based on the coding in Tables 5 through 7. Because the theory of symbolic politics maintains that attitudinal predispositions affect individuals' policy positions, two ethnic identity variables and two party identification variables are created. The island citizens with a *Taiwanese identity* or a *Chinese identity* are coded 1 in the relevant categories and 0 otherwise, while respondents with a dual identity serve as the baseline group. To tap respondents' psychological attachments to political parties, *Pan-Green affiliation* and *Pan-Blue affiliation* are coded 1 for respondents in the relevant categories and 0 otherwise, with nonpartisan voters as the baseline group. Respondents of the Pan-Green camp include those who are identified with the Democratic Progressive Party (DPP) and the Taiwan Solidarity Union (TSU), while respondents of the Pan-Blue camp are those who are identified with the KMT Party, the People's First Party, and the New Party.

To assess the effects of self-interest on respondents' policy positions, two dummy variables, *hurting personal well-being* and *hurting Taiwan's economy*, are created, with 1 indicating responses that personal well-being or Taiwan's economy would be harmed by a less restrictive policy and 0 otherwise. This measurement suggests that the hypothesized effects of both variables are negative if they are coded as 1's. Two dummy variables are created to assess individuals' thereat perceptions: *China's military threat* and *no U.S. defense*. Responses that China will launch military attacks at Taiwan and that the US will not intervene militarily should Taiwan declare itself independent are coded as 1 and 0 otherwise. Such a coding scheme ensures that 1's in both variables represent perceptions of high threats.

Several control variables are also included in the analysis. It is hypothesized that individuals' education level, gender, and age will affect their policy positions. To measure respondents' education level, a dummy variable, *college degree* (*and above*), is created with 1 for those who completed or went beyond a college degree. The variable of *female* is coded 1 according to respondents' gender, and *age* is measured by the number of years since birth.

Because the dependent variable has two categories, a logit model with binary outcomes is employed (Long, 1997; Long and Freese, 2003). Specifically, the regression model takes the form of

$$\ln \boldsymbol{\Omega}(\mathbf{x}) = \ln \frac{\Pr(y=1|\mathbf{x})}{\Pr(y=0|\mathbf{x})} = \mathbf{x}\boldsymbol{\beta}$$

where $\ln\Omega(\mathbf{x})$ is the natural logarithm of the conditional odds of having a response of supporting a less restrictive policy on cross–strait economic exchanges relative to having a response favoring a restricted approach. $\mathbf{x}$ is a vector of independent variables, and $\boldsymbol{\beta}$ is a vector of regression estimates.

Table 8 presents the regression coefficients and corresponding odds ratios after fitting the binary logit model with policy positions as the dependent variable.[5] There are several important findings:

First, all but two regression coefficients associated with the eight key independent variables are statistically significant, which suggests that all three hypotheses based on symbolic politics, self-interest, and threat perceptions provide valid explanations for citizens' policy positions. Specifically, while respondents with a Chinese identity have no appreciable difference from those with a dual identity over cross–strait economic policies, respondents with a Taiwanese identity are reluctant to have an unrestricted policy. The odds of Taiwanese identifiers' supporting an open policy are 42.6 percent smaller by comparison with those with a dual identity. Similarly, comparing respondents of no partisan affiliation, those identified with Pan-Green parties are also unwilling to adopt an unrestricted cross–strait economic policy. These findings are consistent with the hypotheses presented earlier. Because those with a Taiwanese identity or with a Pan-Green partisan affiliation tend to support the island's *de jure* independence, the objection to an unrestricted policy toward trades and investments in China clearly shows their concerns about the possible consequences of economic dependence on the Chinese market. As the island citizens' policy positions are affected by predispositions crystallized in the form of ethnic identity and party identification, the

Table 8: Binary Logit Analysis of Taiwan Citizens' Policy Positions ($N = 611$).

	Coeff. (S.E.)	O.R. (% change)
Symbolic politics variables		
Taiwanese identity	–0.55*	0.57
	(0.30)	(–42.6%)
Chinese identity	0.79	2.20
	(0.51)	(120%)
Pan-Green affiliation	–0.68*	0.51
	(0.39)	(–49%)
Pan-Blue affiliation	0.40	1.50
	(0.31)	(50%)
Self-interest variables		
Hurting personal well-being	–1.62**	0.20
	(0.41)	(–80%)
Hurting Taiwan's economy	–1.86**	0.15
	(0.36)	(–85%)
Threat perceptions variables		
China Military Threat	0.50*	1.64
	(0.27)	(64%)
No US Defense	0.50*	1.65
	(0.29)	(65%)
Demographic variables		
College degree	0.31	1.36
	(0.30)	(36%)
Female	–0.60*	0.55
	(0.28)	(–45%)
Age	0.01	1.01
	(0.01)	(1%)

Note: O.R. = Adjusted Odds Ratio; Coeff. = Maximum Likelihood Coefficient; S.E. = Standard Error.
* Significant at .05; ** Significant at .01, one-tailed test.

findings empirically prove that symbolic attitudes do exert statistically significant effects on individuals' policy positions.

Also consistent with the hypotheses of self-interest, both related regression coefficients are statistically significant and bear negative signs. Respondents who feel that an unrestricted approach would hurt Taiwan at both personal and societal levels are 80 percent and 85 percent smaller in odds, respectively, to support an open policy toward cross–strait economic exchanges. Clearly, rational calculations of costs and benefits of policy outcomes are also a part of Taiwan residents' policy decisions.

Meanwhile, both regression coefficients associated with threat variables are statistically significant but bear positive signs. Compared with citizens with a lower level of threat perception, respondents having a higher sense of threat tend to be more supportive of an unrestricted approach to trades and investments in China. The odds of supporting an open policy are 1.6 times larger for both respondents who perceive military threats from China and who foresee no American intervention in a cross–strait conflict on Taiwan's behalf. As indicated earlier, this finding contradicts the hypothesis that individuals with a higher level of threat perception tend to be more cautious about economic dependence. Apparently, Taiwan citizens with a higher sense of threats support incumbent President Ma Ying-jeou's policy of expanding economic interactions with China to ease cross–strait tension that was aggravated during the 8-year rule of former President Chen Shui-bian.

Only one of the three demographic variables is statistically significant. That is, female citizens on the island are more cautious about the potential negative effects of trades and investments in China. Because the regression coefficients associated with the other two demographic variables are not statistically significant, it means that education and age have no effects on the island citizens' positions on cross–strait economic exchanges.

As this study includes three competing theoretical frameworks of symbolic attitudes, self-interest, and threat perceptions, it begs the question which one of the three explanations is more powerful in accounting for citizens' policy preferences. Table 9 shows the changes in predicted probabilities of policy position for the change of each independent variable. Specifically, when respondents have concerns about the negative effects of cross–strait economic exchanges on personal and societal well-being, the probability of supporting an unrestricted policy

Table 9: Predicted Probabilities of Change in Policy Positions by Elements of Symbolic Politics, Self-Interests and Threat Perceptions ($N = 611$).

Symbolic politics variables	
Taiwanese identity	–0.14
Pan-Green affiliation	–0.17
Self-interest variables	
Hurting personal well-being	–0.38
Hurting Taiwan's economy	–0.44
Threat perceptions variables	
China military threat	0.12
No US defense	0.12
Demographic variables	
Female	–0.14

is 0.38 and 0.43 smaller than for those who do not have such concerns. This is far larger in size than the effects of those variables associated with threat perceptions and symbolic attitudes, which range from 0.12 to 0.16. While all three theoretical frameworks provide valid explanations, it is clear that self-interest variables are the most powerful factors in accounting for Taiwan citizens' policy positions on economic interactions with China. As will be detailed below, these findings also have important policy implications for politicians in Taiwan who have repeatedly manipulated the issue of identity for political gains.

CONCLUSION

This study aims to examine three competing hypotheses on citizens' policy decision making processes in democratic systems. Employing survey data collected in Taiwan, the above analysis shows that the islanders' positions on cross–strait economic exchanges are a function of symbolic politics, self-interest, and threat perceptions. When individuals take a stand on a given issue, they are influenced by both the symbolism evoked by the issue as well as the costs and benefits of associated policy outcomes. In the case of Taiwan, which is a democratic polity under external threats, citizens' analytical minds are also affected by both their perception of military threats from across the Taiwan Strait and Washington's uncertain security commitment. While all three competing theories provide valid explanations for citizens' policy preferences, cost-benefit assessment clearly plays a dominant role in individuals' decision-making processes. This finding contradicts the previous conclusion that symbolism has overriding effects on individuals' policy preferences (Sears *et al.*, 1979, 1980). The conclusions may be inconsistent because the effects of the cross–strait economy have become increasingly more extensive, immediate, and concrete in Taiwan citizens' daily life, as data in Tables 1–3 have demonstrated. Without denying the importance of symbolic politics, which has repeatedly shown considerable effects on Taiwan citizens' political life (Chang and Wang, 2005), the theoretical implication of this finding is that self-interest may also play a significant role in individuals' decision-making processes. More research is needed on the conditions under which self-interest, symbolic politics, and threat perceptions affect citizens' policy positions.

The above findings also have important policy implications for both Taipei and Beijing. First of all, symbolic politics have played an important role in Taiwanese politics during the past decade. Treating China as an inherent enemy, the island's politicians repeatedly manipulated the "identity card" to garner electoral support. As patriotism has been formulated in such slogans as "Loving Taiwan", disagreements on policy issues have frequently been labeled as "betraying Taiwan" or "selling out Taiwan" which deepened animosity between rival politicians, impeded the development of a "loyal opposition", and stifled rational debates on various policy issues, including cross–strait economic exchanges. The above analysis shows that symbolism is not the most important factor in citizens' opinions on issues that would affect their livelihood. As Taiwan has become a full-fledged democracy, the island's politicians need to confront the issue not by affective symbols but by rational analysis of the cost and benefits of each policy outcome in order to win the majority's support.

Beijing leaders also need to take heed of the above analysis because symbolic attitudes are generally stable while self-interests and threat perceptions are more malleable. Contexts conducive for certain policy positions may thus be created through manipulating these factors. Indeed, cross–strait economic exchanges are not merely economic in nature. Unlike former President Chen who implemented a series of policies aiming to distance Taiwan from China, Taipei's newly elected President Ma is now pursuing a policy of expanding economic engagement with China, expecting that this policy could reduce cross–strait tension and sustain stable relations with China (Ma, 2007, 2009). The policies of Ma's and Chen's administrations thus represent two different strategies of dealing with cross–strait relations. As Ma's policy is a significant departure from Chen's pro-independence policy, it represents a turning point for cross–strait relations which have been deadlocked during the past eight years.

While Ma can claim the legitimacy of his policy of rapprochement on his landslide victory in the 2008 presidential election, it is important to know that his policies only acquire the support of the plurality on the island. As shown above, a substantial number of Taiwan citizens are expressing reservation about an unrestricted approach to cross–strait economic exchanges, fearing that economic dependence on the Chinese market may harm the island country's national security. After all, the Beijing government has refused to renounce the use of force against Taiwan and has constantly threatened the island with its military might. Many Taiwan citizens, though sensing external threats from Beijing's military posture and Washington's uncertain security commitment, are willing to support Ma's relaxed policy toward cross–strait economic interactions hoping that it could sustain cross–strait stability. It is important to bear in mind that Taiwan has a full-fledged democratic system, and Ma's policy of engagement could falter if it loses the majority's support. Thus, Ma's policy success will need Beijing leaders' help. If Chinese leaders continue their tactics of isolating Taiwan internationally and threatening the island citizens with military force, the tide of public opinion may turn against Ma's rapprochement policy. Polls taken after the eight-month-long

Missile Crisis began by China in 1995–1996 showed that the crisis had only deepened popular resentment against Beijing. China's attempts to isolate Taiwan internationally, as demonstrated by Beijing's repeated blocks to Taipei's bid for World Health Organization membership and its recent attempt to downgrade the island's World Trade Organization representation in Geneva, only hardened the determination of Taiwan residents to resist China's claim to the island. Chinese leaders will need to be creative in their proposals to Taiwan residents if they are truly committed to resolving the cross–strait conflicts peacefully.

REFERENCES

Chang, GA and TY Wang (2005). Taiwanese or Chinese? Independence or unification? An analysis of generational differences in Taiwan. *Journal of Asian and African Studies*, 40 (1–2), 29–49.

Chen, S-B (2006). President Chen's new year message. Office of the President, the Republic of China, January 1, at *<http://www.president.gov.tw/en/>*.

Cheng, T-J (1993). On Taiwan-Mainland Dyad. *Issues and Studies*, 29, 36–55.

Christensen, TJ (2002). The contemporary security dilemma: Deterring a Taiwan conflict. *The Washington Quarterly*, 25(4), 7–21.

Cooper, JF (1997). The origins of conflict across the Taiwan strait: The problem of differences in perceptions. *Journal of Contemporary China*, 6(15), 199–227.

Downs, A (1957). *An Economic Theory of Democracy*. New York: Harper-Row.

Enav, P (2007). Taiwan leader Riles China, U.S. *Washington Post*, September 9, *<http://www.washingtonpost.com/wp-dyn/content/article/2007/09/09/AR2007090900579.html>*.

Gordon, C and A Arian (2001). Threat and decision making. *Journal of Conflict Resolution*, 45(2), 196–215.

Keng, S, L-H Chen and K-P Huang (2006). Sense, sensitivity, and sophistication in shaping the future of cross–strait relations. *Issues & Studies*, 42(4), 23–66.

Long, JS (1997). *Regression Models for Categorical and Limited Dependent Variables*. Thousand Oaks, CA: Sage Publications.

Long, JS and J Freese (2003). *Regression Models for Categorical Dependent Variables Using STATA*. Revised Edition. College Station, TX: STATA Corporation.

Lu, M (2008). Presidential election 2008: Referendum: Referendums fail to meet thresholds. *Taipei Times*, March 23, *<http://www.taipeitimes.com/News/taiwan/archives/2008/03/23/2003406756>*.

Ma, Y-J (2007). A vision for peace and prosperity in East Asia: A Taiwan perspective. Speech delivered at Doshisha University, Kyoto, Japan, November 21, at *<http://www.kuomintangnews.org>*.

Ma, Y-J (2009). New year's day celebratory message. Government Information Office, Republic of China, January 1, *<http://www.gio.gov.tw/ct.asp?xItem=44972&ctNode=2462>*.

Mainland Affairs Council (Various Years). *Liang-An Jing-gi Tong-gi Yue-bao* (*Monthly Report on Cross-Straits Economy*), *<http://www.mac.gov.tw/>*.

New York Time (2002). New China-Taiwan battle: 3 words on passports. January 15, at *<http://www.nytimes.com>*.

Riker, WH and PC Ordeshook (1973). *An Introduction to Positive Political Theory.* Englewood Cliffs: Prentice-Hall.

Ross, R (2002). Navigating the Taiwan strait: Deterrence, escalation dominance, and U.S.–China relations. *International Security*, 27(2), 48–85.

Schelling, T (1966). *Arms and Influence.* New Haven: Yale University Press.

Sears, DO, CP Hensler and LK Speer (1979). Whites' opposition to "busing": Self-interest or symbolic politics? *American Political Science Review*, 73(2), 369–384.

Sears, DO, RR Lau, TR Tyler and HM Allen, Jr (1980). Self-interest vs. symbolic politics in policy attitudes and presidential voting. *American Political Science Review*, 74(3), 670–684.

Schafer, M (1999). Cooperative and conflictual policy preferences: The effect of identity, security and image of the other. *Political Psychology*, 20(4), 829–844.

Taiwan Affairs Office and the Information Office of the State Council, the People's Republic of China (2000). The one-China principle and the Taiwan issue. *People's Daily Online* (*Renmin Ribao*), *<http://www.peopledaily.com.cn>*.

Taiwan Affairs Office & Information Office State Council, the People's Republic of China (1993). The Taiwan question and reunification of China. 1993, Beijing, *<http://english.peopledaily.com.cn/whitepaper/7.html>*.

Su, J (2005). Anti-secession law troublesome: MAC. *Taipei Times*, March 13, *<http://www.taipeitimes.com/News/taiwan/archives/2005/03/13/2003246046>*.

Wang, TY (2002). Lifting the "No Haste, Be Patient" policy: Implications for cross–strait relations. *Cambridge Review of International Affairs*, 15(1), 131–139.

Wang, TY (2005). The perception of threats and pragmatic policy choice: A survey of public opinion in Taiwan. *Issues & Studies*, 41(1), 87–111.

Wang, TY and A Chang (2006). External threats and political tolerance in Taiwan. *Political Research Quarterly*, 59(3), 377–388.

Xinhuanet (2005). Anti-secession law (*fan fenlie guojia fa*). March 14, *<http://news.xinhuanet.com/tai_gang_ao/2005-03/14/content_2694168.htm>*.

ENDNOTES

1. A part of the title of this study is taken from Sears *et al.* (1980).
2. During the past decade, Taiwan's political landscape has been divided into two political camps: the Pan-Green and the Pan-Blue camps. The former includes the DPP and the Taiwan Solidarity Union, while the latter comprises of KMT, the People's First Party, and the New Party.

3. Probably the most significant event that Washington demonstrated its resolve of deterring Beijing's use of force against Taiwan was the 1995–1996 missile crisis (Cooper, 1997).
4. For an analysis of the "no haste, be patient" policy, see Wang (2002).
5. Because all VIF scores are less than 1.85, it is thus determined that there is no significant evidence of multicollinearity in the analysis.

Chapter

8

Beijing's Shifting Positions in the New Era of Cross–Taiwan Strait Relations

Quansheng Zhao and Guoli Liu

Beijing's policy toward Taiwan has been evolving since 1978, and the most recent changes have attracted growing attention from around the world. We examine Beijing's shifting positions with a focus on the recent development in the new era of cross–strait relations.[1] 1 January 2009 was the 30th anniversary of the "Message to Taiwan Compatriots" issued by the Standing Committee of the National People's Congress of the People's Republic of China. At the meeting to commemorate the important message that announced China's shift from a strategy of armed "liberation of Taiwan" to "peaceful reunification", President Hu Jintao made an important speech on 31 December 2008 and proposed six-point policy for improving the cross–Taiwan strait relations. The "six-points" outlined in Hu's speech are (1) firm adherence to the "one China" principle; (2) strengthening commercial ties, including negotiating an economic cooperation agreement; (3) promoting personnel exchanges; (4) stressing common cultural links between the two sides; (5) allowing Taiwan's "reasonable" participation in global organizations; and (6) negotiating a peace agreement (*Renmin ribao*, 1 January 2009). Compared with Beijing's previous policy statements, Hu's speech is more pragmatic, flexible, and people-oriented. President Hu puts aside difficult disputes and stresses cooperation in economic and other areas. This important speech is a clear indication that Beijing's policy toward Taiwan has undergone significant shifts and is likely to continue to evolve in the positive direction of peaceful cooperation for mutual benefits. This policy will contribute to building mutual trust, enhancing cooperation, and promoting regional peace and prosperity. In this key speech, Hu emphasizes that the main theme of cross–strait relations is peace and development. This policy of actively developing peaceful cross–strait relations will help to realize national unity, harmony, and prosperity. The political foundation of peaceful development of cross–strait relations is maintaining that both the mainland and Taiwan belong to one China.[2]

The responses from Taiwan and the outside world to Hu's speech have been overwhelmingly positive.[3] Taiwan responded positively to Chinese President Hu's call for a truce with the island, saying it reflects China's new thinking and pragmatic approach on cross–strait ties. Hu's speech sets the tone for Beijing's Taiwan policy for the coming years. It could also signal that Beijing is ready to elevate cross–strait dialogue to the next level, which could touch on military and political issues.

Although Taiwan leader Ma Ying-jeou has not provided a comprehensive response to Hu's six-point proposal, Ma has commented several times about Hu's positive proposal and suggested that Taiwan is willing to engage in detailed talks with Beijing on economic cooperation, cultural exchange, and numerous other issues.[4] Before the Taiwanese delegation left for the April 2009 Boao Forum for Asia, Ma met with the members of the delegation and stated that the two sides of the Taiwan Straits should be "forward looking, sailing in the same boat (*tongzhou gongji*), and helping each other to overcome the global financial crisis".

The Taiwanese delegation attending the 2009 Boao Forum for Asia met with Chinese Premier Wen Jiabao on April 19. In his welcoming remarks at the meeting, Wen urged the two sides of the Taiwan Strait to "face the future, bury old grudges, cooperate with each other and move forward together", and he called for them to seize the precious opportunity to achieve peace in the strait. Taiwan's delegation head, former Control Yuan President Fredrick Chien, said he noticed that Wen proposed the ideas of seeking "peaceful development" between the two sides and boosting cross–strait cooperation in the fields of trade, the economy and investment, in a report he made March 5 to the annual session of the National People's Congress. Chien also called for mainland China to boost the daily number of Taiwan-bound tourists, purchase more household electrical appliances from Taiwan, and encourage Chinese enterprises to actively invest in Taiwan. On another front, Chien noted that Taiwan can also do some things for mainland China, such as helping set up new communities accommodating hospitals, factories, and schools, and transform slums into tourist spots.[5]

More significantly, the mainland and Taiwan have signed nine agreements in less than one year since cross–strait talks between the Straits Exchange Foundation (SEF) and the Association for Relations Across the Taiwan Strait (ARATS) resumed. In the latest round of talks in Nanjing on April 25–26, Straits Exchange Foundation (SEF) Chairman Chiang Pin-kung and his counterpart, Association for Relations Across the Taiwan Strait President Chen Yunlin signed a joint statement on opening Taiwan to Chinese investment after their meeting. Taipei and Beijing inked three agreements, agreeing to launch additional regular cross–strait passenger flights, establish a financial cooperation mechanism and join forces to combat crime. These agreements represent full normalization of the "three links". In his opening speech, Chen Yunlin raised the issue of Taiwan's proposed signing of an economic cooperation framework agreement (ECFA) with China, but avoided mentioning the term, saying that the two sides should "establish a cooperation mechanism or framework on cross–strait economics". Chen elaborated, "The two sides should set up systemized regulations for economic development.

I believe we will create a win-win situation that benefits both sides if we overcome difficulties hand in hand". Chen said China would expand its purchases of Taiwanese products and push for Chinese companies to invest in Taiwan, while encouraging Taiwanese companies to invest in China. Chiang echoed Chen's remarks on the establishment of an economic cooperation mechanism, and urged China to help Taiwan gain more international space in seeking economic and trade cooperation with other countries. Thus, Taiwan not only needs to strengthen economic cooperation with mainland China, but also needs to join other major trade partners in regional economic cooperation.

As a result of Chen and Chiang's meeting, the SEF and ARATS agreed to increase the number of scheduled cross–strait flights from 108 weekly flights to 270 and add six more Chinese destinations. The financial cooperation pact will allow financial organizations to set up offices on each side, and the two sides will also work together on currency management. On cross–strait crime fighting, the pact includes white-collar criminals on the list of those eligible for repatriation, allowing the two sides to help each other by providing evidence and making it possible for Taiwan to repatriate fugitives. The fourth round of talks will be held in Taiwan sometime this year. The two sides will address fishing industry cooperation, quality checks of agricultural products, cross–strait cooperation in inspection and certification, and the prevention of double taxation in the next round of cross–strait negotiation, among other issues.[6]

Under the agreements signed by Chen and Chiang on 26 April 2009, the two sides will launch regular passenger and cargo flights across the Taiwan Strait, indicating the normalization of cross–strait air transport service. Before the pact, direct cross–strait flight services were only provided on weekends and during four major traditional festivals. Under the agreement on financial cooperation, the two sides agreed to boost mainland investment in the island and facilitate financial institutions to set up branches on each other's side. The mainland and Taiwan will continue to discuss issues concerning market access of financial institutions on the other side, the agreement stated. According to the agreement on mutual assistance in criminal matters, the two sides will collaborate in civil and criminal fields and take measures to jointly crack down on crimes, with a special focus on major crimes involving kidnapping, weapons, drugs, human trafficking, and cross–strait organized crimes. Economic cases of fraud, money laundering, forging or falsifying currencies, and securities would also be targeted, according to the agreement. The two sides agreed to exchange crime-related information and help each other investigate cases and collect evidence. Each side is also responsible for helping the other to identify witnesses, seize, and repatriate criminals and suspects.[7]

Such warm and cordial exchanges between the two sides of the Taiwan Strait contrast sharply with the often tension-filled days under Chen Shui-bian administration between 2000 and 2008. When dealing with the DPP regime under Chen Shui-bian, Beijing faced two very different scenarios: "economic integration-based unification" (EIU) versus "Taiwan independence-led war" (TIW). Indeed, Beijing confronted the dilemma of choosing war or peace. With the transition of power in Taiwan from Chen to Ma Ying-jeou in May 2008, a precious new opportunity for cross–Taiwan Strait peace and cooperation has emerged. The danger of war in the Taiwan Strait has been significantly reduced. Accordingly, Beijing's policy has further shifted from preparing for the worst case scenario to building mutual trust and enhancing cooperation. As a result, EIU has become more likely, and TIW has been reduced to a minimum level. In the foreseeable future, armed conflict is almost totally out of question.

This paper examines Beijing's shift of policy toward Taiwan with an emphasis on the interaction of three variables. (1) Changes inside Taiwan. (2) Beijing's changing ideas and domestic situation in the PRC. (3) Changes in international environment and political change inside the United States.

CHANGES INSIDE TAIWAN

Since spring 2008, significant political change has taken place in Taiwan which has favored the peaceful development of cross–strait relations. From May 2000 to May 2008, the Chen Shui-bian administration frequently challenged mainland China. Chen's pro-Taiwan independence policies created serious crises in cross–Taiwan Strait relations. Chen's strategy aimed at gaining local support backfired in the end. In the January 2008 parliamentary election the Democratic Progressive Party (DPP) only won 27 seats. Smaller political parties allied with the KMT and the DPP were marginalized. The DPP's focus on Taiwan identity politics (which emphasize that Taiwan is not part of China) was overplayed in the run-up to the December 2004 legislative election, which limited the increase in its share of the vote. However, the DPP still reached a peak in its level of support in the 2004 legislative election by securing 38% of the vote. In the January 2008 legislative election, it was largely Chen's unpopularity that resulted in the Nationalist Party (KMT)'s two-thirds majority in parliament. The 2008 election was conducted under a new electoral system of single-member districts/two ballots system, which replaced the multi-member districts/single non-transferable vote system (SNTV) used in the 2004 election. This new electoral system was actually "unfriendly" to small parties or the DPP. It is reasonable to say that the new electoral system might have partially led to the DPP's loss/defeat in the 2008 legislative election (Wang, 2008).

In the March 2008 presidential election, voters in Taiwan handed opposition candidate Ma Ying-jeou a landslide victory, raising hopes of détente with China after eight years of pro-independence brinksmanship that had strained ties with the United States. The result was a rebuke to President Chen Shui-bian, whose candidate, Frank Hsieh, lost by two million votes out of 13.2 million cast. Analysts said it signaled a prioritizing of economic interests over ethnic identity and the anti-China rhetoric of Chen's ailing party, which also lost heavily in January's legislative elections. "Taiwan should be united without using ethnicity as an issue for political purposes... I will be symbol of national unity, not a source of social division", said Ma at a victory press conference, taking a swipe at the opposition Democratic Progressive Party's campaign ads that highlighted his roots on the mainland, in contrast to Taiwanese-born opponents. Ma said that he wanted Taiwan to be a "responsible stakeholder" in international circles and to restore "mutual trust" with the United States, Taiwan's closest ally. He said he would seek to restore direct air links with China and bring more Chinese tourists to Taiwan as his first steps toward economic cooperation that may eventually yield a "common market" for goods and services (Montlake, 2008). With no national elections taking place until 2012, the DPP will remain marginalized at least until then. As a result of the KMT's dominance, Ma Ying-jeou will have solid backing from parliament. This is in contrast to Chen's administration, which had to promote its policies in a hostile legislative environment (*The Economist* Intelligence Unit, 5, 6).

Power transition from DPP to KMT and from Chen Shui-bian to Ma Ying-jeou created a historic opportunity for improving cross–Taiwan strait relations. Since the Kuomintang administration came to power in May 2008, cross–Taiwan Strait policy has been significantly relaxed, and tensions across the strait have eased, heightening expectations for a normalization of economic and trade exchange between the two sides.

Since taking office in May 2008, the Ma administration has focused on relaxing cross–strait policy and normalizing economic and trade relations. In June 2008, the Strait Exchange Foundation and the Association for Relations Across the Taiwan Strait formally resumed negotiations after a 10-year hiatus (*Renmin ribao*, 13 June 2008). They held two meetings in June and November 2008, during which several agreements were signed, including ones on allowing more mainland Chinese tourists to visit Taiwan, opening up direct passenger and cargo charter flights between the two sides, promoting food safety, and expanding postal cooperation. As we mentioned above, the April 2009 meeting between the two sides achieved three additional significant agreements.

From the Ma administration's perspective, one of the top priorities is to repair cross–Taiwan Strait relations. Ma resurrected Frederick Chien's proposition that "cross–strait relations are higher than diplomatic relations". In September 2008, Ma proposed that the relationship between Taiwan and the mainland is a "special relation" but not "state to state relation". Ma's expression of special relation overturned the so-called "state to state relation" emphasized by both Lee Teng-hui and Chen Shui-bian for more than ten years. Ma's new proposition has had remarkable effect on positive transition of cross–strait relations.

The divisions and struggles between pan-Blue and pan-Green continue in Taiwan. Taiwan politics are most likely to be pluralistic, and no one party can totally dominate political agenda. If Ma goes too far in any direction, he is likely to alienate a significant portion of the electorate and thus risks losing the next election. As a result, the Ma administration tends to walk a fine line in seeking a balance between the contending political forces in Taiwan. Ma is sharply different from Chen. Chen Shui-bian became deeply involved in scandals. The on-going legal case against Chen is a testimony to the maturity of Taiwan's legal system and democratic practice. That is, DPP and Taiwan independence forces are still active. Though they are temporarily in retreat, Taiwan identity is still strong, and the Taiwan tendency towards independence continues to exist. It is significant that Beijing has clearly recognized that "love Taiwan and love home" feelings in Taiwan do not equal the Taiwan independence tendency. Beijing is willing to develop relations with all political forces in Taiwan as long as they do not pursue Taiwan independence. The most recent example is that the Mayor of Kaohsiung, Chen Chu, became the first top government leader of the opposition Democratic Progressive Party (DPP) to visit Beijing and Shanghai in May 2009.

With the passing of the old generation of mainlanders, the new generation of KMT leaders no longer holds a deeply rooted view on the reunification of China. In the 2008 Presidential campaign, even KMT proposed that Taiwan independence could be one of the options for Taiwan's future. This type of statement might be a campaign tactic. Nevertheless, it is a deeply alarming signal for Beijing.

Ma Ying-jeou is much more acceptable to Beijing than Chen Shui-bian. Although Ma is not interested in unification, at least not in his term as President, he is the best Beijing can hope for under the circumstances. Furthermore, Ma has promised to improve Taiwan's economy by resuming ties with the mainland. Here the two sides have found common ground. What followed from this consensus has been remarkable, not the least of which was the joining of the Taipei Zoo by Tuan Tuan and Yuan Yuan, the two giant pandas from Sichuan Province that charmed Taiwan's children and their parents.

According to Wu Yu-shan, Taiwan wants to achieve three major goals with its new course: economic revitalization, diplomatic truce and expanded international space, and peace agreement. Beijing is perfectly willing to help Taiwan achieve the first goal, but what ultimately transpires may not be enough to meet inflated expectations, especially amidst the international financial crisis. The second and third goals are more troublesome for Beijing. The Ma administration is definitely not for Taiwan independence, but nor is it in favor of unification. It has moved from the traditional KMT position of gradual unification to sticking to the status quo, with national future to be determined. Given this lack of commitment to ultimate unification, how far is Beijing willing to go to grant Taipei international space that may later be used to pursue independence or name change? Beijing is also worried about the DPP making a comeback in three or seven years and taking advantage of Taiwan's improved diplomatic and security positions. Before making concessions, Beijing may want to receive concrete promises from Ma's government that it is committed to unification. Failing that, there could be little progress on the diplomatic or security front. At this point euphoria may dissipate and give way to bitter disappointment (Wu, 2009).

The expansion of Taiwan-owned factories in China, as well as increasing domestic demand on the mainland, has led to a rapid increase in cross–strait trade in recent years. Trade between Taiwan and China was banned until the early 1990s, and despite a subsequent easing of restrictions, many goods leaving the island for China are still recorded as heading elsewhere, usually to Hong Kong. Data from the Ministry of Finance show that in 2007 mainland China (including Hong Kong) took 42.8% of Taiwan's exports, whereas the United States took 13.6%. These figures notwithstanding, the long-standing position of the United States as the most important overseas market for Taiwan firms remains unchanged: a high, although indeterminate, proportion of the finished products manufactured by Taiwan factories on the Chinese mainland are re-exported to the US as well as to other developed economies, including the EU and Japan (*The Economist* Intelligence Unit, 25).

As an open market economy that relies heavily on export, Taiwan has been hit particularly hard in the global financial crisis. During his videoconference speech to the Center for Strategic & International Studies on April 22, Ma Ying-jeou stressed the need to build close ties with the mainland:

> We are fully aware that for Taiwan to maintain its strength *vis-à-vis* the mainland, Taiwan must strengthen its international competitiveness. As mainland China becomes the workshop of the world, normalizing economic relations with the other side is a crucial step in achieving this goal. The prospective creation of the Cross–Strait Economic Cooperation Framework Agreement (ECFA) is at the heart of this idea. The spirit of ECFA conjoins Taiwan's interest with the ideals of liberalization and globalization. By concluding the ECFA with the mainland, while also building Taiwan into an innovation and logistic center for multinational companies, we will surely bolster and safeguard Taiwan's competitive edge in the mainland market, and, in turn, the greater global market. The benefits of ECFA to the international community, including American investors are more than obvious. Opening the Three Links — and the goodwill behind them — have made flying, shipping or mailing across the Strait a feasible option now. Together with a more stable political environment, there will be more incentives for foreign business to include Taiwan in their regional operations (Ma, 2009).

In 2008, trade between Taiwan and mainland China exceeded \$129.22 billion. Taiwan's import from the mainland was \$25.88 billion, and Taiwan's exports to the mainland reached \$103.34 billion. Taiwan enjoyed a trade surplus of \$77.46 billion. By the end of 2008, the total amount of Taiwan investment in mainland China reached \$47.66 billion, which ranks Taiwan's investment fifth in the world (*Renmin Ribao* overseas edition, 5 February 2009, p. 3). Data from Taiwan are different but also very impressive. Mainland-bound cumulative investments by Taiwan companies surged to \$68.9 billion as of May 2008 from \$15.3 billion in 2000. Taiwan's cross–strait trade turned to surplus \$35.4 billion in 2008 from deficit \$2 billion in 2000 (Lin, 2009). Even so, the global financial crisis is hurting both Taiwan and the mainland. From Taipei's view, however, the economic emergency also gives the government unprecedented power and legitimacy to pursue policies that it deems necessary to salvage the economy. Bold actions can be taken that could hardly be imagined in normal times, including cross–strait initiatives. In short, Ma's new course is being tested in an environment of high crisis and high capacity. Its success hinges on avoiding the mid-1990s scenario and delivering at tolerable costs in a timely fashion (Wu, 2009).

Leaders in both Beijing and Taipei have publicly pledged to enhance cultural and economic exchanges and financial cooperation. Interestingly, Beijing has declared that it is willing to provide financial assistance to Taiwan if it is necessary to overcome the financial crisis. Such cooperation is certainly mutually beneficial and will contribute not only to economic development across the Taiwan Strait but also to regional stability and prosperity. Ma wants to "end Taiwan's isolation from the world by putting our economic relations with the Chinese mainland on a more normal footing. At the same time, the more contentious political issues will be left on the back burner. We will put off political talks until after a firm foundation on economic, cultural and educational exchanges have been established and buttressed by reciprocal trust and confidence on both sides".[8]

Meanwhile, Ma Ying-jeou has adopted a foreign policy style of "surprise free and low key". In line with "flexible diplomacy", the Ma administration has taken the "first steps towards reconciliation with the mainland by declaring a diplomatic truce. This truce will bring about the end of diplomatic belligerency so that we can concentrate on issues that will yield more real and substantial rewards". Reflecting Taiwan's popular wish, Ma is working to expand Taiwan's international space. Specifically, Ma is actively pursuing Taiwan's role in the World Health Assembly. Interestingly, Ma also perceives the existence of "the gross military imbalance across the strait". He urges the

United States to "provide Taiwan with the necessary defensive arms as stipulated in the TRA" (Taiwan Relations Act) (*Taiwan Journal*, 17 April 2009, p. 7). The Ma administration is simultaneously trying to build closer ties with the mainland and trying to stabilize and strengthen its relations with the United States. Such policies reflect the wish of the majority people in Taiwan and are likely to contribute to the stability of cross–strait relations. How Beijing and Washington respond to such calls will be critical in deciding the future of cross–Taiwan strait relations.

History clearly indicates that internal changes in Taiwan can have significant impact on cross–strait relations (Su, 2008). The recent changes in Taiwan have created a much more favorable environment for improving cross–strait relations. Next we will turn to Beijing's changing ideas and policies. After that we will address the international situation with a focus on the evolving and complex relations among Beijing, Taipei, and Washington. It is important to point out that all parties have a growing common interest in maintaining peace and promoting prosperity across the Taiwan Strait.

BEIJING'S CHANGING IDEAS AND SITUATION IN THE MAINLAND

The dynamics of Chinese foreign policy have been fundamentally influenced by changes in its domestic politics (Zhao, 1996). China's national interest in Taiwan is present in at least two forms. First, Beijing's desire for national unification with Taiwan, Hong Kong, and Macao is at the top of China's national goals. Since matters relating to Hong Kong and Macau were resolved in 1997 and 1999 respectively, the Taiwan issue has become more salient. Second, ever since China's reform and opening policy began in 1978, modernization has been a national priority. Beijing thus considers Taipei not only critical to its national interest in terms of sovereignty and legitimacy, but also important because it can accelerate the mainland's economic drive. Taiwan, like South Korea, is one of the four East Asian tigers, and is therefore also able to provide China with capital, technology, and markets. Furthermore, because of a shared culture,

Taiwan is in a position to provide the mainland with capitalist know-how to help China develop a market economy and integrate itself further into the world economy (Zhao, 2006, 48, 49). Beijing's Taiwan policy is partially driven by rising nationalism. Reinforcing Chinese national confidence and turning past humiliation and current weakness into a driving force for China's modernization, nationalism has become an effective instrument to enhance the legitimacy of the communist state.

Beijing's dilemma with Taiwan is twofold. First, Beijing would like to achieve national reunification with Taiwan through a peaceful path, but it must be prepared for a war scenario if Taiwan insists on breaking from the mainland for its independence. Second, there has been a consensus among China's elite since 1978 when Deng Xiaoping began his reform and openness policy that economic development should be the top priority for China. The modernization drive, however, has in turn produced greater nationalistic sentiment among Chinese people, which makes a compromise with Taiwan's demand for separation virtually impossible for any leader to grant. Fear of the following scenarios makes it difficult for Beijing's leadership to make a choice: if Beijing concentrates solely on economic modernization without preparing to use military force with Taiwan, then Taiwan may move toward a permanent separation; on the other hand, if war manifests over Taiwan, there will almost certainly be a great economic setback, if not a disaster, to both sides of the Taiwan Strait (Zhao, 2005a).

Instead of political and military pressure, the means Beijing has increasingly relied upon to promote its integration with Taiwan in recent years have been economic. Whatever the outcome, Beijing's overall strategy remains clear. A particularly important factor in Taiwan's politics is the business sector, as profit-driven business people generally have viewed the mainland as a desirable market and location for investment. Indeed, Taiwan's extensive trade and economic relations with the mainland have been responsible for generating Taiwan's huge trade surplus. Thus, Taiwan's business community has pressured its politicians to allow for enhanced ties across the Taiwan Strait (Zhao, 2005a, 222). It seems that this economic strategy has had many positive effects.

A key element in analyzing Beijing's Taiwan policy is to look at the PRC's domestic considerations. There are three critical factors. First, since modernization has become the PRC's top international and domestic priority, Beijing would like to promote economic integration within the so-called "Greater China" — namely, the mainland, Taiwan, and Hong Kong. Taiwan has made significant contributions to the PRC's modernization in terms of providing investment, trade, and managerial know-how to speed up China's economic modernization. Second, with nationalism on the rise within the mainland, Beijing's leadership has been acutely sensitive to the issues of sovereignty and regime legitimacy (Zhao, 2004; Gries, 2004). No Chinese leader can afford to become a person condemned by history for not acting to prevent the split of the nation. Third, China's rapid economic growth and rise in status within the international community has allowed Beijing to become more assertive in its foreign policy, as well as in its policy toward Taiwan (Zhao, 2005a, 224).

Beijing began a new strategy of peaceful reunification by promoting economic and cultural exchange across the Taiwan Strait in the 1980s, although it never ruled out the use of force. Beijing's peaceful reunification offense started with the publication of a "Message" to the Taiwan people from the Standing Committee of the National People's Congress on January 1, 1979, and was further elaborated on 30 September 1981, by the NPC leader Ye Jianying in a nine-point proposal for peaceful reunification. In his plan, Ye suggested talks between the CCP and the KMT, and specifically proposed *santong* (three links: commercial, postal, and travel) and *siliu* (four exchanges: academic, cultural, economic, and sports) as the first steps to "gradually eliminate antagonism between the two sides and increase mutual understanding"(*Beijing Review*, 5 October 1981, 11).

In 1983, Chinese leader Deng Xiaoping put forward the "peaceful unification, one country, two systems" formula. The key points of Deng's formula are six fold. (1) Peaceful reunification would be achieved through cooperation between the Chinese Communist Party (CCP) and the Kuomintang (KMT). (2) After reunification, Taiwan and the mainland would pursue different political systems. (3) After reunification, Taiwan would maintain its judicial discretion, legislative power, its court of final appeal, and armed forces. The mainland would neither send civilian nor military personnel to Taiwan. (4) The mainland would not agree to "total autonomy" of Taiwan because that would mean "two Chinas". (5) Peaceful reunification does not mean annexation of Taiwan by the mainland, nor vice versa. (6) Peaceful reunification talks would be conducted on equal footing, not between the central government and local authorities. China would brook no foreign interference.[9]

A significant breakthrough in cross–strait relations was the "1992 Consensus" that can be explicated as "both mainland and Taiwan belong to one China". Unlike his predecessor Chen Shui-bian who denied the existence of the 1992 Consensus, Mao Ying-jeou has clearly recognized the existence of the 1992 Consensus. According to Ma, "the 1992 Consensus seemed to become a nightmare to the DPP government, which tried desperately to deny its existence. In fact, many who were directly involved in preparing and conducting the November 1992 negotiations in Hong Kong that led to the consensus — including Chairman Koo Cheng-fu of the SEF; Chin Chin-yi, former vice chairman and secretary of the SEF; Dr. Kao Kung-lian, vice chairman of MAC; and the author (Ma), who was MAC's senior vice chairman and spokesman — remember clearly that such a consensus on the one-China principle was reached and that each side had agreed in correspondence that the meaning of one China, on which they disagreed, was to be interpreted orally by each side. Although no written agreement was signed, correspondence between SEF and ARATS following the November meeting attested to the existence of such a consensus" (Ma, 2003, 46). Since Ma came into office in May 2008, his administration has "set into motion elements that will not only defuse cross–strait tension, but more importantly embed a new foundation for stability. At the center of this new cross–strait rapprochement is 'the 1992 consensus'. That is, both sides recognize that there is only one China but agree to differ on its definition. Past negotiations with the mainland over 15 years ago were also founded upon this premise, so a common understanding has existed ever since" (Ma, 2009).

In January 1995, then CCP General Secretary Jiang Zemin made an important policy proposal to Taiwan. Jiang's proposal contained the following new elements. (1) The cross–strait talks would not be conducted between the CCP and the KMT alone, but between the CCP and representatives of all political parties and influential groups and organizations in Taiwan. (2) As the first step, the two sides across the strait would negotiate an official ending of hostility. (3) The mainland would separate politics from economics in handling cross–strait affairs. (4) The mainland would not take issue with Taiwan's nonofficial economic or cultural exchanges with foreign countries. (5) The mainland would regard cultural links across the strait as an important basis for reunification.[10] Jiang's goodwill proposal was met by Taiwan leader Lee Teng-hui's challenge. In 1995, Lee paid a well publicized "private visit" to the United States. Beijing reacted strongly and conducted military exercises in 1996. It was indeed a serious crisis in the Taiwan Strait (Suettinger, 2006; Niu, 2004).

The "One China" principle was officially rephrased in August 2000 when Vice-Premier Qian Qichen stated for the first time that "there is only 'One China' in the world, Taiwan and the mainland are both parts of China, and China's territory and sovereignty brook no division". At his meeting with Wu Po-hsiung on November 23, 2000, Qian stated, "saying the mainland and Taiwan are both a part of 'One China' shows that Beijing is pragmatic and accommodating". Indeed, this rephrase softened Beijing's insistence on a single definition for the "One China" principle and suggested a "One China" that is ambiguous enough to allow a resumption of relations based on the 1992 understanding between Beijing and the KMT administration (Zhao, 2008, 204). It is interesting to compare Qian's rephrase with the standard description of the Taiwan issue in the Shanghai Communique of 1972: "the Government of the People's Republic of China is the sole legal government of China; Taiwan is a province of China which has long been returned to the motherland; the liberation of Taiwan is China's internal affair in which no other country has the right to interfere" (http://www.china.org.cn/english/china-us/26012.htm).

Beijing's policy shift flows from the political–economy paradox. From the late 1980s the steady growth of trade, investment, and personnel exchanges has formed powerful linkages across the Taiwan Strait. As the two sides are getting closer economically, they are moving further apart politically. Political changes on both sides appear to widen the Strait, though economic ties continue to bridge it. Beijing's Taiwan policy has always been a combination of *Fang Du* (prevention of Taiwan independence) and *Cu Tong* (promoting reunification). Preventing and even coercing Taipei from *de jure* independence is a constant and sometimes urgent task that could even lead to the use of force. Chinese leaders have a positive reading of the paradox of political alienation *cum* economic integration in cross–strait relations. Beijing is confident that growing economic interdependence will translate in its favor in the long run (Hu, 2006).

Beijing has always been prepared for two scenarios: EIU and TIW. When Chen Shui-bian was in power, there were genuine worries in Beijing that Taiwan's tendency toward independence might grow further with the DPP regime. The hard-liners in Beijing emphasize that only military preparation can stop Taiwan's growing tendency toward independence. In contrast, soft-liners have generally believed that sufficient pressure has been placed on Taiwan, including the military means indicated in the White Paper of February 2000, to ensure that Taipei is unlikely to make an official declaration of *Taidu* (Taiwan independence). Therefore, the PRC should emphasize an EIU direction and avoid making military threats toward Taiwan. In this way, China's modernization drive will continue, and economic developments, particularly along the east coast, will not be damaged.... To be sure, soft-liners also tend to believe that China's national sovereignty is the major principle at stake, and consequently, China would use military force if that sovereignty were violated. However, they also sound a note of caution and emphasize the importance of first engaging Taiwan peacefully. While maintaining military pressure, Beijing's leadership still maintains high hopes of finding a peaceful resolution to the Taiwan issue. During much of the reform era in the 1980s and 1990s, the EIU scenario seemed more attractive to Beijing leadership and proved to be an effective way to deal with the issue of Taiwan (Zhao, 2005a, 228–230).

In March 2005, Chinese leader Hu Jintao made an important policy proclamation on the Taiwan issue. Hu emphasized four points. (1) Never sway in adhering to the one China principle. (2) Never give up efforts to seek peaceful reunification. (3) Never change the principle of placing hope on the Taiwanese people. (4) Never compromise in opposing "Taiwan independence" secessionist activities (*Renmin Ribao*, 5 March 2005). An interesting interpretation of Hu's approach to Taiwan is "the tough side is tougher and the soft side is softer." The hard-line approach was further strengthened with the promulgation of the Anti-Separation law in February 2005. The law is explicitly aimed at Taiwan and legitimizes Chinese military intervention in the case of Taiwanese independence or when all peaceful options for reunification are exhausted. The Anti-Secession Law represents just another case of making a war threat to win peace, and it grew out of Beijing's frustration with Chen Shui-bian's pushing the envelope, particularly his attempt to change the ROC constitution (Zhao, 2008, 208; You, 2006). The law clearly draws a line that, should Taiwan ever cross it to seek independence, would risk the mainland resorting to any necessary means to stop Taiwan from moving toward independence. "Prescribing the conditions for possible use of force, the Anti-Secession Law has not changed Beijing's rationality of threatening war for peace. This seemingly contradictory strategy of talking tough but acting in a calculated manner showed that pragmatic leaders were aware of the danger of being a victim of emotional nationalism. China's Taiwan policy has not been dictated by the emotional voice of nationalism but based on careful calculation of China's national interests" (Zhao, 2008, 211).

On the soft (a better translation of "soft" is perhaps "attraction") side, Hu has taken active steps to improve both political and economic conditions for improving cross–strait relations. The highly publicized visit by Taiwan's opposition parties leaders Lien Chan and James Soong in April–May 2005 indicated a new stage in cross–strait relations. The visit clearly demonstrated Beijing's renewed conciliatory efforts with Taiwan to work towards an EIU direction. Lien Chan's visit took place between 26 April and 3 May 2005. The two most important events during Lien's trip to China were his speech at Beijing University and his meeting with the CCP chairman and PRC president Hu Jintao. These events were truly historic in the China-Taiwan framework, since they marked the first time a KMT chairman set foot to mainland China since 1949. Lien's talks with Hu resulted in a CCP–KMT communiqué issued by the parties right after the meeting. The emphasis of the communiqué was on peace promotion and increasing communication. It contained what was later dubbed the "three agreements" and "five promotions". The three agreements included recognition of the 1992 consensus, opposition to Taiwan independence, and seeking of peace and stability across the Taiwan Straits. The five promotions included: endorsing cross–strait talks and consultations on the basis of the 1992 consensus; promoting a formal end to the state of hostility across the Taiwan straits and taking steps toward a peace accord; promoting economic cooperation and the "three links"; discussing Taiwan's participation in international activities after the resumption of cross-straits talks; and establishing a regular platform for exchanges between the two parties. Such high level meetings and agreements provided hope for cross-strait cooperation and prepared the foundation for further improved relations as pro-status quo forces in Taiwan gained the upper hand against the pro-Taiwan independent forces. More significantly, the resumption of CCP–KMT relations facilitated cross–strait communication and cooperation when the KMT gained popular support and came into power after the March 2008 elections.

Compared with Jiang Zemin's eight-point proposal, Hu Jintao's Taiwan policy contained the following new elements. (1) Hu set opposition to "*de jure*" Taiwan independence, not reunification, as the policy goal for the foreseeable future. (2) He set peace and development as the axis of cross–strait relations. (3) For the first time, Hu defined "status quo" across the strait — the mainland and Taiwan belong to one China. (4) He adopted a "forward-looking" stance toward the DPP and other "pro-independence" parties in Taiwan and was willing to talk with them, regardless of past statements and actions, as long as the One China principle was met one way or another. (5) He insisted on the policy of pinning hope on Taiwanese compatriots. This reflects Hu's thinking that the human factor is the basis for policy-making and that, to achieve reunification, the mainland should win the hearts and minds of the Taiwanese people. (6) Hu upheld the position that the Taiwan issue should and could only be solved by all the Chinese on both sides of the strait; neither side should seek a unilateral solution (Xu and Vogel, 2008, 110).

The 17th CCP Congress in 2007 proposed "building a framework of peaceful development of cross–strait relations and open[ing] a new situation of peaceful development of cross–strait relations". This is the most authoritative statement of the official position of Beijing's policy. It seems that this policy has taken root and will last into the foreseeable future.

However, Beijing is still divided about how to see Ma Ying-jeou. There are at least two schools of thinking in Beijing about Ma. Whereas one school is positive and optimistic, the other is more cautious and takes a wait-and-see attitude about Ma. That is, there is a hard line and there is a soft line.[11] The hard-liners in Beijing believe that the PRC has made too many concessions to Taiwan. The toughest challenge to Beijing's management of cross–Taiwan strait relations is how to prevent Taiwan independence on the one hand and how to prevent war on the other hand. The military balance across the Taiwan Strait has developed in favor of the mainland (Fisher, 2008). Interestingly, mainland China's need to use force has actually declined because of both the improved political environment and its growing military capability. The increased capability provides Beijing's leaders great confidence and more flexibility in managing the Taiwan issue. According to PLA general Luo Yuan, now is the time to establish military security and mutual trust across the Taiwan Strait. Confidence-building measures should involve multiple dimensions. Both sides should think comprehensively and act concretely. They can begin by dealing with less demanding issues and then move toward approaching consensus on fundamental issues as mutual trust increases. Building confidence on military security issues will help end the hostility between the two sides, reach a peace agreement, stabilize the Taiwan Straits relations, reduce military security concerns, and avoid accidental military conflicts. An additional benefit will include reduced military spending, and the defense savings could be used to enhance people's living standards.[12]

A key issue in Beijing's current internal debate about Taiwan's international space is whether to grant Taipei's access to the World Health Organization (WHO). In May 2009, with Beijing's consent, Taiwan was for the first time invited to attend the 62nd World Health Assembly (WHA) as an observer under the name "Chinese Taipei". The timing was excellent because the threat of H1N1 flu was growing in April and May of 2009. The mainland is still debating whether Taiwan should be invited to attend the WHA on an annual basis or should it be made a permanent member. Part of the concern is what Beijing can or should do if the DPP returns to power in Taiwan in the future. Another part of the debate involves whether or not Beijing should make further accommodations for Taipei's participation in the WHO itself in addition to the WHA.[13] If cross–strait relations continue to evolve in the positive direction they have taken since May 2008, it is likely that Taiwan will be able to formally participate in the WHO in a format acceptable to both Beijing and Taipei.

Chen Kongli, a senior expert on the Taiwan issue, has examined the benefits of a peaceful development strategy. According to Chen, peaceful development and ultimate peaceful unification entail the following benefits: promoting the warm feelings of compatriots on both sides of the Taiwan Straits; sharing peace and security; saving defense expenditures; enhancing cultural and educational exchange; promoting common and peaceful development in the Asia–Pacific region. However, contending voices in the mainland argue for "the benefits of armed unification". People who advocate this approach tend to believe that peaceful unification will take too long. The longer the separation lasts, the more likely it becomes that the United States might intervene in a conflict in the Taiwan Strait and the more destructive a war might become. Additionally, a war might stimulate the domestic economy, and an armed conflict might provide a chance to destroy the Taiwan independence forces (Chen, 2009). The Taiwan issue is one of the most contentious issues among scholars and policymakers in China. Under the Hu leadership, the peaceful development strategy has clearly dominated the policy agenda. Beijing will not give up this strategy as long as there is hope for peaceful development in cross–strait relations. This peaceful strategy is driven by China's domestic situation and supported by a changing international environment that tends to favor a peaceful orientation. Next we will turn to the changing international environment as it relates to cross-Taiwan Strait relations.

CHANGES IN INTERNATIONAL ENVIRONMENT

Since the beginning of the new century, three major changes in the international environment have had significant impacts on the cross–Taiwan Strait relations. First, the terrorist attacks on the United States on 11 September 2001 produced dramatic shifts in United States national security strategy and related transformation in international strategic situation. Second, the U.S.-led invasion of Iraq created a more complex situation in the Middle East and a stronger demand for peace in other regions of the world. Third, the global financial crisis that began in 2008 has deepened and affected all countries in the world. This crisis has had profound impact on bilateral and multilateral relations and might lead to drastic changes in international economic relations. Before we examine these changes in details, it is necessary to look at the international context of the Taiwan issue in historical perspectives.

The Taiwan issue itself is the product of a combination of factors, including domestic rivalry (the civil war of 1946–1949 between the CCP and KMT), the intervention of external powers, and changing international relations in the Asia-Pacific region. The dynamics of the international environment frequently and significantly affect Beijing's policy considerations toward Taiwan. Beijing regards the United States as a major obstacle to its goal of reunification with Taiwan. The issue can be traced back historically to the Chinese civil war period when the United States supported the Chiang Kai-shek regime and, at the cessation of the Korean War in the early 1950s, signed a Mutual Defense Treaty with Taiwan which effectively prevented the PRC from taking over the island. In the early 1970s, both Beijing and Washington were willing to normalize their relations due primarily to their mutual concern about the threat from the Soviet Union. While Washington has recognized Beijing officially and ceased its official relations with Taipei, Beijing still views the "Taiwan Relations Act" and US arms sales to Taiwan as unwarranted "intervention in internal affairs" (Zhao, 2005a, 230). Taiwan has long been the most sensitive issue in United States–China relations and will likely remain so for the foreseeable future. The area of the greatest danger of potential conflict between China and the United States concerns security involving the Taiwan issue.

Taiwan leader Lee Teng-hui's moves in the 1990s caused Beijing to worry about growing tendencies toward separatism. Some months after Lee visited the United States in 1995, Beijing fired missiles near Taiwan to warn about pressures toward separatism. The United States responded by sending two carrier task forces to the area around Taiwan (Garver, 1997). Since the standoff in the Taiwan Strait in 1996, U.S. officials have shown great concern for avoiding conflict with mainland China over the Taiwan issue.

During his visit to China in 1998, President Bill Clinton publicly affirmed for the first time the so-called Three No's policy of the United States toward Taiwan: no support for Taiwan's independence; no support for "two Chinas" or "One China, One Taiwan"; and no support for Taiwan membership in international organizations that require statehood.

Strategic planners in the Pentagon, however, made it clear that Taiwan was crucial to US security interest in its Quadrennial Defense Review (QDR) in 2001. The QDR makes pointed reference to the "East Asian littoral", defined as the region stretching from south of Japan into the Bay of Bengal, including Japan, Taiwan, the Philippines, Indonesia, and Australia, as an area of core strategic interest. This is one of a few statements from Washington that undoubtedly reveal the importance of Taiwan to its strategic interests.

As we now understand very well, September 11 significantly changed perceived strategic interests in Washington. China was no longer regarded as a challenger or rival, but rather a partner in many key U.S. interests, such as the war against terrorism and the North Korea nuclear crisis. Maintaining stability and peace in the region became a top priority for the Bush administration. Moreover, avoiding military confrontation with China over the issue of Taiwan has become essential so the United States can concentrate on the war in Iraq and other anti-terrorism priorities. Therefore, one can sense that although supporting Taiwan as a democracy and maintaining Taiwan's separation from China is still important to US interests, at this juncture, it is not necessarily a high priority interest (Zhao, 2005b).

President George W. Bush opposed both Taiwan independence and any side unilaterally trying to change the status quo. Since the late 1990s the United States has found itself more actively involved in cross–strait affairs to prevent potential miscalculation or perceived provocations by either side from spilling over into confrontation (Bergsten *et al.*, 2008, 180).

In recent years, particularly after the terrorist attacks of 11 September 2001, when US national priority shifted to the fight against international terrorism, there has been growing recognition that both China and the Untied States have an interest in the maintenance of peace in the Taiwan Strait. Xu Shiquan and Ezra F. Vogel summarize the positive development in the following four areas. First, China is absolutely firm on the One China principle but over the years has shown flexibility in its definition. The Anti-Secession Law passed in March 2005 stated: "There is only one China in the world. Both the mainland and Taiwan belong to one China. China's sovereignty and territorial integrity brook no division". The second positive development is the maintenance of the status quo. China and the United States have different definitions of the status quo across the Taiwan Strait. China stresses the "*de jure*" side of the status quo, whereas the United States emphasizes the "*de facto*" side of it. So long as the status quo meant by both is not unilaterally changed, no serious problems should arise between the two countries over the issue. Third, cross–strait exchange is a positive development. This is the least problematic, since the two sides have a common understanding. The United States has no objection to China's growing links with Taiwan as they are achieved peacefully. Fourth, China and the United States might develop a mutual understanding about an ultimate solution to the Taiwan issue. The United States insists on a peaceful solution to the Taiwan issue, while China refuses to renounce the use of force if peaceful efforts should be obstructed. China's position is that the ultimate solution of the Taiwan issue has to be decided by all its 1.3 billion people — including the 23 million Taiwanese compatriots. The United States' position is that in the final analysis, the Taiwan issue is for people on both sides of the Strait to solve. If the positions of both countries remain unchanged, the risk of misunderstanding is reduced (Xu and Vogel, 2009).

In his meeting with Chinese Premier Wen Jiaobao in 2003, United States President George W. Bush made a clear statement of America's position on the Taiwan issue: "We oppose any unilateral decision, by either China or Taiwan, to change the status quo of Taiwan's relations with the mainland" (Lawrence and Dean, 2003). This referred to Taiwan President Chen Shui-bian's call for an unprecedented referendum — asking voters to demand that China moves its missiles — on the day of the 2004 presidential election. President Bush, for the first time, rebuked Chen's referendum action as a move that would change the status quo. At the same time, he warned Beijing that the United States will intervene if the mainland attacks Taiwan. Several days later Chinese President Hu Jintao, in a telephone conversation with Bush, warned that "China would not tolerate the island's independence" (Pan, 2003). It seems that the One China policy has taken deep root in both Beijing and Washington.

After 11 September China formed a close partnership with the United States in the international struggle against terrorism. It might be reasonable to say that anti-terrorism has become a new common ground for the two countries to achieve strategic cooperation. However, the U.S.-led war against Iraq in 2003 divided the international community. Unlike the first Gulf War that received the broad support of the United Nations Security Council, the new Iraq war did not received UN support. The former UN Secretary General Kofi Annan said that the Iraq war was not a legitimate war under international law. The initial quick U.S. military success against Sadam Hussein's Iraq was followed by long, bloody, and painful conflicts between U.S. forces and insurgent forces inside Iraq. The Iraq war has become extraordinarily costly both in human sacrifice and in political economic terms. The war has divided the world community and has dominated U.S. foreign policy agenda.

Although China is against the war, Beijing did not assume a world lead against the U.S. war in Iraq. In fact, Beijing has tried both to work with the new Iraqi government and to participate in the re-building process in Iraq. Knowing that Beijing has different interests and a different perspective, the Bush administration could not expect Beijing's full cooperation on the Iraq issue. It is reasonable to suggest that President Bush was satisfied that China did not instigate stronger opposition to the US policy in Iraq. As a result of the overwhelming demand of the Iraq war on the United States, the Bush administration adopted a more moderate approach in dealing with East Asia.

China's policy toward Korea has shifted from a bilateral approach to a multilateral approach. During the Cold War and the first year of the post-Cold War era, China maintained its traditional bilateral approach with regard to Korea, conducting separate talks with Tokyo, Pyongyang, and Washington. In the past few years, however, Beijing's position has moved toward a multilateral approach to co-manage the issues related to the Korean peninsula (Zhao, 2006, 53–60). The Six Party Talks have achieved mixed results. There is no doubt that any meaningful future solution to the North Korean nuclear crisis will require close cooperation of all parties involved, especially Pyongyang, Beijing, and Washington.

The nature of the North Korean problem is different from the Taiwan issue. However, a co-management approach to the latter issue can also be discerned in the interactions between Beijing and Washington (and to a lesser degree Tokyo). Nevertheless, the nascent Chinese and American co-management approach to the Taiwan issue is implicit at best, far from the explicit style of the Six Party Talks on the North Korean nuclear crisis. One should bear this in mind when analyzing the Taiwan policy case. Beijing has long considered the Taiwan issue its own internal affair from both the history-embedded perspective and the national interest-driven approach. China, therefore, is very attentive to any signs of involvement by major powers on the issue of Taiwan. One can nevertheless observe some subtle changes in Beijing's approach that suggest Beijing has begun to move toward a co-management approach with Washington at the beginning of this century (Zhao, 2006, 60–62).

A clear official signal from Washington came in October 2004, when then U.S. Secretary of State Colin Powell stated: "Those who speak out for independence in Taiwan will find no support from the United States". Powell made the U.S. position even clearer by further saying, "Taiwan is not independent; it does not enjoy sovereignty as a nation, and the two sides should improve dialogue" and "move forward to that day when we will see a peaceful unification" (Powell, 2004). This view reflects a fresh look at the scenarios across the Taiwan Strait by advocating a detached policy toward Taiwan. Washington's clear statement and its willingness to co-manage the Taiwan Strait situation with Beijing has exerted enormous influence on Taipei and effectively curbed the island's independence campaign.

The nature of this co-management is fragile, however, since the Taiwan case is still in its initial stages and is largely composed of implicit understandings rather than the explicit co-management style represented by the Six Party Talks. Beijing's and Washington's indirect arrangements over Taiwan have increased stability in the region, but the potential for serious conflict has not been totally removed (Zhao, 2006, 72, 73). It seems that America's intervention in Taiwan's movement towards independence has considerably impacted the island. Beijing's coordination and cooperation with Washington in this regard needs to be further strengthened. Beijing should not be afraid to discuss the issue of Taiwan in the international arena (although it considers the issue a domestic affair) since the situation has already been internationalized. In other words, China should recognize that the involvement of the United States (and Japan) in the issue of Taiwan is unavoidable; thus, the Chinese should attempt to manipulate this involvement in their favor (Zhao, 2005b, 21, 22). The call for co-management is also supported by other American scholars. According to Bonnie Glaser and Brad Glosserman, "a crisis in the Taiwan Strait can become the most serious challenge to Beijing's grand strategy of peaceful development. The interesting fact is that neither Beijing nor Washington wishes to see a crisis in the Taiwan Strait. Perhaps a "co-management" of the Taiwan issue could reduce risks of misperception and dangerous behaviors in the region. The bottom line of Beijing is to deter Taiwan independence at any cost. If a major military confrontation breaks out in the Taiwan Strait, the peaceful development strategy will become a victim of the crisis. Beijing needs to demonstrate a deep commitment to a peaceful approach without losing credibility to deter against separatist movement" (Glaser and Glosserman, 2008).

With frustration in Iraq and some other areas, it is interesting that President Bush's main foreign policy accomplishment is that he was able to build a solid relationship with China. President Bush and his secretary of state Condoleezza Rice have both claimed that U.S.-China relations achieved unprecedented progress and stability. Under the Bush administration, U.S.-China trade grew significantly. China became a "stakeholder" in the existing international system. Additionally, the United States and China conducted multiple rounds of Strategic Economic dialogue, and the two sides achieved a good understanding of the One China policy. President Bush helped to curb the Taiwan independence movement by stating unequivocally that the United States "opposes Taiwan independence", and "opposes any unilateral efforts to change the status quo" in the Taiwan Straits.

Since coming into the White House in January 2009, President Obama has made it clear that he is determined to change American foreign policy in the Middle East by initiating an orderly withdrawal of combatant troops from Iraq. On China policy, however, it seems that there will be more continuity than change from the Bush administration to the Obama administration. In their first meeting at the G-20 economic summit in London on 1 April 2009, President Obama and President Hu agreed to work together to build a "positive, cooperative and comprehensive relationship in the 21st century". Hu said during the meeting that no matter how the situation across the Taiwan Strait evolves, China will steadfastly adhere to the one-China policy and resolutely oppose "Taiwan independence", "One China, one Taiwan", and "Two Chinas". Obama said the U.S. government is committed to the one-China policy and the three Chinese–U.S. joint communiques, adding that this stand will not change. The United States welcomes and supports efforts to improve relations across the Strait and hopes for greater progress in the relations.[14]

The global financial crisis that began in 2008 is one of the most significant developments in the international community, the full impact of which will be felt for a long time to come. The global financial crisis originated in the United States and has created world-wide repercussions. Both Taiwan and the mainland are facing the tough challenges. It is clear that there is no escape from the crisis, and all countries are in the same boat of globalization. Furthermore, the crisis has led to a much deeper interdependence between China and the United States. The weakening international economy has negatively impacted the development of cross–strait economic and trade exchanges. Export-oriented economies such as Taiwan and the mainland have been hard hit by the global crisis as exports to the United States and Europe fall. The economic downturn is likely to give rise to trade protectionism, adding to the woes of mainland-based Taiwan enterprises and hampering cross–strait economic and trade relations.

In response to the global financial crisis, Beijing has shifted from a fiscally conservative position to a more aggressive policy, with four trillion yuan (US$588 billion) for infrastructural projects to pump up domestic demand. Beijing has publicly welcomed Taiwan enterprises to participate in stimulus programs. This should create new business opportunities and energize cross–strait economic and trade exchange. In response to the weakening economy, Taipei and Beijing are adopting looser economic policies aimed at expanding domestic demand by stimulating private consumption and investment, as well as expanding public infrastructure investment. Moreover, the normalizing of bilateral economic and trade relations has become a focal point for authorities on both sides, and this will have a positive impact on the future development of cross–strait exchanges (*Taiwan Journal*, 20 February 2009, p. 7).

Beijing is keenly aware of the key role that is played by the world's only superpower, the United States. The PRC is expected to intensify its efforts to gain Washington's forbearance so that the United States will not play a one-sided role in the cross–strait relationship. Nevertheless, the fate of the cross–strait relationship remains primarily in the hands of Beijing and Taipei. Clearly, a peaceful settlement is in the interest of both sides. International dynamics have always played a crucial role in Beijing's Taiwan policy calculations. The United States remains the most important international actor, as it is not only the sole superpower in the world but also the only major power that would be able to provide substantial political, economic, and military assistance to Taiwan should another cross–strait military crisis arise. Therefore, one cannot totally rule out the possibility of a major military confrontation between the United States and China over the issue of Taiwan in the case of TIW scenario. There is a danger that unintentional action or rhetoric may have severe consequences due to miscommunication and misunderstanding. Therefore, confidence-building measures and crisis management mechanisms should be established. This is particularly crucial for China and the Untied States (Zhao, 2005a, 237).

One of the measures, as some U.S. scholars and officials have suggested, is to set up a mid-range arrangement to stabilize the situation. That is, during a certain period, say in 20, 30, or 50 years, the two sides would make a pledge: Taiwan will not seek independence; China will not use military force; and the United States would act as a moderator. This would provide a period of peace for both parties to engage in economic construction, arms reduction, and increased dialogue and engagement (Lieberthal, 2005). Further economic integration may indeed push the cooperation of the two sides to a new level, which may ultimately lead to a political settlement.

On the economic front, China's persistent trade surplus with the United States hit a record $266.3 billion in 2008 and has been a source of tension between Beijing and Washington. However, the global recession has hurt both countries' exports and increased the temptation for governments around the world to raise import barriers to protect local companies. The size and importance of the

United States–China trade, which totaled $409 billion in 2008, means both countries have a stake in making sure it is "fair, sustainable and mutually beneficial", U.S. Trade Representative Ron Kirk said in a statement after meeting with Chinese Minister of Commerce Chen Deming.[15]

Chinese and U.S. firms signed 32 trade and investment contracts worth some $10.6 billion on 27 April 2009, which the U.S. Chamber of Commerce said will support U.S. economic growth and job creation. "With businesses in both countries struggling, these deals come at a critical time and will help create jobs and stronger commercial bonds between the United States and China", said Myron Brilliant, the chamber's senior vice president of international affairs, who presided over the signing ceremony. Chen Deming said that China "will continue to encourage Chinese companies to import more from the United States, and we will also welcome U.S. companies and trade-promotion agencies to be more active in China".[16]

Some U.S. analysts believe that the financial crisis may have significant long-term effects that would make it harder for the United States to remain the world's financial superpower. The financial crisis contributes indirectly to the rise of mainland China, since poor U.S. management of the American financial system is widely blamed as the trigger for the crisis. Accordingly, U.S. soft power and moral authority are reduced, and U.S. influence declines with them (Roy, 2009). Nevertheless, the United States will remain the only superpower in the near future. American interests and policy will continue to affect the evolution in cross–strait relations.

According to Richard C. Bush, Director of Center for Northeast Asian Policy Studies, and Alan Romberg, Distinguished Fellow of Henry L. Stimson Center, the goal of the United States since the mid-1950s has been the maintenance of peace and stability in the Taiwan Strait, including the peaceful resolution of issues between Beijing and Taipei. Maintaining a balance of power and influence has been a means to that end, and not a trivial one. But it is not the only way that Washington has pursued its underlying goal. Diplomacy is another means. Fostering a good relationship with Beijing has been another, and encouraging cross–strait cooperation is yet another.

The point here is that we should not confuse means and ends. U.S. actions during the Chen Shui-bian administration demonstrated this approach at work. Of course, China's growing military power provided a context, but the key challenge was the danger that the deepening antagonism between Chen and Beijing could, through miscalculation, result in a conflict that would involve the United States. Such an outcome would have been fundamentally at odds with U.S. goal of promoting peace and preventing war and highly damaging to U.S. strategic national interests. The Bush administration then used diplomacy to reduce the chance of conflict.[17] Since he took office more than a year ago, President Ma's initiatives toward Beijing and Beijing's positive response have been a boon to U.S. interests because they have reduced the mutual fear that has poisoned cross–strait relations for the last 15 years.

The solution to the Taiwan issue will involve compromise among the key parties (Bush, 2005). As Robert Scalapino points out, in the long run it may be possible to achieve a political relationship between China and Taiwan "based on federation or confederation, setting the issue of sovereignty aside" (Scalapino, 2004, 299). For now, both Beijing and Taipei seem to be focusing on the easier questions in economic cooperation and cultural exchange and have left the more difficult political issues involving sovereignty to future negotiations. This pragmatic approach of dealing with "economics ahead of politics" and addressing "easier questions ahead of tougher issues" has been working in the mutual interests of both sides. Leaders in both Beijing and Taipei have endorsed this approach. Progress in economic and cultural areas may lead to growth in goodwill and mutual trust. Such progress will pave ways for the two sides to take up tougher political challenges in the future.

CONCLUSION AND PROSPECT OF CROSS–STRAIT RELATIONS

The above analysis indicates that the recent shifts in Beijing's policies toward Taiwan are the result of interactions of three variables: (1) political and economic changes inside Taiwan; (2) political and economic changes inside mainland China; and (3) changes in the international environment and related changes in the United States–China relations. Leaders in Beijing and Taipei may wish to seize the historical opportunity presented by power transition in Taiwan and a relatively stable regional environment to enhance mutual understanding, consolidate the gains of anti-Taiwan independence, and actively promote the three links.

Taiwan's political transition from the pro-independent DPP administration to the pro-status quo KMT administration has certainly contributed to the return to the "1992 consensus" about one China. This has provided a good foundation for both sides of the Taiwan Strait to resume meaningful and productive dialogue. The three rounds of talks between the two sides have led to the signing of nine agreements which resulted in the full normalization of the "three links" of flying, shipping, and postal services. For the first time in six decades, cross–strait communication and transportation have been normalized. The three links have opened new channels for both people-to-people interaction and much more productive economic cooperation.

The international space for Taiwan has become a key issue in recent discussions between Beijing and Taipei. Xu Shiquan, former director the Institute of Taiwan Studies of the Chinese Academy of Social Sciences, recognizes that Taiwan's international space is a complex and sensitive issue. Because this issue involves national sovereignty and territorial integrity, the mainland has always taken this issue very seriously. In principle, Beijing has consistently maintained the one China policy. Considering the fact that the two sides of the Taiwan Strait are not united yet, Taiwan cannot be completely kept out of the political, economic, and social aspects of international society. The mainland has rationally and pragmatically managed issues relating to Taiwan's participation in international life. Beijing and Taipei have compromised on Taiwan's participation in the Olympics Games, Asian Development Bank, Asia-Pacific Economic Cooperation, and the World Trade Organization. Xu has proposed that Beijing and Taipei could consider the following "rules of game" in dealing with future diplomatic relations with other countries. (1) The passive principle: both sides pledge that neither side will actively take actions to undermine the other's existing diplomatic relations. If there is change in "diplomatic" relations, such change should be proposed by the third party. (2) The principle of separation of politics and the economy: both sides will pledge not to buy "diplomatic" relations with money, nor to induce "diplomatic" relations by providing economic assistance. Economic relations with countries with "diplomatic" relations should be discussed after, rather than before, diplomatic relations are established. (3) The communication principle: if there are changes in "diplomatic" relations, the affected side should be notified in advance to avoid surprise. Such measures will help confidence building. (4) And, the principle of considering compatriots' interests as a top priority: both sides pledge to take the responsibility of defending the interest of all compatriot regardless of whether they are from Taiwan or the mainland in any countries with "diplomatic" relations (Xu, 2008).

Fundamentally speaking, mainland China's modernization, reform, and opening policy have contributed to Beijing's policy shift from "liberation of Taiwan" to "peaceful development". The growth of cross–strait relations has been and will remain an essential component of mainland China's grand strategy of peaceful development. China has developed friendly and cooperative relations with almost all of its neighbors. The issue of Taiwan is perhaps the single most explosive issue for China. Therefore, from Deng Xiaoping to Jiang Zemin and now Hu Jintao, Chinese leaders have attached great significance to peaceful unification. Hu has made it clearer than ever that as long as there is any hope for peaceful development, China will not resort to the use of force on Taiwan.

The six-point proposal announced by Hu on the eve of New Year 2009 represents the most systematic and authoritative statement of Beijing's new thinking for peaceful development in cross–strait relations. Hu's policy has produced tangible results in the CCP–KMT dialogue and cooperation. Under the more favorable environment, the productive talks between the Straits Exchange Foundation (SEF) and the Association for Relations Across the Taiwan Strait (ARATS) have led to the full normalization of the three links. Hu Jintao and

Ma Yingjeou are seizing the historical opportunity to build peace and prosperity across the Taiwan Strait. Currently they are focusing on economic cooperation and people-to-people exchange. As the cross–strait socioeconomic ties grow stronger and mutual understanding as well as mutual trust are improved, Beijing and Taipei may gradually discuss and manage more challenging political and security issues in the future.

The international environment has experienced significant changes. (1) September 11 transformed the global strategic environment. Terrorism has become the common enemy of the United States, China, and the world community at large. The joint struggle against terrorism requires unprecedented cooperation among great powers, including China and the United States. This strategic shift has resulted in a transformation of the U.S. perception of China as a competitor to the new thinking of China as an essential partner and stakeholder in existing international political and economic systems. The growth in common interests between Beijing and Washington has also made it easer for the two sides to settle their differences on the Taiwan issue and defend the One China policy. (2) The U.S.-led war in Iraq has exhausted the power of unilateralism and increased demand for global cooperation. This has increased the possibility for China and the United States to co-manage the North Korean nuclear crisis and cooperate in other areas. Furthermore, such success in the formal co-management of North Korea could encourage informal co-management of the Taiwan issue. This point was made clear by President Bush's public declaration against Taiwan independence. (3) The global financial crisis has exposed the vulnerability of the United States and also made it clear that no country can escape the negative effects of the global financial crisis. With a relatively fast growing economy and the world's largest foreign currency reserve of two trillion dollars, China has emerged as an indispensable partner in the common struggle against the financial crisis. At the same time, both Taiwan and the mainland have powerful incentives to strengthen economic cooperation in a joint effort to fight against the financial crisis. Tough economic times have created an urgent demand for enhanced cooperation. Closer economic interaction between Taiwan and the mainland as well as closer economic interdependence between China and the United States are likely to create a more favorable political environment for the key parties to reach better mutual understanding of each others' needs and concerns. Cooperation in the economic arena might create more good will and political trust and ultimately lead to improved political relations.

To borrow a phrase from Charles Dickens, this is the best of times, and this is the worst of times. In a deep global financial crisis, there is hope for cross–strait relations to be improved because both Taiwan and the mainland have powerful incentives to help each other overcome the tough challenges ahead. There is hope for China and the United States to forge stronger ties economically and politically. In the foreseeable future, cross–strait relations are likely to grow in the basic framework of peace and development. Of course, some uncertainties remain, and dangers continue to exist. Only wise political leadership, prudent policies, and skillful management by all key parties involved can reduce the risks, overcome the obstacles, and move toward a bright future of cross–strait relations.

REFERENCES

Bergsten, CF, C Freeman, NR Lardy and DJ Mitchell (2008). *China's Rise: Challenges and Opportunities.* Washington, DC: Peterson Institute for International Economics and Center for Strategic & International Studies.

Bush, RC (2005). *Untying the Knot: Making Peace in the Taiwan Strait.* Washington, DC: Brookings Institution Press.

Chen, K (2009). Challenges to the principle of peaceful unification. http://www.tecn.cn/data/detail.php?id=24443, May 1, 2009.

Fisher, RD Jr (2008). One China and the military balance on the Taiwan Strait. *The "One China" Dilemma*, Chow, PCY (ed.), 217–256. New York: Palgrave Macmillan.

Garver, JW (1997). *Face Off: China, the United States, and Taiwan's Democratization.* Seattle: University of Washington Press.

Glaser, B and B Glosserman (2008). Promoting confidence building across the Taiwan Strait. In *A report of the CSIS International Security Program and Pacific Forum CSIS*, September.

Gries, PH (2004). *China's New Nationalism: Pride, Politics, and Diplomacy*, Berkeley: University of California Press.

Hu, W (2006). The political–economic paradox and Beijing's strategic options. *China's Rise, Taiwan's Dilemmas and International Peace*, Friedman E (ed.), 22–38. New York: Routledge.

Lawrence, S and J Dean (2003). A new threat. *Far Eastern Economic Review*, December 18, 16–18.

Lieberthal, K (2005). Preventing a war over Taiwan. *Foreign Affairs*, 84(2), 53–63.

Lin, A (2009). Government sees need for cross-strait economic deal. *Taiwan Journal*, March 6, 1.

Ma Y-J (2003). Cross-strait relations at a crossroad: Impasse or breakthrough?" *Breaking the China-Taiwan Impasse*, Zaoria DS (ed.), pp. 39–65. Westport: Praeger.

Ma Y-J (2009). Video conference speech at the center for strategic and international studies, April 22. http://www.csis.org/media/csis/events/090422_ma_speech.pdf, April 29, 2009.

Montlake, S (2008). Taiwan president-elect's bold mandate: Improve ties with China, U.S. *The Christian Science Monitor*. http://www.csmonitor.com/2008/0324/p04s01-wosc.html, March 24, 2009.

Niu, J (2004). Chinese decision making in three military actions across the Taiwan strait. *Managing Sino-American Crises: Case Studies and Analysis*, Swaine MD and Z Tuosheng (eds.), 293–326. Washington DC: Carnegie Endowment for International Peace.

Pan, PP (2003). China thanks Bush for Taiwan stance. *The Washington Post*, December 22, A22.

Powell, C (2004). Interview with Mike Chinoy of CNN international TV and "Interview with Antony Yuen of Phoenix TV," October 25. www.state.gov/secretary/rm/37366pf.htm, November 2, 2004.

Roy, D (2009). New circumstances strain old arrangement. *Taiwan Journal*, April 24, 7.

Scalapino, R (2004). Asia–Pacific security issues and US policy. *American Foreign Policy Interests*, 26, 297–308.

Su, C (2008). *Taiwan's Relations with Mainland China: A Tail Wagging Two Dogs*. London: Routledge.

Suettinger, RL (2006). U.S. 'Management' of Three Taiwan 'Crises'. *Managing Sino-American Crises: Case Studies and Analysis*, Swaine MD and Z Tuosheng (eds.), 251–292. Washington DC: Carnegie Endowment for International Peace.

The Economist, Intelligence Unit (2009). *2009 EIU Taiwan Country Profile*.

Wang, V (2008). The impact of Taiwan's 2008 elections on cross-strait relations: A game-theoretical analysis, *Asian Perspective*, 32(2), 145–172.

Wu, Y-S (2009). Back to future for cross–strait relations. *Taiwan Journal*, March 20, 7.

Xu, S (2008). Taiwan's international space's issue in cross-strait relations. In *Paper presented at the conference on cross-strait relations co-hosted by the Center for*

Taiwan Studies at Peking University and Global Forum of Chinese Political Scientists, Beijing, September, 21–22.

Xu, S and EF Vogel (2009). Dampening the Taiwanese flash point. *Power and Restraint: A Shared Vision for the U.S.–China Relationship*, Rosecrance R and G Guoliang (eds.), 107–117. New York: PublicAffairs.

Yan, X (2008). Who will maintain peaceful cross–strait relations?" An apology from Yan Xuetong, posted: 2008-6-23; http://en.chinaelections.org/newsinfo.asp?newsid=18155, May 23, 2009.

You, J (2006). China's anti-secession law and the risk of war in the Taiwan strait. *Contemporary Security Policy*, 27(2), 237–257.

Zhao, Q (1996). *Interpreting Chinese Foreign Policy*. New York: Oxford University Press. A revised edition is forthcoming.

Zhao, Q (2005a). Beijing's dilemma with Taiwan: War or peace? *The Pacific Review*, 18(2), 217–242.

Zhao, Q (2005b). America's response to the rise of China and Sino–US Relations. *Asian Journal of Political Science*, 14(1), 1–27.

Zhao, Q (2006). Moving toward a co-management approach: China's policy toward North Korea and Taiwan. *Asian Perspective*, 30(1), 39–78.

Zhao, S (2004). *A Nation-State by Construction: Dynamics of Modern Chinese Nationalism*. Stanford: Stanford University Press.

Zhao, S (2008). Strategic dilemma of Beijing's Taiwan policy: Chinese nationalism and the making of the anti-secession law. In *The One China Dilemma*, Peter Chow (ed.), 199–213. New York: Palgrave.

ENDNOTES

1. We would like to thank Wei-chin Lee for his thoughtful comments and suggestions for our manuscript.
2. The six key points are (1) Firm adherence to the "one China" principle, and increase mutual political trust. Maintaining national sovereignty and territorial integrity is China's core national interest. Although the mainland and Taiwan are not united yet, China's territorial and sovereignty are not split. Cross-strait reunification is not recreating sovereignty but ending political hostility. Under the framework of one China, the two sides can hold equal consultation and negotiations, gradually resolve historical problems and new problems emerging in the process of development. (2) Strengthening economic cooperation and promote mutual development. Expand the three links and build common interests are win-win. Institutionalization of cross–strait economic cooperation will provide solid material foundation for peaceful development of cross–strait relations. The two sides should sign comprehensive economic cooperation agreement, establish the mechanisms for economic cooperation, taking

advantages of each side and maximize the mutual benefits. (3) Strengthening common cultural links between the two sides. The long-lasting and glorious Chinese civilization is common treasure of all compatriots and critical links of national feelings across the strait. Cross–strait cultural and education exchanges should move to a higher level. (4) Promoting personnel exchange. Beijing will actively respond to any constructive suggestions for peaceful development of cross–strait relations. The CCP will continue to work with the KMT to achieve the common vision of peaceful development. If DPP clearly realizes the current situation and stop "Taiwan independence" activities, Beijing will positively react. (5) Defending national sovereignty and negotiation on foreign affairs-related issues. Beijing understands Taiwan compatriots' feeling about participating in international activities and will pay attention to resolving related issues. The mainland and Taiwan should reduce internal struggles and enhance common interest. Under the conditions of not creating "two Chinas", or "one China one Taiwan", the two sides can reasonably arrange Taiwan's participation in international organizations. (6) Negotiating a peace agreement and end hostility. Chinese on both sides of the strait have responsibility to end the history of hostile confrontation and avoid the military conflict. Both sides can pragmatically explore political relations under the special situation of the nation not yet united. In order to stabilize the Taiwan Strait situation and reduce military security concerns, at an appropriate time, both sides can have exchange on military issues and discuss issues of building military security mutual confidence. See *Renmin ribao,* 1 January 2009.

3. In a statement responding to Hu's six point proposal, Taiwan's presidential spokesman Wang Yu-chi said: "We're pleased to see cross–strait ties developing on the axis of 'peaceful development', under which the two sides can negotiate, launch exchanges, and benefit each other. By calling a truce, the two sides "can terminate hostilities, further understanding of each other and bolster cooperation". See http://www.straitstimes.com/Breaking%2BNews/Asia/Story/STIStory_321046.html, accessed 5 January 2009.
4. Professors John W. Garver and Wei-chin Lee have suggested that observers should pay more attention to what Ma has done rather than what he has said in response to Hu's proposal. According to their analyses, Ma has done much more than what he has said. Ma's actions have contributed significantly to improving cross–Taiwan Strait relations. See Dwnews special report on Ma's response to Hu's six point proposal at http://www.dwnews.com/gb/MainNews/Forums/BackStage/2009_4_28_19_49_58_993.html, accessed April 29, 2009.
5. http://www.chinapost.com.tw/taiwan/china-taiwan-relations/2009/04/19/204852/Taiwan-and.htm, accessed 20 April 2009. Chien has previously served as foreign minister and as Taiwan's representative to the United States and his meeting with Wen drew Taiwanese media attention. He is attending the forum

in the capacity of the senior advisor of the non-profit Cross–Strait Common Market Foundation. For Xinhua news report on the Wen-Chien meeting, see http://news.xinhuanet.com/newscenter/2009-04/18/content_11210891.htm.

6. See http://www.taipeitimes.com/News/front/archives/2009/04/27/2003442153, accessed 27 April 2009.

   President Ma Ying-jeou had instructed Chiang to raise the ECFA issue in his meeting with Chen. Ma stated that if Taiwan does not sign an ECFA with China, it would risk being marginalized and losing its competitiveness because China and neighboring countries are planning to sign free-trade agreements.

7. The three agreements are: "The Agreement on Cross–Strait Air Traffic Supply", "The Agreement on Cross–Strait Financial Cooperation" and "The Agreement on Cross–Strait Mutual Assistance in Cracking Down on Crimes". See http://www.chinadaily.com.cn/china/2009-04/26/content_7717293.htm, accessed 28 April 2009.
8. This is a statement that Ma made in Taipei on April 12 and printed in *Taiwan Journal*, 17 April 2009, p. 7. His statement on Taiwan's isolation refers to the following situation. "When Taiwan restricts the flow of commerce from the mainland, it forces foreign companies to exclude us from their regional operations. With such restrictions, multinational firms simply are not able to link up their supply chains if they are headquartered in Taiwan". Therefore, it is in Taiwan's interest to allow the "three links" of flying, shipping, and postal services with the mainland.
9. See detailed discussion in "Thoughts on Peaceful Reunification between Chinese mainland and Taiwan", in *Deng Xiaoping Wenxuan*, vol. 3, Beijing: Renmin chubanshe, 1993, pp. 30, 31.
10. For details of Jiang's eight-point proposal, see *Renmin Ribao*, 31 January 1995.
11. Tsinghua University professor Yan Xuetong once predicted that there could be a war in the Taiwan Strait in 2008. He was very critical of scholars who took a more moderate view of Taiwan. It is interesting that Yan made a new prediction stating that there would be no conflict in the Taiwan Strait before 2016: "The stable trend of peace beginning from 2008 will undoubtedly promote peace and development in the Taiwan Strait, although no one can foresee if such a trend will effectively prevent Taiwan independence and further reunification. During the past 30 years, the Taiwan Strait has remained peaceful; reunification has yet to be achieved; and Taiwan independence forces have been strengthened. I hope that my forecasts on relations in the coming eight years will not be proven wrong, as were the false predictions about a military conflict in the Strait that I previously made" (Yan 2008).
12. See http://news.xinhuanet.com/herald/2009-01/05/content_10605084.html, accessed on 27 February, 2009.

13. This is based on information learned from an international conference on Sino-U.S. relations and security issues jointly sponsored by the Center of American Studies of Fudan University and the Pacific Forum based in Honolulu, Hawaii, Fudan University, Shanghai, 8, 9 May 2009.
14. http://news.xinhuanet.com/english/2009-04/02/content_11116139.htm, accessed 1 May 2009.
15. http://www.nytimes.com/reuters/2009/04/27/business/international-usa-china-trade.html?_r=1, accessed 28 April 2009.
16. http://www.chinadaily.com.cn/china/2009-04/28/content_7724271.htm, accessed 28 April 2009.
17. http://www.brookings.edu/opinions/2009/0312_cross_strait_relations_bush.aspx, accessed 22 April 2009.

Chapter

9

Sound and Fury: The United States–Taiwan Relations under Chen Shui-bian in the 2000s

Wei-Chin Lee

> Life's but a walking shadow, a poor player
> That struts and frets his hour upon the stage.
> And then is heard no more. It is a tale
> Told by an idiot, full of sound and fury,
> Signifying nothing.
>
> Act 5, Scene 5 of Shakespeare's *Macbeth*

Unlike the cozy relations of the early 2000s, a certain wariness crept into the United States–Taiwan interaction prior to the change of Taiwan's government in 2008. In any likely deliberation of war or peace, Taiwan has only one powerful ally in the world — the United States — in facing China's threats. However, one cannot help but notice a steady stream of bilateral disagreements between Taiwan and the United States during the second term of Chen Shui-bian's presidency, 2004–2008. The purpose of this chapter is, therefore, to explore why the initially intimate friendship turned lukewarm and indifferent, what factors as well as events contributed to the course of change, and what implications can be drawn for our understanding of the United States–Taiwan informal alliance. The core argument is that Taiwan's indigenization drive not only proclaimed its own identity, but also attempted to reformulate the United States–Taiwan alliance portfolio. The disputes in the United States–Taiwan bilateral relations began with both the Chen government's vigorous and unyielding attempts to propagate its version of self-identity in the international community and the firm U.S. stand on its original understanding of Taiwan's status at the time of alliance formation. Chen's government attempted to exploit the Bush Administration's strong commitment to Taiwan in order to test the relationship boundaries for Taiwan's identity formulation. The difference in policy stands has caused significant strain between allies due to the dynamic interaction of fears of abandonment and entrapment. The contention also arose in conjunction with Taiwanese ruling elites' effort to use the identity issue to discredit opponents and mobilize electoral solidarities for domestic gains.

This analysis begins with theoretical arguments that center on fears of entrapment and abandonment in an asymmetrical alliance. It also examines how identity politics in the domestic sphere shapes a country's policy behavior outward. This study attempts to show the order of events that had a critical impact on the United States–Taiwan alliance relations since 2000 by focusing on three issues: Taiwan's referendum issue; the United States–Taiwan arms transfers; and Chen Shui-bian's transit stops in the United States. While the first two issues provide diplomats and politicians with substance for bickering and debate, an examination of U.S. approvals of Chen's transit stops offers a unique angle to examine the cohesion of the United States–Taiwan bilateral relations. The study ends with an elaboration of the persistence, or erosion, of the United States–Taiwan relations by drawing out the reasons behind the Taiwanese government's consistent employment of identity in its interaction with the United States and the limitations and implications of Taiwan's foreign policy. Since there have been numerous works on U.S. policy toward Taiwan, this study will delve more into Taiwan's perspective and policy objectives.

INFORMAL ALLIANCE AND IDENTITY POLITICS

Countries form an alliance for deterrent, defensive, and preclusive reasons — deterring the targeted opponent from rushing into military attacks, raising the level of defensive capability, and precluding allies from making another alliance with one's opponent (Snyder, 1997, 56). Alliances come with costs, including the emergence of counter-alliance by the opponent for balance, the restraint on one's freedom of action in order to maintain the alliance, and the heightened possibility of entrapment in an unwanted war caused by the ally's reckless moves and uncompromising policy stands with the opponent (Snyder, 1997, 43, 44).

Naturally, a weak state would feel relieved when a powerful ally stands on the same side and shoulders the security burden against a presumed opponent (Olson and Zeckhauser, 1966). The willingness of a strong power to step in adds significant weight in the superior opponent's strategic calculation. The situation is delicate if the relationship is based on convergence of mutual interests, tacit understandings, and alliance member's domestic requirements, rather than on a formal, written international agreement. As long as the informal alliance relation is managed well, the mutual expectations and behavioral coordination for security assistance between allies will be sufficiently similar to those in a formal alliance.[1] While the informal alliance is a far less specific form of security arrangement than a formal alliance, the possibility remains that an opponent's actions against any party of the informal alliance may lead to grim results.

Even so, the lack of a security treaty in an informal alliance heightens the interplay of two opposing fears in an alliance security dilemma for member states — the fear of abandonment and the fear of entrapment (Snyder, 1997, 307). Hence, the credibility of an informal alliance requires constant identification of the potential opponent, a shared commitment to ensure that the perceived adversary will not endanger their security, and repeated collaborations to establish standardized procedures of mutual assistance to "comrades in arms".[2] These repeated, habitualized interactions in reciprocal practice iron out differences and reconfirm mutual commitments to prevent the alliance from faltering and eventually falling apart (Berge and Luckmann, 1967, 53–55). As Baier (1986, 234) elaborates, one actor's tolerance of the other actor's deviation from some specified conditions and "dependable habits" defines one's assessment of the trustworthiness of the other. In order to maintain the alliance, allies may convey signals and use reciprocal threats to punish deviations from their mutual understandings (Axelrod, 1984; Morrow, 2000, 68–71). Regular military collaboration and cordial diplomatic exchanges have been signs of robust alliance cohesion.

However, the initially converged security interests in the informal alliance might diverge as each alliance member readjusts its perception and assessment of the opponent's threat level due to shifting international and domestic political environments and policy priority over time. A resolution or concession of previous disputes between rivals could soften the policy stand of a member of the informal alliance and affect alliance cohesion and unity. Any signal of degradation or wavering in commitments on the stronger partner's side could lead to the weaker ally's grave concern of possible abandonment. Defection is actually quite appealing to the stronger ally if the targeted adversary is no longer a threat to the stronger ally, but the adversary may remain a serious challenge to the weaker member. Undoubtedly, the stronger ally will face moral criticism and international credibility loss for its inaction or delayed response, but the unfavorable public reaction could be brushed aside by claiming a lack of legal obligations in an informal alliance.

Hence, the fear of abandonment would be less overtly prominent to the stronger ally than the fear of entrapment caused by the weaker ally's potentially haphazard and careless acts that might lead the stronger ally into an unnecessary conflict. Due to aggravated exasperation over the fear of entrapment, the stronger state can choose quietly to rescind its previously permitted acts, withhold support for its ally, or explicitly qualify the conditions of its security pledges in its alliance partner's specific disputes with the adversary. Quiet rescission of formerly permitted acts, such as transit permits to Taiwanese leaders, certainly creates bumps and bruises for both members of the informal alliance. Such diplomatic acts could signal that the perceived informal alliance has seen cracks, though is not unraveling. The explicit expression of newly qualified conditions of involvement strikes at the core of the informal alliance, which relies on the essence of ambiguities in commitments, reciprocal understandings, and mutual trusts cultivated and nurtured in the long-term process. Deliberately stepping forward into the limelight to switch the code from ambiguity to clarity might be read as a warning that the alliance cohesion and sustainability are at risk.

In the area of military collaboration, the stronger state acts cautiously in arms transfer. Should the weaker ally eventually be defeated or negotiate a peaceful solution with its adversary, weapons previously transferred to the weaker ally could change hands and be employed by the former opponent against the original donor. Close security collaboration might also emanate a signal of security guarantee and embolden its weaker ally to initiate a radical move that might be detrimental to the stronger partner's interests in differing policy issues or geographic areas. Concerns of this nature may lead the powerful ally to become selective in its security contribution with respect to weapons and technology to sustain its alliance commitments, as the past United States–Taiwan security relations have demonstrated.

In such an asymmetrical alliance, a logical, rationalistic generalization is that the weaker state will try its best to consolidate its security relationship in order to lessen the likelihood of the stronger ally's abandonment. However, this generalization may require reconsideration, particularly when a weaker ally like Taiwan is engaging in volatile construction of state identity.

Since a new identity takes time to develop, both established elites and emerging elites often compete in a spiral of nationalist outbidding to win support. For instance, in Taiwan's case, the rising Democratic Progressive Party (DPP) elites have opted for an ethnic line by criticizing old Kuomintang (KMT, Nationalist Party) elites of previous regimes for favoring one particular ethnic or cultural group — "mainlanders" and China-centered identity supporters — and suppressing the long-held indigenous desire for a new distinctive identity separated from China. The dispute over identity had led to the polarization of political space and identity discourse. The Taiwan situation could be worse, however, if DPP governmental elites with abundant political resources actively attempted to monopolize the identity discourse when they encountered a legitimacy crisis in governance or faced an uphill battle in electoral campaigns. By whipping up mass enthusiasm threatened DPP elites hope to use their own version of identity to mobilize supporters to "forgive and forget" their governance failures and incapacity in non-identity issue areas in order to maintain their political survival and regime sustainability. The cost-effective strategy for threatened DPP elites is to consolidate power by marketing and perpetuating their identity discourse to solid supporters, rather than trying in vain to cross the aisle and persuade their opponents. In doing this, they minimize their political audience costs by reaffirming their identity pledges among core domestic constituents, even though the increasingly non-negotiable stance concerning Taiwan's state identity might both trigger its ally's entrapment concerns and heighten international audience costs (Snyder and Ballentine, 2001, 70–78; Fearon, 1994, 577–592; Chan, 2003, 120–122). After all, the legitimacy of governance comes primarily from domestic supporters through elections. The rationalistic interplay of entrapment–abandonment dynamics in alliance management is hence qualified by domestic developments.

Moreover, identity as a variable in political interaction not only refers to the content of a collective identity, but also strongly indicates the process of contestation among related actors (Abdelal *et al.*, 2006, 700, 701). When an identity construction movement gains massive awareness of *different-ness* in domestic political space, it seems natural for the weaker ally like Taiwan to transform its domestic momentum into an international demand for *separate-ness* from its previous affiliated entity (Johnston, 2004, 65).[3] In foreign affairs, a combination of the fear of abandonment with domestic pressures often generates incentives for threatened elites to take a belligerent approach to international identity recognition with a hope to shore up their legitimacy and prestige at home by seeking victories or subtle concessions abroad. Even if the signal of a new state identity appears provocative to China and has not been well received by its allies, Taiwanese political leaders can use such unpleasant news to divert domestic attention. Indeed, the playing of the identity card introduces complications into the management of alliance relations. It should come as no surprise that the United States has had to re-evaluate the potential costs of conflict relative to the value of its alliance commitment. After all, the emergence of a new Taiwanese identity has challenged the status quo, which has been the basis for alliance formation. Any attempt to change the status quo places strains on alliance cohesion because the new identity represents new game rules, duties, and responsibilities. Unfortunately, allies tend to be conservative. They are only willing to take risks in a relatively stable environment.

In this case, why did Chen's government decide to risk challenging the U.S. policy stand? Surely calculated courses of action may take unexpected turns. While it may have been a miscalculation or irrational act on Taiwan's part to cause alliance friction by adopting a policy to change the status quo, the Bush administration's strong commitment to Taiwan's security and democracy might have led Chen and the DPP to believe that they would be bailed out even if things did not proceed as planned. The support of democracy has been a U.S. core interest in foreign policy; thus, referendum in a democracy becomes a subtle, legitimate way for Taiwan to redefine the status quo. On the domestic front, national identity has also been a salient issue in previous elections, as the pursuit of identity politics helped consolidate the power base of partisan supporters and potentially gain swing votes tilting toward the DPP. Chen has thus danced dialectic steps in his attempt to manipulate identity in his management of the United States–Taiwan alliance. The combination of thesis — Chen's provocative identity proposition — and anti-thesis — the U.S. responses — resulted in a synthesis, a mutually compromising position. Even though the new synthesis might not have moved far away from the initial stand, Chen and the DPP government have anticipated that the shocking, provocative effect of an unorthodox proposal would diminish somewhat in their next attempt and recede in several attempts. Eventually the proposal would be treated just like any regular political issue, losing its political steam. That is to say, Taiwan's independent status could be summed up as part of an international social construct achieved through repetitive, gradual steps taken over a long period of time. The cyclical repetitions of provocation–compromise–reiteration–retention through referendums offer an opportunity to "socialize" the international community to accommodate Taiwan's identity discourse. As a weaker state burdened heavily by the anxiety of abandonment due to the rise of China and shifting U.S. global strategies, Taiwan has argued constantly that the United States–China jointly defined status quo no longer corresponds to the evolving international reality. The entrapment-abandonment dilemma is therefore connected tightly to identity politics.

Therefore, both the surge and mobilization of Taiwan's indigenous identity to assist democratic transition and the repeated reframing of non-Chinese political constructs have closely connected identity to security interests. With political survival and electoral gains in mind during his tenure, Chen's radical and uncompromising policy moves have overly heightened the fear of entrapment on the United States and added considerable strains to the interactive web of alliance politics. Taiwan's vigorous quest for an international identity represents a good case to demonstrate the interplay between domestic politics and foreign relations as elaborated in various studies by Putnam (1988), Gourevitch (2001), and others (Keohane and Milner, 1996; Schweller, 2006, 11–13). Conventional wisdom about fears of abandonment and entrapment in alliances requires further exploration when identity politics is involved, as exemplified in the analysis of Taiwanese government's use of identity-oriented referendums in recent years.

THE FOUNDATION OF THE UNITED STATES–TAIWAN INFORMAL ALLIANCE

U.S. recognition of the People's Republic of China in 1979 precipitated the termination, in 1980, of the formal United States–Taiwan alliance based on the 1954 United States–Taiwan Mutual Defense Treaty.[4] As a salvaging act for the future, the 1979 Taiwan Relations Act (TRA, Public Law 96-8) has become the capstone of the United States–Taiwan informal alliance. In it, the United States pledges "to resist any resort to force or other forms of coercion that would jeopardize the security, or the social or economic system, of the people on Taiwan" (Sec. 2(b)(6)) for a peaceful resolution of the Taiwan issue. In order to implement the United States provision of "defense article and defense services in such quantity as may be necessary to enable Taiwan to maintain a sufficient self-defense capability", the United States President and the Congress have a joint responsibility "to determine the nature and quantity of such defense articles and services" in light of the security situation (Sec. 3). Through the years, even strong Congressional supporters of Taiwan have later conceded that the TRA served U.S. national interests well by maintaining U.S. foreign policy flexibility and achieving an appropriate balance in the United States–China–Taiwan triangular relations (Koenig *et al.*, 1985).

The TRA also upholds the U.S. policy of "strategic ambiguity". It reaffirms U.S. support of one China, of which Taiwan is a part, but does not necessarily accept China's claim that Taiwan is part of the PRC. Additionally, the TRA's security assurance remains open-ended without specifying what action might be taken if Taiwan is attacked by China. Although the United States agrees to support Taiwan's defense, the transfer of defensive articles and services to Taiwan's security remains a U.S. prerogative and open to deliberation. As a domestic law, the TRA is one-sided in the United States–Taiwan informal alliance, allowing the United States to make unilateral interpretation and implementation. It provides the U.S. administration with legal grounds to help Taiwan's self-defense capability to deter China's military threat and aggression. While the TRA is a product of various compromising constituencies, its ambiguous nature about possible U.S. responses has added unpredictable risks to China's strategic calculation of military options. At the same time, the assurance to offer defensive articles and services and a vague reaction to Taiwan's crisis has served as an effective instrument both to check

Taiwan's impetuous move toward independence and to reduce U.S. fear of entrapment. Unlike the precise wording of alliance obligation in the 1954 United States–Taiwan Mutual Defense Treaty, the ambiguity of U.S. responses makes Taiwan think twice before rushing to declare independence. The TRA offers no inviolable security obligations and outlines no concrete action as most alliance treaties do.[5]

When the United States signed a communiqué with China on 17 August 1982 to pledge the gradual reduction of arms sales to Taiwan without a final time table, the Reagan Administration provided Taiwan with "Six Assurances" to reaffirm the U.S. alliance commitment. These six "not to do" pledges (no cutoff date for arms sales; no amendment of the TRA; not pressure on Taiwan to accept the PRC unification; no serving as a mediator; no prior consultation of arms sales; no recognition of the PRC sovereignty over Taiwan) surely soothed Taiwan's anxiety of abandonment and lessened the possibility of U.S. entrapment by not providing Taiwan with a list of concrete United States "to do" actions in a crisis (Holdridge, 1997, 232; Lee, 2000, 183–188; Ross, 1995, 177–200; U.S. Senate, 1982, 16, 17). Even when the United States dispatched two aircraft carrier battle groups to the Taiwan Strait in accordance with the TRA provisions to tackle China's threats in the 1995–1996 Taiwan Strait crises, the U.S. government repeatedly declined to comment on what specific actions it would undertake in the future.

In essence, the U.S. principles of "peaceful resolution" of the Taiwan issue and "strategic ambiguity" in concrete alliance plans have created a delicate equilibrium across the Taiwan Strait. The effectiveness of this informal alliance has been contingent upon mutual understanding of the nature and extent of the opponent's threat and the maintenance of the status quo that Taiwan will not declare independence and China will not resolve the Taiwan issue with force. The consensual understanding of the status quo remained relatively stable and acceptable to both allies until Taiwan's democratic transition in the 1990s, when Lee Teng-hui began to actively promote Taiwan's independent identity. Following his predecessor's footsteps, Chen Shui-bian accelerated the drive for independence. The ebb and flow of the United States–Taiwan alliance is best captured by the examination of two key issues of their disputes — referendum proposals and arms sales — with Chen's transit permit as a barometer to evaluate the alliance cohesion.

DIPLOMACY OF *BON VOYAGE*: YEARS OF ACCORD, 2000–2003

In 2000, both Taiwan and the United States encountered a change of political landscape through presidential elections. Taiwan's breathtaking presidential election in March 2000, which ended with a victory for Chen Shui-bian and his Democratic Progressive Party (DPP) and the ousting of the long ruling Nationalist Party (Kuomintang, KMT), symbolized a new era for Taiwan's democratic consolidation.

In a gesture to lessen domestic worries about his political inclination for Taiwan independence, to stabilize cross–strait relations, and to lessen the US fear of entrapment, Chen announced the "Five No's" (or "Four No's and One Without") in his 2000 inaugural speech. He pledged not to declare independence, not to change the national title, not to promote the inclusion of (Lee Teng-hui's) "two states theory" into the constitution, not to promote referendum on unification, and not to abolish the National Unification Council and National Unification Guidelines ("One Without'). With a moderate rhetoric on independence, Chen won warm support from the Clinton Administration, and his first overseas visit in August 2000, during the final year of the Clinton Administration, received a transit permit in Los Angeles. However, the United States simply treated Chen as a transit passenger and did not allow him to meet U.S. legislators. Consequently, one U.S. Congressman had to sneak through a hotel's kitchen area to meet Chen to avoid public exposure.

Then Republican George W. Bush won the U.S. election in late 2000. Upon taking office in early 2001, the Bush Administration adopted a relatively high profile "lean-to-one-side" policy toward Taiwan, and the United States–Taiwan relations entered an era greatly departing from the former Democratic administration. Announcing a major arms sales package in April 2001, Bush boldly expressed his commitment to Taiwan by indicating that the United States would do "whatever it took" to help Taiwan defend itself.

Bush's amity toward Taiwan extended to his visit to Beijing in February 2002, when he reiterated firm U.S. stands on the TRA, even after China had constantly criticized U.S. neglect of its pledges stipulated in the 1972, 1978, and 1982 United States–China Communiqués. Bush's public confirmation of the TRA to honor U.S. commitments to Taiwan's security contrasted with his private pledges to those bilateral Communiqués given only in closed conversations with Chinese leaders (Romberg, 2003, 25). Bush's statement was seen as a swing back in favor of Taiwan's position, in contrast to Clinton's 1998 public statement of a U.S. "Three No's" policy in Shanghai (not to support Taiwan's independence; not to support two Chinas, or one Taiwan-one China; not to support Taiwan's membership in international organizations) (Clinton, 1998). Sailing in the favorable wind of U.S. policy, Annette Lu, Taiwan's Vice-President, and some Taiwanese officials urged the United States to abrogate those three United States–PRC Communiqués, which had been considered the "sacred texts" of the "one China" policy. The abrogation of them would free the United States from its adherence to the "one China" policy, though it would not necessarily dismantle the explosive Taiwan issue (Lin and Lin, 2003).

The Bush Administration's policy, more supportive and solicitous than former administrations, welcomed the Chen Shui-bian government's pragmatic and realistic view of Taiwan's security. The uplifting of bilateral relations was evident in the U.S. approval of Taiwan's senior leaders' transit through U.S. territories en route to visit diplomatic allies in the Southern Pacific, Central America, and Africa. While the U.S. State Department emphasized their "safety, comfort, and convenience while respecting the dignity of the traveler", the choice of cities for stopover and refueling and the permission for media coverage and meeting with dignitaries frequently required extensive negotiations between Taiwan and the United States.

Indeed, Taiwan has perceived transit permit as an important gauge to assess the closeness of the United States and Taiwan alliance, and transit permit was an indication of U.S. support and recognition of Chen's leadership. Domestically, Chen used the U.S. transit permit to boost his political legitimacy in Taiwan, compensating for his perceived lack of legitimacy after his less-than-50 percent majority in the 2000 presidential election, an unresolved failed assassination attempt against him during the 2004 election, and unending corruption scandals during his second term. Strong U.S. patronage gave his administration a powerful instrument to ward off the critical attacks by the pan-blue legislative majority coalition (KMT and the People First Party).

Contrary to the Clinton Administration, the Bush Administration gave more liberal latitude to Chen's transit flights through New York and Houston in May 2001. The U.S. then upgraded the transit treatment of Chen's second trip to Africa in 2002 and his third trip to Panama in 2003 by allowing a stopover in New York and permitting public interactions with local and national public figures.

The third trip was the climax of all Chen's U.S. transit visits. His appreciative remark that "U.S. is the best friend of Taiwan" corresponded well with an exuberant statement of "Bush is Taiwan's guardian angel" by Therese Shaheen, then the Chair of the Board and Managing Director of the American Institute in Taiwan (AIT) (*United Daily*, Nov. 3, 2003, A3; Nov. 17, 2003, A13). Unfortunately, the enthusiasm was quickly dampened by the diplomatic storm over Chen's advocacy of a referendum law in late 2003 and the combination of referendum and presidential election in 2004 (Kau, 2005).

Actually, Taiwan independence has been a policy goal for Chen and the DPP ever since they assumed power. As early as August 2002, when Chen was at a teleconference of the World Federation of Taiwanese Association, he stated his view of "one country on each side" (*yibian yiguo)* of the Taiwan Strait, a slogan similar to Lee Teng-hui's "Two States Theory". That act partially fulfilled the expectation of his electoral constituencies, but it also tested the limits of U.S. tolerance. Chen's bold proclamation naturally drew criticism from China for his blunt challenge to the one China policy and from the United States because the inappropriate comments deviated from Chen's inaugural promises ("Five No's") in 2000. By responding that it was an exercise of basic human rights in any democratic society, Chen simultaneously addressed the necessity of establishing a referendum law to bypass a possible legislative sclerosis that was dominated by a majority opposition coalition (Bradsher, 2007).

Without prior consultation with the United States, Chen indicated, in September 2003, his plan to draft a new constitution to make Taiwan a normal and complete state (Witter, 2003). In Chen's calculation, the referendum law would be employed to approve the new constitution, which could then be in force at the end of his second term in 2008. No doubt, such a ploy could be seen as an electoral maneuver. It could also be perceived as a strategy to ride the high tide of U.S. alliance support to modify and solidify Taiwan's international status. Meanwhile, since 2001 Chen and the DPP had been reportedly receiving subtle hints and quiet encouragements from some neoconservatives to move toward Taiwan's independence stand and to remain an anti-communist bastion (Stein, 2007). Since the United States had been gradually shifting its strategic focus to the war on terror in the post-9/11 period, China's assistance became crucial on various aspects of U.S. global strategy. It seemed an understandable act for Taiwan to take advantage of U.S. support before China's rise accumulated immeasurable weight in U.S. strategic calculations and Taiwan's fear of abandonment increased.

As a result, the Chen government and the DPP proposed packaging the call for referendum with the presidential election in 2004. The proposal put the United States in an awkward position. Realizing that referendum was undoubtedly a usual democratic practice, the United States was worried that Chen might employ the referendum law passed on 27 November 2003, to win an endorsement of his party's agenda for Taiwan independence. This, in turn, would push China into a corner with no choice but to resort to a military solution and could lead the United States down an unpleasant and potentially confrontational path in dealing with China's military threat against Taiwan.

Repeated efforts to dissuade Taiwan from such an aggressive push for a "defensive referendum" were to no avail. President Bush finally had to step forward and oppose Taiwan's referendum during a meeting with Chinese premier Wen Jiabao on 9 December 2003

(FoxNews, 2003). Bush's stern opposition resulted in a face-saving alternative. The referendum vote was still held on 20 March 2004, but the promised referendums were revised to deal with non-provocative and uncontroversial issues concerning the necessity of acquiring advanced anti-missile weapons and the establishment of a "peace and stability" framework for cross–strait relations to which most Taiwanese might not vehemently object.[6] Amid the heavy partisan politics, electoral campaigning, and the U.S. criticisms and intervention, both referendum proposals failed, though Chen successfully won a razor-thin margin of less than 30,000 votes in his 2004 reelection after a failed assassination attempt against him on the eve of the presidential election. The mass rallies and debates caused by the referendum issues and the U.S. pressures appeared to help the DPP in electoral mobilization in Chen's second presidential campaign (Huang, 2005; Mattlin, 2004).

A RIFT WITHIN THE ALLIANCE: YEARS OF DISCORD, 2003–2007

After the electoral hoopla settled and Chen had been reelected, the United States reiterated that its policy toward Taiwan based on the TRA remained unchanged (Copper, 2006, 152, 153). Peaceful resolution of the Taiwan issue and the "one China" policy remained U.S. guiding principles in cross–strait relations. Hoping to better harness Taipei's policy discretion, the United States expressed that it "does not support" independence for Taiwan or any unilateral moves that would change the status quo as the United States defined it. The United States also urged Taiwan and Chen Shui-bian to exercise prudence and restraint in dealing with cross–strait relations (Kelly, 2004; Kan, 2007).

While the referendum controversy temporarily vanished along with the 2004 presidential election, Chen was busy answering public inquiries about the failed assassination attempt against him and his Vice President the day before the presidential election.[7] In March 2005, China passed an anti-secession law to curb Taiwan's propensity toward independence. Then, Lian Zhan, Chairperson of the KMT, and James Soong, Chairperson of the People First Party (PFP), visited China one after another in May 2005, attracting extensive media coverage and stirring up a "China fever" in Taiwan. In order to preempt any surprise from the scheduled meeting between Bush and Hu Jintao, China's President, in April 2006, Chen rescinded one of his inaugural pledges by abolishing the National Unification Council in February 2006. The Council was initially set up in 1990 to convince the PRC that Taiwan was committed to reunification, though it had not been convened since 2000. Through the elimination of the Council, the National Unification Guidelines also ceased to apply (Regan, 2006). In addition to China's harsh criticisms, Chen faced tremendous pressures from the United States, who considered such a move unhelpful and dangerous to the cross–strait status quo. Apparently, the valuation of Taiwan's state identity had moved beyond simple consideration of military security.

Learning that the 2003 referendum controversy had not tempered Chen's provocative style of diplomacy, Bush was reportedly furious over Chen's inconsiderate, brinkmanship move, particularly at the crucial moment of U.S. global security layouts that desperately needed multiple levels of China's cooperation in the war on terrorism, the "quagmire" in Iraq, and the North Korean crisis. Besides demanding a reasonable explanation for such a sudden move, the United States wanted Taipei to correct the record of the news, replacing the original "abolishment" (*feizhi*) with "ceasing activity" (*zhongzhi*) in regard to the National Unification Council. The United States also expected Taiwan to "unambiguously affirm" that the status quo remained intact and Chen's pledges in 2000 were unchanged (Kelly, 2006; Ereli, 2006).

In a *quid pro quo* fashion, the United States showed its unhappiness to Chen's unpredictable manner and provocative behavior by reciprocating with "punishments", lowering the level of transit treatment in response to his deviations from the United States–Taiwan consensual understanding of the status quo. Immediately after the "National Unification Council" controversy, on a "take it or leave it" condition, Bush allowed Chen to stop over only at Hawaii and Alaska for resting and refueling without overnight stay in his May 2006 trip to Paraguay and Costa Rica (Snyder and Tsao, 2006). Rather than accepting such a humiliating condition, Chen's trip detoured through Amsterdam, Abu Dhabi, and Libya. As Chen decided to forego the designated U.S. transit stop after his departure, his flight received extensive media frenzy and speculation of his whereabouts in his "star trek" journey of searching for landing sites for his aircraft. The trip not only prompted a domestic storm of criticism, including dissenting opinions from Chen's own party, but also triggered the United States anger over his unorthodox style of diplomatic protocol.

As U.S. Deputy Secretary of State Robert Zoellick testified in a Congressional Hearing on 11 May 2006, the decision to offer stopovers only in Anchorage or Honolulu was in retaliation for Chen's failure to carry out the "Five No's" he had pledged and his intent to redefine Washington's "one China" policy. Such a unilateral move deepened U.S. fear of entrapment. In Zoellick's concise testimony of United States concerns over its fear of entrapment, Taiwan's "independence means war. That means American soldiers, sailors, airmen, and marines.... Where lives can be lost" (Snyder, 2006; *China Post*, 2006). The Chen Administration was angry with the U.S. handling of the matter of transit stops, as it was best summarized in one Taiwanese senior official's exclamation, "Taiwan is not a U.S. *gui erzi* (appendage)" in response to perceived "disgraceful and improper" treatment.[8] However, the commotion about stopovers temporarily ended with a mutual agreement to gloss things over on good terms. Since then, Chen's employment of transit visits to test U.S. commitment and garner domestic support appeared to lose its glamor, particularly when he was caught in a series of corruption allegations and scandals threatening his legitimacy and governance. The United States–Taiwan alliance relations have since been tense.

In September 2006, the United States granted a transit stop at Guam for Chen's trip to Palau and Nauru, but his insistence on riding a military aircraft, Taiwan's "Air Force One", was denied. Upon request for information about this trip, the U.S. State Department's replies played down the transit stop by calling the trip as a "private, unofficial" trip and referring reporters to "his" (i.e., Chen's) office for itinerary confirmation, avoiding proper diplomatic protocol addressing him as "President Chen" (*United Daily*, Sept. 2, 2006, A5).

On the domestic front, public perception viewed Chen's overseas trip as a deliberate move to stay away from month-long massive "Red Shirt Army" (*hongshan jun*) demonstrations in Taipei because demonstrators had demanded his ousting for unending scandals involving him, his wife, and other family members. When the scandals got rough, Chen became tougher and chose a policy of entrenchment in dealing with the United States, though he later reportedly gave in to U.S. pressure by permitting U.S. officials to pre-screen his New Year speech to ensure that it contained no surprising announcement of a new Taiwan constitution challenging the United States "one China" policy. In exchange, the United States permitted Chen's trip to Nicaragua in January 2007 to stop over in Los Angeles and San Francisco with some restrictions. Chen also softened his stand, stating that he would be willing to accept the "consensual foundation" of the 1992 Hong Kong negotiation, a hint of thawing the cross–strait relations (*United Daily*, January 9, 2007, A2).

Chen's retreat from his adventurous behavior reflected his concern over a possible U.S. policy shift from the "Six Assurances" in light of China's economic rise and global weight in the 2000s. Among these six assurances, Taiwan was particularly concerned about the one concerning U.S. non-recognition of China's sovereignty over Taiwan and another one about the United States not pressuring Taiwan to the negotiation table. When Raymond F. Burghardt, the Chairman of the American Institute in Taiwan, met with President Chen in mid-June, 2007, Chen surprisingly requested that the United States reaffirm its six assurances. Burghardt trod lightly, simply expressing that the six assurances remain intact and that the United States would not support Taiwan's membership in international organizations requiring statehood (Wang, 2007; Hsu, 2008). While Burghardt was cautious in his comments about the United States–Taiwan relations to avoid unnecessary over-reading into his statements, extensive media coverage and comments on his visits showed signs of distrust and concerns over the United States–Taiwan alliance relation on both sides.

In fact, Taiwan's fierce party competition has increased U.S. fear of entrapment. Expecting opposition and warnings from the United States, Chen still launched another referendum proposal in mid-2007 to "join the UN by using the name of Taiwan", intended to influence 2008 presidential election — a repeat of his 2004 electoral maneuvering of combining referendum with the presidential election. Numerous corruption accusations and scandals within the Chen Administration began to take a toll on the legitimacy of Chen's political authority and depleted his administration's already weak capabilities in governance. The emotionally loaded, identity-oriented referendum became a convenient instrument not only to inspire and unify the ruling party's mass backers, but also to divert public attention and debates from domestic forums to international arena. The U.S. opposition offered Chen and the DPP a chance to play the "identity" card for domestic electioneering by expressing Taiwan's misery and sadness over a lack of status recognition in the international community (*China Times*, June 21, 2007, A6; June 23, 2007, A4). Craving voters' support and competing to claim its representation of Taiwan's identity, the KMT had no choice but to wade into the identity outbidding process by proposing its own referendum proposal to seek UN membership as the Republic of China in a campaign analogous to a chicken game. Had the KMT remained lukewarm or silent on Taiwan's identity issue, the DPP would have assumed the pivotal role in identity discourse and condemned the KMT's attitude of indifference to Taiwan's future.

Surely, Chen's extreme move did not appeal to all swing voters who had an inclination toward the status quo. The 2003–2004 referendum controversy clearly showed that any extreme departure from the status quo would incite U.S. acrimonious rebuttals and disciplinary action. Yet, in 2007 Chen and the DPP again loudly appealed to the public by claiming that the UN bid referendum was simply an inspirational assertion of Taiwanese identity and status in the world. In September 2007, Chen even tried to calm his critics by saying that "nothing is likely to happen" even if the UN bid referendum is approved in the 2008 election (*Liberty Times*, 14 September 2007).

Why did Chen and his DPP elites adopt such a provocative strategy to challenge the status quo and risk heightening the U.S. fear of entrapment? There are several explanations of Chen's aggressive move. First, as a political leader receiving electoral mandates during his second and last term, Chen might have felt personally inclined to fulfill his ideological conviction of Taiwan independence. This would become his political legacy after he leaves the office. His adamant position also suited well the political objectives of those staunch supporters of Taiwan independence, such as "deep green" party elites Gu Kuanmin, Yao Jiawen, and You Xikun. Although Chen's political legitimacy was severely challenged amid his corruption scandals, "deep green" supporters felt that the supremacy of Taiwan independence outweighed all other political considerations. Therefore, Chen's fight for political survival and the Taiwan-independence fundamentalists wish for Taiwan's ultimate independence joined together to suppress intra-party adversaries and hijacked the party toward an irreconcilable approach to identity politics.

Second, with the joint force of Chen and the "deep green" supporters, the DPP became less tolerant of different views and more demanding on uniformity in political agenda. By adopting a "blue-excluding opinion poll" in the DPP primaries for the 2008 legislative election, the DPP excluded "pro-blue" (or pro-KMT) respondents from the opinion survey that served as a base of nomination. Hence, "deep green" candidates with extreme partisan views favoring Chen's agenda won the nomination, though they had limited chance to expand the DPP's electoral base. On the other hand, moderate DPP primary contenders with a broad appeal to swing voters with "light green or light blue" political inclination had no way to win party primaries. As a result, DPP moderates lost their clout and voice in the agenda-setting process within the party and were unable to counterbalance Chen's policy.

Third, the push for identity-embedded referendum generated useful domestic audience effects. Given Taiwan's dependence on China for trade and economic sustainability, an identity-driven referendum reminded voters of China's threat and slowed opposition parties' calls for more opening toward China. At the same time, Chen's frequent emphasis on Taiwan's identity and status answered the calls of ardent Taiwan independence supporters, reignited the enthusiastic spirit of previously lukewarm independence-oriented supporters, and lastly, retooled the train of thought of Chen's opponents by decrying "bullying and arrogant" U.S. behavior, as evidenced by his manipulation of U.S. harsh criticism in his push for a "UN membership bid" (*United Daily*, 21 June 2007, A4). With careful agenda presentation and public discourse, some swing voters might feel dignified and justified in supporting Taiwan's claim of UN eligibility. If Taiwan's Legislative Yuan elections in 2001, 2004, and 2008 are a guide to Taiwan's party vote shares, the gap between the pan-blue camp (49.8 percent, 46.85 percent, and 55.18 percent respectively) and the pan-green camp (41.2 percent, 43.51 percent, and 40.14 percent) has been hovering between 10 percent and 15 percent.[9] In an attempt to compound the effects of the identity-oriented referendum to favor the pro-independence DPP presidential candidate, Chen and his party hoped to gain some swing voters' support to accept their referendum initiative and eventually compensate the difference in vote shares for a winning majority over the pan-blue camp in the presidential election. The wishful thinking was: voting for the DPP referendum initiative constitutes "loving Taiwan", and the DPP is the only guardian of Taiwan's independent status. As demonstrated in the 2008 presidential election, one cannot rule out the referendum's inspirational impact in election. Amid widespread public dissatisfaction of Chen's governmental performance and corruption scandals, Frank Hsieh, the DPP candidate, still received 41.55 percent of votes, a vote share more or less reflecting and maintaining the DPP power base.

Fourth, although it might seem delusional for Chen and the DPP to try to use such a referendum to modify as well as socialize the United States and the world to have a favorable status quo policy toward Taiwan, one should not forget that the DPP has long believed that persistence and patience would eventually pay off through the painstaking task of reframing social constructs and discourses. Inspired by their favorite song, "We Shall Overcome", they have been convinced that their long-term laborious drive for Taiwan's independence will eventually prevail over all obstacles as evidenced in their past struggles with the KMT prior to the DPP's rise to power. Stated differently, the whole UN bid campaign has been orchestrated by a mix of liberalist conviction that a democratic Taiwan deserves a right of self-determination and a constructive postulate that, given time, the endless call for Taiwan's identity will reach a tipping point to create a cascade effect and gain widespread support (Finnemore and Sikkink, 1998, 901–905). Concurrently, if China reacts strongly, it could give Chen and the DPP a wonderful opportunity to stir up the passion of their supporters and harden the DPP's determination toward independence.

In the end, Chen and the DPP have eagerly donned the mantle of identity politics to maximize their chances of winning the next presidential election against a strong KMT opponent, Ma Ying-jeou, and retain legitimacy in governance. The problem is that identity is not one dimensional. Taiwanese voters' choices of identity have been constructed in various dimensions, including self-consciousness of *different-ness* in national identity from China, preferences regarding Taiwan's statehood in the future, and a pragmatic view of identity realization in light of China's security threat and economic interdependence across the Strait (Chu and Nathan, 2007–2008, 80, 81; Bush, 2005, 180; Wu, 2002, 209–213). Individual identification with Taiwanese identity has grown from 17.2 percent in June 1993 to 43.7 percent in July 2007. However, the increase in Taiwanese identity has not translated necessarily into a strong support for an independent statehood in immediate policy demands. In fact, a significant percentage of Taiwanese surveyed, either 71.9 percent in December 1994 or 80 percent in June 2007, has continuously preferred the status quo — neither immediate independence nor unification with China.[10] Even the former DPP legislator Lin Cho-shui has acknowledged that the utility of the constant employment of "Taiwan identity" as an electoral agenda has seen its diminishing utility with the support of "Taiwanization" among voters declining from 73 percent in 1997 to 20 percent in 2008 ("Ex-lawmakers", 2008).

Politicians in competitive elections, regrettably, have chosen to compress these various dimensions into one simple policy spectrum in order to differentiate themselves from their opponents and urge voters to stay with the politician's proposal. Frequent employment of identity issues has been likely to generate a diminishing return of utility after voters become fed up with endless verbal thuggery. Even so, Chen refused to retreat from its UN bid referendum in the 2008 presidential election and his overwhelming concerns about domestic politics have surely deepened U.S. fear of entrapment.

Certainly, the United States has worried about a mutual bidding process of referendum politics as it could harden Taiwan's position against the United States wishes and heighten the risk of entrapment. Different from the first referendum controversy in 2003–2004, Chen has appeared to be resolute in his second referendum effort. This prompted Thomas Christensen, Deputy Assistant Secretary of State for East Asian and Pacific Affairs, to send a stern message to Taiwan in September 2007, criticizing Chen's government for its provocative "Taiwan for UN" referendum move, which could become a "legally binding popular vote" to change the U.S.-defined status quo in the event of a change in national title. On the contrary, the KMT's "odd and unproductive" referendum proposal of "ROC (Republic of China) for Taiwan" without invoking a name change would, in Christensen's view, be considered a domestic political posturing rather than a provocative external move to disrupt the status quo (Christensen, 2007).

Christensen's statement signaled U.S. willingness to accept a sub-optimal option — the KMT referendum — should the referendum be unstoppable in Taiwan's presidential elections. In different ways, the United States and the KMT have joined together to adopt a pincer maneuver to hinder Chen's adventurous move.

As U.S. pressures continued in December 2007, U.S. Secretary of State Condoleezza Rice expressed openly that the "UN bid" referendum was a "provocative" move that did not deliver any benefit to the Taiwanese people (Rice, 2007). Again, the United States only permitted Chen's transit through Alaska in January 2008 for his trip to

Guatemala. Still, any reasonable U.S. explanation of its opposition to referendum proposals would be branded by the DPP as an intervention in Taiwan's domestic politics and employed as an easy argument to arouse nationalistic sentiment.

In the end, through repeated challenges, Chen attempted to accumulate sizeable political gains. Chen's referendum proposal appeared to "entrap" the KMT into following his lead to evoke a KMT-initiated referendum of Taiwan's legitimate right of UN membership. However, he failed to change the U.S.-defined status quo. While the referendum issue and transit visits have caused serious strain, the arms sales issue — the usual bond for alliance collaboration — has not offered much relief to US fear of entrapment either.

THE FEUD OVER ARMS SALES: COORDINATED DEFENSE AND ARMS TRANSFER

During the era of Chen's governance, bilateral arms sales — a solid pillar of the United States–Taiwan alliance — also led the United States to question Taiwan's commitment and contribution to the alliance. Encountering China's rise in the international community, the United States has adopted a dual-pronged approach, an "engaging and hedging" military strategy, to deal with China's rise in military capability (Foot, 2006). While "engaging" promotes a "positive-sum" perspective by encouraging China to be a responsible "stakeholder and force" in the world, a precautionary mood of "hedging" China's potential threat to U.S. interests leads both the U.S. and Taiwan to the coordinated arrangement of forces in areas close to China and to the introduction of advanced weapon systems in the region to offset Beijing's power (Christensen, 2006, 95–104; U.S. Department of Defense, 2006, 29). Other efforts involve the incorporation of India, Japan, Mongolia, and Pakistan into a "hub-and-spoke" security arrangement to prepare for a worst case scenario and to create a subtle deterrent effect. In this regional scheme, Taiwan's geopolitical location in the western Pacific and its uncompromising stand against China's unification serve U.S. "hedging" strategy well.

Taiwan's security also relies on a firm U.S. commitment to swift and forceful intervention. Even so, the 9/11 terrorist attack in 2001 and the 2003 war on Iraq have changed U.S. global strategy, which now requires assistance and support from other countries, including China — a major player in world politics and a permanent member of the UN Security Council. In addition to China's appeal to the U.S. business community for its huge potential in market shares and profit earnings, China has played a crucial role as mediator in the North Korean nuclear issue, particularly while U.S. forces have been tied down in wars in Afghanistan and Iraq. The overstretching of U.S. troops has been so serious that one could question the U.S. ability to deliver and deploy a "ready brigade" to any hot spot anywhere in the world, including Taiwan, within 72 hours (Thompson, 2007). Moreover, given growing interdependence between China and the United States, it is unlikely that the United States could reach a quick and easy resolution among the various domestic constituencies of its policy toward Taiwan at the time of a potential military crisis. As a result, Taiwan has reasonable concerns over U.S. commitment to its security. Fears of abandonment have prompted Taiwan to look for constant security assurances either in words or in deeds. It is no wonder that Taiwan would also like to explore various options on its own, such as the development and deployment of medium to long-range missiles to counter China's security threat.

If direct U.S. intervention is difficult, U.S. arms supply is another way to confirm US alliance commitments and soothe Taiwan's fear of abandonment. After all, what would be a better index of U.S. alliance support than a steady supply of arms for Taiwan's defense? On this point, the United States has demonstrated its alliance commitments with the delivery of arms and equipment exceeding US$11.4 billion in value to Taiwan and concurrently concluded numerous arms purchase agreements totaling around US$9 billion with Taiwan between 1998 and 2005 (Grimmett, 2006, 2–7).

While arms supplied by the United States are intended to increase Taiwan's security, they may also have a detrimental effect on the status quo in the region. On one hand, arms transfer creates a "coupling" effect — an impression of alliance between Taiwan and the United States. On the other hand, Taiwan's increased self-confidence and security through arms transfers may boost its pro-independence stance and potentially drive cross–strait relations into a collision course. Stated differently, a substantial improvement in Taiwan's security through the steady supply of arms could reinforce its yearning for independence and, thus, increase U.S. fear of entrapment should Taiwanese authorities choose to disregard U.S. concerns and warnings. It is imperative for the United States to maintain a delicate balance and ensure Taiwan's security without giving it the illusion of unconditional security that might cause Taiwan to endanger U.S. interests.

Accordingly, the United States does not necessarily agree to whatever Taiwan demands. Even if an arms sale is approved, the weapons transferred will not necessarily fulfill Taiwan's wish list. For instance, when Taiwan requested four U.S.-made Arleigh Burke-class destroyers equipped with the Aegis battle management system, the United States would agree to sell only second hand Kidd-class missile destroyers. Similarly, Taiwan acquired F-16s with restrictions on their air refueling capability. As a stronger ally and the supplier of military technology and end products, the United States sets up the terms for arms transfer to dictate the alliance relationship.[11]

If the weaker state remains a meek follower and the stronger state has a steadfast and unwavering commitment, then one would expect a high level of alliance cohesion. While the United States faces domestic pressures to achieve a sensible policy toward China, Taiwan encounters divergent societal pressures, vigorous party competition, and volatile political changes in its policy deliberation and design. The persistent internal disputes over Taiwan's identity and the increasing economic ties between Taiwan and China have led to disagreements among parties and elites on their assessment of China's threats, priorities of security arrangements, and how to allocate scarce resources for best results (Schweller, 2006, 11, 12).

Legislative scrutiny adds complexity to U.S. arms sales to Taiwan. While Taiwanese legislative critical review can be a useful ploy and justification for Taiwan's negotiators to make a better deal, the legislature's powerful interference in foreign policy can bring a hard bargained deal to a complete halt. For example, legislators' adamant demand to reduce the price of the Kidd-class warships by 15 percent almost scuttled the entire deal. The same applies to the proposed special arms procurement package of NT$610.8 billion (US$18.2 billion) in 2004, which included the acquisition of twelve P-3C Orion submarine-hunting aircraft, eight diesel-electric submarines and six PAC-3 (Patriot Advanced Capabiility-3) missile batteries.

Since Chen's pan-green coalition, including the DPP and Taiwan Solidarity Union (TSU), was in a legislative minority, the special arms proposal failed to pass through the Procedure Committee in Legislative Yuan in a total of 70 attempts. It was finally approved with a deep budgetary cut in its original proposal. This special arms procurement proposal has become an impediment to the United States–Taiwan security alliance in recent years. The resistance has come from primarily the pan-blue opposition parties (KMT and PFP), military veterans, and an ad hoc coalition of NGOs who are against huge arms purchases on various grounds. For example, critics have questioned the quantity, effectiveness, and reliability of Patriot missiles, the suspicion of price gouging by U.S. suppliers, the over reliance on the United States, the necessity of proposed weapons, the priority of weapons, and the likely repercussion of a security dilemma effect on the Taiwan–China arms race. Furthermore, Taiwan's first-ever nationwide referendum proposal regarding the purchase of advanced anti-missile weapons (i.e., PAC-3 missiles) failed to pass in March 2004. Based on arms purchase opponents' interpretation of Article 33 of the 2003 Referendum Law, a defeated proposal has to wait for three more years before resubmission. Consequently, any "resubmission" of a missile purchase proposal prior to 2007 would be illegal and unacceptable.[12] Thus, the use of referendum for electoral campaigns had apparently backfired to restrain Chen's government's arms request.

Opponents' criticisms were not completely unjustified. For example, without knowing of the model of promised diesel-electric submarines, Taiwan's 2006 estimated cost for purchasing one submarine was US$657 million. This was much higher than other countries' costs, because the United States no longer built diesel-electronic submarines and no other country was willing to sell submarines to Taiwan due to political and diplomatic factors (Dumbaugh, 2006, 7; "MND Estimated", 2006). In addition to their doubts about the suitability of PAC-3 missile defense in the Taiwan theater, opponents also questioned the wisdom of acquiring used P-3C anti-submarine aircraft in the initial proposal to extend their service life. Some critics were also concerned about the unending arms race between Taiwan and China and questioned whether U.S. sales motives benefited the commercial interests of its military industrial complex and was merely a shrewd ploy of using Taiwan to pin down China in regional conflicts.

As a result of strong opposition, the government had to revise the initial proposed budget from NT$610.8 billion in April 2004, to NT$448 billion in March 2005, and, finally, to NT$340 billion in September 2005. In June 2007, the Taiwanese legislature approved NT$25.7 billion (US$790 million) to fund an upgrade plan for PAC-2 Patriot Missile Batteries, P-3C Orion aircraft, and the first phase budget for the acquisition of F-16 C/D fighter planes (pending U.S. approval). As for the "feasibility study" budget for submarines, the legislature drastically reduced the revised budget request from NT$4.537 billion (US$136 million) to a meager amount of NT$200 million (US$6 million) (Shih 2007a). Since U.S.–Taiwan relations were at a low ebb, the United States declined to accept Taiwan's arms requests for F-16 C/D four times in 2007 as a signal to convey its displeasure over Chen's refusal to withdraw Taiwan's UN bid referendum (Minnick, 2008). This intentional postponement prevented Chen from gaining political advantages by using the approval of F-16 C/D sales as a vindication of U.S. tacit approval of his UN referendum plan (Shih, 2007b). In a similar fashion, by delaying the approval of the arms package during the period of 2004–2007, Taiwan's opposition parties hindered Chen's active independence agenda and subtly lessened U.S. fear of entrapment.

Nevertheless, the legislative stall on arms purchases tested U.S. patience and caused tensions in alliance cohesion. The U.S. officials began to raise issues of Taiwan's eroding military capability, questioned its willingness to defend itself, and put further strains on the collaborative mechanism in the United States–Taiwan alliance. In 2005, Edward Ross, a senior Pentagon official, even suggested reassessing the U.S. defense assistance to Taiwan, "if Taiwan is not willing to properly invest in its own self-defense" (Agence France-Presse, 2005). Steve Young, the AIT Director in Taipei, bordered on intervening in Taiwan's domestic politics by publicly warning in October 2006 that "the United States is watching closely and will judge those who take responsible positions on this as well those who play politics" in objection to the proposed arms deals (AIT, 2006). Of course, Taiwan should not take the complete blame for the delayed arms purchases. Worrying that a revival of the diesel–electrical submarine program for Taiwan might divert resources away from the U.S. nuclear-powered submarine program, U.S. Navy bureaucracy deliberately slowed down the cost estimation process of Taiwan's deal and over-inflated the production cost in order to sabotage the deal (Minnick, 2006).

Whether or not Taiwan's subordination is annoying or repulsive to those who argue strongly for state autonomy in the United States–Taiwan interaction, U.S. arms transfer has become an integral part of the informal alliance. Taiwan's national security configuration is in no position to rule out U.S. military assistance, if it believes in the strategy of "peace-through-strength" in dealing with China. At the same time, the United States is also bonded to Taiwan's security, if the United States continues its value-oriented foreign policy of promoting and protecting Taiwan's democracy and maintains its "hedging" defense profile in East Asia. Although arms sales packages have been affected by the controversy of identity-oriented referendums, in the end arms transfers have remained relatively stable in the United States–Taiwan alliance.

BRING IDENTITY INTO SECURITY: TAIWAN'S ART OF ALLIANCE MANAGEMENT

The United States has appeared to adopt a don't-rock-the-boat mentality so profound that any proposed deviation from its "one China" policy and the principle of peaceful resolution of the Taiwan issue would have to be assessed for its impact on the United States–China–Taiwan strategic situation. As the stronger partner, the United States is determined to maintain its perceived status quo, even though the United States might intervene in Taiwan's domestic affairs. Without "intervention", the United States would be unable to maintain peaceful resolution as a feasible option. Failure to keep the peace would increase the likelihood of an extremely costly conflict with China, should China choose a military solution. Hence, it becomes a top priority for the United States to carefully monitor Taiwan's domestic development, as Chen's government has adopted incessant, provocative tactics to assert its sovereign claims of a new identity critically challenging China's position. As the weaker counterpart, Taiwan has realized that the United States prying into its internal affairs and foreign policy is an inescapable part of the informal alliance. On the issue of arms transfers, the interaction between alliance partners has appeared to work, though it has been fraught with disruptions and tensions since 2004. The U.S. assistance and involvement in Taiwan's security arrangement continues to be helpful and useful to counter China's military threat.

Since there is no written treaty spelling out the United States–Taiwan security relations, Taiwan is relatively free to reinterpret the game rules to fit its situational needs, to expand the permeability of those rules, and to intentionally preempt the United States from tilting further toward China. The persistent acts of Chen's government in the past several years have been efforts to redefine the status quo and reconstruct Taiwan's international identities through the process of signaling, interpretations, responses, and negotiations (Alexander and Wiley, 1981). Although these moves have seemed inconsequential for immediate impact and might have been counterproductive to the United States–Taiwan relations, they have offered an opportunity for both sides to purposively manipulate, re-orient, and transform identities in ongoing interactions.

Besides the fear of abandonment as an impetus to Taiwan's referendum initiatives, internal balancing has clearly acquired more weight in Taiwan's approach to the United States–Taiwan alliance relations during Chen's second term. Chen has encountered constant partisan divisions on the issues of state identity, diverse assessments of the nature and extent of China's threats, and regime vulnerability plagued by corruption scandals and allegations. Under siege from irate public criticism, Chen's unruly and sudden moves demonstrated his determination to "dig in" deep and hard to stay in power until the end of his second term in 2008. Unfortunately, he has not taken into account the multiplicity and complexity of identity consciousness in Taiwan and the necessity of a pragmatic approach to reach a balance between identity and security in the delicate Taiwan–United States–China relation. While continuous U.S. arms transfer would relieve Taiwan's fear of abandonment, Taiwan's aggressive identity reformulation in foreign policy has increased U.S. fear of entrapment.

An addition of identity politics to security consideration could potentially tear apart the formerly well-cultivated United States–Taiwan alliance. In an asymmetrical alliance, the weaker ally's bargaining power is limited because the weak usually acquiesces to the rules imposed by the strong. If handled unwisely, frequent flip-flops in alliance promises could become a political liability. Any indication of political opportunism could cause doubt in the seriousness of alliance commitment and, thus, endanger alliance cohesion and bilateral trust. As Taiwan edges near or beyond the fuzzy "red line" drawn by the United States, the trusting relationship diminishes and the unity and cohesion of the informal alliance could be severely compromised.

In sum, if the United States persistently resists the initiations, Taiwan's aggressive attempt to create a new identity role in the alliance only self-perpetuates a narcissism without the other's recognition (Mitzen, 2006, 359, 360). Rhetoric which greatly departs from realistic vision can be perceived as hypocrisy in the eyes of others. The failure to receive positive responses hurts the sincerity and seriousness of identity transformation, because an alliance presupposes that trust and empathy are essential to its bilateral management and cohesion. Naturally, Taiwan is expected to employ continuously identity reformulation as part of its alliance management. However, Taiwan's repeated incorporation of identity into its security discourses has not received positive feedback from the United States. While it is understandable for Chen to pursue more changes than what the United States would accept in the alliance portfolio, his frequent unorthodox approach to the United States–Taiwan alliance relations has actually backfired and harmed Taiwan's long-term interests. How to reconstruct the mutual trust between the United States and Taiwan is therefore a crucial task for the new Ma Ying-jeou administration in the coming years. In stark contrast to Chen's confrontational posture, Ma's low-key profile in his first state visit to Latin America in August 2008 with transit stops in the United States has shown Taiwan's change of course to bolster its relations with the United States. Whether the prudent approach will contribute positively to Taiwan's security and diplomacy deserves further examination.

*Parts of this chapter are based on a paper presented at the conference on Taiwan, University of South Carolina, Columbia, SC, September 25–27, 2009. The conference paper will appear in a forthcoming issue of *Issues and Studies*.

REFERENCES

Abdelal, R, YM Herrera, AI Johnston and R McDermott (2006). Identity as a variable. *Perspectives on Politics*, 4(4), 695–711.

Agence, F-P (2005). Pentagon official warns Taiwan on defense spending, <*DefenseNews.com*>. September 21.

AIT (American Institute in Taiwan) (2006). Press conference: Stephen M. Young, Director, American Institute in Taiwan. October 27. OT-0617E. <www.ait.org.tw/en/news/officialtext/viewer.aspx?id=2006102702>.

Alexander, CN Jr and MG Wiley (1981). Situated activity and identity formation. In *Social Psychology: Sociological Perspectives*, Rosenberg, M and RH Turner (eds.), 269–289. New York: Basic Books.

Axelrod, RM (1984). *The Evolution of Cooperation*. New York: Basic Books.

Baier, A (1986). Trust and antitrust. *Ethics*, 96(2), 231–260.

Berge, PL and T Luckmann (1967). *The Social Construction of Reality: A Treatise in the Sociology of Knowledge*. New York: Anchor Books.

Bradsher, K (2007). Defying China, Taiwan leader backs a vote on sovereignty. *New York Times*, August 3, 4.

Bush, R (2005). Taiwan faces China: Attraction and repulsion. In *Power Shift*, Shambaugh, D (ed.), 170–186. Berkeley, CA: University of California Press.

Cha, VD (2000). Abandonment, entrapment, and neoclassical realism in Asia: The United States, Japan, and Korea. *International Studies Quarterly*, 44(1), 261–291.

Chan, S (2003). Extended deterrence in the Taiwan strait. *World Affairs*, 166(2), 109–125.

China Post (Taipei) (2006). Taiwan independence means war for US, Zoellick Says. May 12, 1.

China Times (*Zhongguo* Shibao, Taipei). <www.chinatimes.com)>.

Christensen, TJ (2006). Fostering stability or creating a monster? The rise of China and US policy toward East Asia. *International Security*, 31(1), 81–126.

Christensen, TJ (2007). A strong and moderate Taiwan. Speech to US–Taiwan Business Council, Defense Industry Conference, Annapolis, MD, September 11. <www.state.gov/p/eap/rls/rm/2007/91979.htm>.

Chu, Y-H and AJ Nathan (2007–2008). Seizing the opportunity for change in the Taiwan strait. *Washington Quarterly*, 31(1), 77–91.

Clinton, W (1998). Remarks by the president and the first lady in discussion on shaping China for the 21st century. <forums.chinatimes.com/report/meeting/01-18.htm>.

Copper, JF (2006). United States Taiwan policy: How the 2004 (Taiwan) presidential election put it to the test. In *Sources of Conflict and Cooperation in the Taiwan Strait*, Zheng Y and RR-K Wu (eds.). Singapore: World Scientific.

Dumbaugh, K (2006). Taiwan: Recent developments and US policy choices. *CRS Issue Brief for Congress*. Updated June 8, 2006, order code IB98034.

Ereli, A (2006). Taiwan-senior Taiwan officials comments on national unification council, March 2. <merln.ndu.edu/archivepdf/china/State/62488.pdf>.

Ex-lawmakers blame DPP downfall on 'Taiwanization' (2008). *China Post*, April 24. <www.chinapost.com.tw/taiwan/2008/04/24/153327/Ex-lawmakers-blame.htm>.

Fearon, J (1994). Domestic political audiences and the escalation of international disputes. *American Political Science Review*, 88(3), 577–592.

Finnemore, M and K Sikkink (1998). International norm dynamics and political change. *International Organization*, 52(4), 887–917.

Foot, R (2006). Chinese strategies in a US-hegemonic global order: Accommodating and hedging. *International Affairs*, 82(1), 77–94.

FoxNews (2003). Bush opposes Taiwan independence. December 9. <www.foxnews.com/story/0,2933,105239,00.html>.

Gourevitch, P (2001). Domestic politics and international relations. In *Handbook of International Relations*, Carlsnaes W, T Risse and BA Simmons (eds.). pp. 309–328. London: Sage Publications.

Grimmett, RF (2006). *US Arms Sales: Agreements with and Deliveries to Major Clients, 1998–2005*, CRS Report for Congress, order code RL33758, December 15.

Holdridge, JH (1997). *Crossing the Divide: An Insider's Account of Normalization of US–China Relations*. Lanham, MD: Rowman & Littlefield.

Hsu, A (2008). AIT chairman reaffirms US commitment. *Taiwan Journal*, June 22, 1.

Huang, C (2005). Referendum and mobilization in Taiwan. 2005 Meeting of the American Political Science Association, Washington, DC, September 1.

Johnston, AI (2004). Beijing's security behavior in the Asia–Pacific: Is China a dissatisfied power? In *Rethinking Security in East Asia: Identity, Power, and Efficiency*, Suh, JJ, PJ Katzenstein and A Carson (eds.), 34–96. Stanford, CA: Stanford University Press.

Kan, SA (2007). *Taiwan: Major US Arms Sales Since 1990*, CRS Report for Congress, updated July 12, order code RL30957.

Kann, RA (1976). Alliances versus ententes. *World Politics*, 28(4), 611–621.

Kau, MYM (ed.) (2005). *Direct Democracy Practices in Taiwan*. Taipei: Taiwan Foundation for Democracy.

Kelley, S-P (2006). US–Taiwan relations at low ebb, insider report indicates. February 2. <agonist.org/story/2006/2/2/151221/9739>.

Kelly, JA (2004). Assistant secretary of state for East Asian and Pacific affairs, "Overview of US Policy toward Taiwan", Testimony at a hearing on Taiwan, House International Relations Committee, Washington, DC, April 21.

Keohane, R and H Milner (1996). *Internationalization and Domestic Politics*. Cambridge: Cambridge University Press.

Koenig, LW, JC Hsiung and K-Y Chang (eds.) (1985). *Congress, the Presidency, and the Taiwan Relations Act*. New York: Praeger.

Lee, DT (2000). *The Making of the Taiwan Relations Act: Twenty Years in Retrospect*. Hong Kong: Oxford University Press.

Liberty Times (*Ziyou Shibao*, Taipei). <www.libertytimes.com.tw>.

Lin, JW (2004). Taiwan's referendum act and the stability of the status quo. *Issues and Studies*, 40(2), 119–153.

Lin, MC and CY Lin (2003). Lu asks US to beef up Taiwan ties. *Taipei Times*, March 30, 3.

Mattlin, M (2004). Referendum as a form of *Zaoshi*: The instrumental political functions of Taiwan's referendum ploy. *Issues and Studies*, 40(2), 155–185.

Minnick, W (2006). Taiwan claims US navy is sabotaging SSK plans. *Jane's Defense Weekly*. February 10. <www.janes.com/defence/news/jdw/jdw060210_1_n.shtml>.

Minnick, W (2008). Taiwan fears China is chipping away at US support. January 7. <www.defensenews.com>.

Mitzen, J (2006). Ontological security in world politics: State identity and the security dilemma. *European Journal of International Relations*, 12(3), 341–370.

MND Estimated Submarine Price at US$657 million (2006). *Central News Agency*, March 20.

Morrow, JD (1991). Alliances and asymmetry: An alternative to the capability aggregation model of alliances. *American Journal of Political Science*, 35(4), 904–933.

Morrow, JD (1999). The strategic setting of choices: Signaling, commitment, and negotiation in international politics. In *Strategic Choice and International Politics*, Lake, DA and R Powell (eds.), 77–114. Princeton, NJ: Princeton University Press.

Morrow, JD (2000). Alliances: Why write them down? *Annual Review of Political Science*, 3, 63–83.

Putnam, RD (1988). Diplomacy and domestic politics: The logic of two-level games. *International Organization*, 42(3), 427–460.

Olson, M and R Zeckhauser (1966). An economic theory of alliances. *Review of Economics and Statistics*, 48(3), 266–279.

Regan, T (2006). Taiwan's president abolishes China reunification committee. *Christian Science Monitor*, February 27. <www.csmonitor.com/2006/0227/dailyUpdate.html>.

Rice, C (2007). Press conference by secretary of state Condoleezza rice. December 21. <www.state.gov/secretary/rm/2007/12/97945.htm>.

Romberg, AD (2003). Some thoughts on cross–strait relations. In *Breaking the China–Taiwan Impasse*, Zagoria, DS (ed.), pp. 23–38. Westport, CT: Praeger.

Ross, RS (1995). *Negotiating Cooperation: The United States and China, 1969–1989.* Stanford, CA: Stanford University Press.

Schweller, R (2006). *Unanswered Threats: Political Constraints on the Balance of Power.* Princeton, NJ: Princeton University Press.

Shih, HC (2007a). Six-year saga. *Taipei Times*, June 16.

Shih, HC (2007b). KMT says Chen's UN bid has derailed US sales of F-16s. *Taipei Times*, July 17.

Snyder, C (2006). US congress members defend Chen. *Taipei Times*, May 12, 3.

Snyder, C and N Tsao (2006). US decides on transit plan: Source. *Taipei Times*, May 3, 3.

Snyder, J and K Ballentine (2001). Nationalism and the marketplace of ideas. In *Nationalism and Ethnic Conflict*, Brown, ME *et al.* (eds.), 61–69. Cambridge, MA: MIT Press.

Snyder, GH (1997). *Alliance Politics.* Ithaca, NY: Cornell University Press.

Stein, J (2007). Defense officials tried to reverse China policy, says powell aide. *CQ Home Security*, June 1. <public.cq.com/docs/hs/hsnews110-000002523531.html>.

Thompson, M (2007). Broken down. *Time*, April 16.

US, Department of Defense (2006). *Quadrennial Defense Review Report.* Washington, DC: Office of the Secretary of Defense, Department of Defense.

US Senate, Committee on Foreign Relations (1982). U.S. policy toward China and Taiwan. 97th Congress, 2nd Session, Hearing, August 17.

United Daily (*Lienho Bao*, Taipei).

Walt, SM (1987). *The Origins of* Alliances. Ithaca, NY: Cornell University Press.
Wang, E (2007). AIT chief to meet with both 2008 candidates. *China Post*, June 16. <www.chinapost.com.tw/taiwan/112487.htm>.
Witter, W (2003). New constitution, referendums demanded. *Washington Times*. October 25. <www.washtimes.com/world/20031025-111019-3506r.htm>.
Wu, R-R (2002). Toward a pragmatic nationalism, democratization and Taiwan's passive revolution. In *Memories of the Future: National Identity Issues and the Search for a New Taiwan*, Corcuff, S (ed.), 196–218. Armonk, NY: M.E. Sharpe.

ENDNOTES

1. Still, in a formal alliance, members may deliberately leave some areas of mutual obligations and commitments vague for future interpretation (Morrow, 2000, 73; Morrow, 1999, 94, 95).
2. It is certainly debatable whether the United States–Taiwan security relationship should be treated as an alliance or an alignment. However, I decided to use informal alliance to describe their security relations during this period of time. For the difference between alliance and alignment, please see Kann (1976), Walt (1987, 12), and Cha (2000, 265–269), Snyder (1997, 6, 21, 61–62), and Morrow (1991, 906, 907; 2000, 64, 65).
3. Of course, the existence of Taiwanese identity does not automatically lead to a quest for independence.
4. Article 10 of the 1954 Mutual Defense Treaty stipulates that the treaty ceases to function one year after notice has been given to the other party. The United States served its notice in 1979 and the treaty was officially terminated in 1980.
5. Such a cautious approach was clearly evident in the floor debates about the use of the language "of grave concern" or "security interest" in the TRA to express U.S. seriousness in maintaining a peaceful settlement of the Taiwan issue. Under heavy White House lobbying pressures and some legislators' doubts, the phrase "of grave concern" (TRA, Sec. 2 (b)(4)) was adopted to avoid jeopardizing U.S. policy toward China and conveying an overblown message of US commitment to Taiwan (David Lee, 2000, 142–145).
6. The two questions listed for the "peace" referendum in place of previously claimed "defensive" referendum are: (1) Should mainland China refuse to withdraw the missiles it has targeted at Taiwan and to openly renounce the use of force against us, would you agree the government should acquire more advanced anti-missile weapons to strengthen Taiwan's self-defense capabilities? (2) Would you agree that our government should engage in negotiation with mainland China on the establishment of a "peace and stability" framework for cross-strait integrations in order to build consensus and for the welfare of the peoples on both sides? (Lin, 2004).

7. On the final day of his presidential campaign in March 2004, both Chen and his Vice President were wounded by an apparent assassination attempt. The bullet created a surface wound on his belly. Another bullet hit the Vice President's knee. The incident remains unresolved.
8. The term *gui erzi* literally means "son of turtle" in Chinese. It can be used as a swear word. Yet, it is occasionally used in a non-abrasive way. In this particularly context, it implied that Taiwan was not a subordinate to the United States.
9. The pan-blue camp includes the KMT, the People First Party, and the New Party. The pan-green camp includes the DPP and Taiwan Solidarity Union.
10. Here Taiwanese identity does not include those with "both Taiwanese and Chinese identity". Status quo supporters include those who support status quo indefinitely and those who support status quo, but may move toward independence or unification in the future. Data about the changes in the Taiwanese/Chinese identity and changes in the unification-independence stances of Taiwanese as tracked in surveys by the Election Study Center, National Chengchi University, can be found in <esc.nccu.edu.tw/eng/data/data03-2.htm> and <esc.nccu.edu.tw/eng/data/data03-3.htm>.
11. Another well-known case to show Taiwan's security dependence is a mobile communication and electronic warfare system called "*Tiequan*" (Iron Fist) after the 1996 Taiwan Strait Crisis. However, the contractual conditions were lop-sided in favor of the supplier with no compensatory clause for the supplier's contractual neglects and failures in meeting Taiwan's technical specifications. The project lasted for five years (1999–2004) and ended with no concrete result except a huge waste of NT$2.2 billion (US$66 million) (*Liberty Times*, August 9, 2006).
12. Regarding the legal effect of the failed proposal on anti-missile weapons in the 2004 referendum, there are different interpretations. One interpretation is that the rejected referendum did not prohibit the government from maintaining the current level of defense since the referendum was phrased to "*acquire more advanced anti-missile weapons to strengthen Taiwan's self-defense capabilities*". Moreover, the law requires the referendum proposal not be proposed again as a referendum proposal for at least three years, but does not prevent the government from submitting it as a regular policy proposal. Opponents argue that the law required the proposal on Patriot missiles be put aside for three years.

Chapter

10

Taiwan's Participation in Asia–Pacific Regional Processes: Searching for an Agenda of Cross–Strait Consultations

Chyungly Lee

Recent developments of multilateral cooperation in the Asia–Pacific have suggested a pattern of multilayered (or multitrack) policy communications, ranging from networks of informal consultation among non-state actors (including non-governmental organizations and civil society organizations) to summits of state leaders. Trends have indicated an increase of confidence among regional actors to make collective responses to their common concerns. In spite of their overlapping memberships and agenda, however, these multitrack mechanisms do not seem to converge toward regional unity, rather they can be considered as compatible processes. The degree and extent of Taiwan's participation in various regional processes are thus indeed subject to the political sensitivity of concerned issues and the different approaches to institution-building of each mechanism.

In terms of membership involving state governments, Asia–Pacific regional processes suggest two clusters: one is the pan-Asia–Pacific model emerging in the wake of the Cold War; the other is the ASEAN (Association of Southeast Asian Nations)-centered East Asian integration processes initiated after the outbreak of 1997–1998 Asian financial crises. The former includes the first region-wide intergovernmental mechanism established in 1989 — the Forum for Asia–Pacific Economic Cooperation (APEC), and the only regional security cooperation mechanism launched in 1994 — the ASEAN Regional Forum (ARF). The members of both mechanisms cover broad geographical areas beyond East Asia. In contrast, the ASEAN Plus Three (APT) process launched in 1997 allowed the ramifications of economic distresses to regional politico-security and socio-cultural developments to be jointly addressed by the ASEAN member states together with Japan, China, and South Korea. In 2005, the footprint of East Asia integration was extended to Australia, New Zealand, and India, when the first East Asia Summit (EAS) was held in Kuala Lumpur, Malaysia.

Taiwan is an important economic and security actor in the Asia–Pacific. However, even though the region has been experiencing multilateral initiatives for the last two decades, APEC remains the only regional inter-governmental organization in which Taiwan has been accepted as a member. Through APEC, Taiwan is able to participate directly in pan-Asia–Pacific economic cooperation. Nevertheless, as for the pan-Asia–Pacific security cooperation processes, Taiwan can only be indirectly involved in the process through informal track two dialog processes, mainly the Council for Asia–Pacific Security Cooperation (CSCAP). Regarding the ongoing state-led integration processes in East Asia, Taiwan thus far has had no chance to join in any of the aforementioned initiatives. Diplomatic obstruction from Beijing has been the main factor in Taiwan's incomplete participation in these regional cooperation mechanisms. The more rising China's strategic leverage over regional developments increases, the more decisive the China factor will be in Taiwan's striving for expanding its international space. Therefore, stabilizing cross–strait relations becomes one of the necessary and sufficient conditions for advancing Taiwan's regional profile.

Since President Ma took office in May 2008, Taipei and Beijing have resumed consultations under the "1992 consensus". Both governments agreed that their respective authority and jurisdiction will be mutually recognized only when the "one China" principle is commonly accepted, even with their respective interpretations.[1] The resumption of talks between the Strait Exchange Foundation (SEF) and the Association for Relations Across the Taiwan Strait (ARATS) facilitated several functional agreements in 2008–2009.[2] As for Taiwan's international participation, in his speech delivered in the 30th Anniversary of the Adoption of China's Peaceful Policy toward Taiwan on 31 December 2008, Hu Jintao proclaimed that Beijing is willing to discuss "proper and reasonable arrangements" for Taiwan's participation in international organizations, as long as the scenario of "two Chinas" or "one China, one Taiwan" will not be implied.[3] In contrast to the complete blockade against the intent of expanding international participation during the administration of the Democratic Progressive Party (DPP), Beijing seems to have softened its position. The notion of "proper and reasonable arrangements" in Hu's speech may not suggest a wide range of possibilities, but at least it implies the hope of searching for a common negotiation agenda.

The objective of this chapter is to highlight a possible negotiation agenda if the issue of Taiwan's participation in Asia–Pacific regional processes is brought up in the cross–strait consultations. According to the current status of Taiwan's regional participation, this chapter discusses three cases: direct participation in pan-Asia–Pacific economic cooperation, indirect participation in pan-Asia–Pacific security cooperation, and no-participation in East Asian integration processes. This chapter briefly reviews the main features of each regional process, summaries the China factor in Taiwan's participation in the past, speculates progress in the new dynamics of cross-strait relations, and concludes with an assessment based on messages cross-delivered by scholars and experts during the first year of President Ma's administration.

DIRECT PARTICIPATION IN PAN-ASIA–PACIFIC ECONOMIC COOPERATION

APEC

Since the first APEC informal Leaders' Summit hosted by the United States in 1993, policy coordination and view exchanges of APEC member economies were elevated to the Summit level. To a great extent, consensus reached among leaders has since become a driving force in shaping regional policies. In 1993, the principle of "open regionalism" was confirmed to assure the process of regional trade liberalization compatible with the pace of the Uruguay Round negotiations. In 1994, the APEC Bogor Declaration targeted the year of 2010 for developed member economies to complete the schedules of trade liberalization, and 2020 for the developing ones. The Osaka Action Plan of 1995 suggested the Individual Action Plan (IAP), which allows individual member economies to adapt their own pace toward the goals set at Bogor.[4] More recently, in response to the proliferation of Free Trade Agreements/Regional Trade Agreements (FTAs/RTAs) in the region, a project of "Best Practices" was initiated in 2005 to suggest a high standard FTAs/RTAs model for member economies' reference when signing FTAs/RTAs.[5] In 2006, the idea of the Asia–Pacific Free Trade Area (APFTA) was discussed at the Hanoi APEC Informal Summit, where members agreed to study the scheme.

In addition to trade liberalization, business facilitation and the Economic and Technical Cooperation (ECOTEC) are the other two pillars of APEC. The former introduced measures to enhance the business incentives of increasing trade flows among APEC member economies. The latter aimed at narrowing the development gap among member economies and was institutionalized in 1998, when the sub-committee on ECOTECH (ESC) was established.[6] In response to emerging transnational security concerns, APEC member economies also took joint actions to prevent non-economic factors from slowing down the pace of trade and investment liberalization and facilitation. After the 9/11 events of 2001, Secure Trade in APEC Region (STAR) was initiated to enhance the safety of cargo, ships, and aviation. In 2003, the Counter-Terrorism Task Force (CTTF) was organized to coordinate the technical assistance and capacity-building process on counter-terrorism issues. Soon after the outbreak of SARS, the Health Task Force (HTF) was established to cope with health-related economic threats. After the 2004 Indian Ocean tsunami, APEC launched a Task Force of Emergency Preparedness to manage losses from natural and man-made disasters.

Taiwan's Incomplete Membership

Taiwan's economic leverage over regional growth in the late 1980s was too significant to be neglected by the APEC founding members. However, the nature of inter-governmental cooperation, even a model of non-binding forum, causes political sensitivity due to Beijing's concerns. In 1991, negotiations on the membership of China, Taiwan, and Hong Kong were facilitated by the APEC host country of the year — South Korea. In late September of that year, all sides came to an agreement including the following points (Funabashi, 1995, 74, 75):

1. The respective designations of the three parties shall be the People's Republic of China, Chinese Taipei, and Hong Kong (as Hong Kong was to be re-designated as "Hong Kong, China" from 1 July 1997 according to the Sino-British Joint Declaration on the Question of Hong Kong signed on 19 December 1984). These designations shall be used in all APEC meetings, activities, documents, materials, and other publications as well as in all APEC administrative and conference arrangements.
2. Without prejudice to the rights of APEC participants to appoint their respective representatives to APEC meetings, Chinese Taipei shall be represented at Ministerial Meetings only by a Minister or Ministers in charge of APEC-related economic affairs, while its "foreign minister" or "vice-foreign minister" shall not attend APEC meetings. Chinese Taipei's delegation may include officials of "foreign" and other ministries at or below the level of department

director. Members of Chinese Taipei's delegation may use their official titles subject to the principles agreed upon in this Memorandum of Understanding.

3. Subject to the aforementioned terms, the three parties will participate in APEC meetings and activities on an equal basis with the current APEC participants.

On 2 October 1991, a memorandum of understanding containing the above agreements was signed. Thereafter, China, in its exchange of notes, added that to assure the smooth progress of the APEC work and the convenience of various member states, Chinese Taipei will not be on the rotation of being a host member economy. Accordingly, on 12 November 1991, China, Chinese Taipei, and Hong Kong attended, as new members, the third APEC ministerial conference held in Seoul. The document, usually called the 1991 Seoul Memorandum of Understanding (MOU), has been used by Beijing as an effective legal basis to monitor Taiwan's intentions to expand diplomatic space through APEC activities.

Since their accession to APEC, Beijing and Taipei have repeatedly collided on protocol and procedural issues. Most of the cases have referred to Beijing's complaints about using "Taiwan" instead of "Chinese Taipei" in APEC documents.[7] Other than the procedural objections, representatives from both sides have seldom interacted with each other. In some cases, China has intentionally dissuaded other member economies from supporting Taiwan's initiatives. Regarding Taiwan's attempts to host conferences, workshops, and other APEC events, in cases in which no other members were interested in doing so and as long as the arrangements suggested in the Seoul MOU were followed, Beijing had few objections to Taiwan's offers.[8]

The provisions included in the 1991 MOU could not possibly address the issue of Taiwan's participation in APEC informal Leaders' Summit, which was initiated after the 1991 MOU. Nevertheless, before the first APEC Summit in 1993, the United States reached an agreement with China and set up the so-called Seattle model, in which the "one China" principle was again stressed as the basis for including delegations from Chinese Taipei. Beijing alleged that as a member economy (not a member state), Chinese Taipei could only send leaders of economic affairs to the Summit. Since then, the special envoy from Chinese Taipei to the Summit has routinely become a common issue to be tackled by Beijing, Taipei, and the APEC host country. In practice, Beijing enjoys the veto power to decline the name suggested by Taipei if it is considered to imply "two Chinas" or "one China, one Taiwan".

The inclusion of the PRC, Chinese Taipei, and Hong Kong was a replay of the experience in the Pacific Economic Cooperation Council (PECC) in 1985–1986 (Woods, 1993: 134, 135). To a great extent, accommodating "three Chinas" at the same time indicated the pragmatism of the international economic community. Even under great diplomatic pressure, the member economies of APEC could not afford to ignore Taiwan's critical economic position in the region. Such arrangements led to some important political implications and consequences. Some argue that Beijing and Taipei, though quarreling over titles and representation, actually have increased contact over substantive issues under the APEC framework. Such a framework has also allowed other countries in the region to engage Beijing and Taipei at the same time and has provided a useful vehicle for mutual behavioral influence (Yang, 1997).

Prospects

The 16th APEC Leaders' Summit held in Lima, Peru, on 22–23 November 2008 was the first APEC Summit after cross-strait consultations were resumed. President Ma, with no objection from Beijing, sent the former Vice President Lien Chan (連戰) as his special envoy to the occasion. In comparison with the delegations holding Ministerial ranks or high-profile businessmen in the past, Lien was the most prominent political figure representing Chinese Taipei in the APEC Summit. In 2001, the DPP government also proposed former Vice President Lee Yuancu (李元簇) as a special envoy to the APEC Summit in Shanghai. However, the request was denied by Beijing. While the DPP and KMT often dispute over cross-strait policies, sending a former national leader to the APEC summit seems to be a shared goal. It was hoped that such a breakthrough can be set as a Peru model to temporarily settle issues of presidential envoy of Chinese Taipei.

Lien visited Hu in Beijing in an ice-breaking trip to China in 2005 and has since spearheaded the KMT's efforts to develop a rapport with the Chinese Communist Party (CCP). Lien's advocacy of improved ties with China won the trust of Beijing. Although Lien and Hu have met three times since 2005, the 2008 APEC Leader's Summit was the first international occasion in which they acted in the capacity of state leaders. The development of the Summit can be considered to have possibly opened a new phase of bilateral ties. In comparison with the rejection of the DPP's earlier attempt at sending the former Vice President Lee to the Summit in 2001, Beijing's acceptance of Lien in 2008 not only manifested how Beijing prioritized the importance of KMT–CCP platform, but also sent a strong message to the pan-green camp in Taiwan that accepting the "1992 consensus" would be necessary to make it possible for the expansion of Taiwan's international space.

Interestingly, while making a public statement on the precedent, China reiterated that as long as the Taiwan government abides by the substance of the 1991 Seoul MOU, China would keep an open attitude toward the name of the Taiwanese delegation.[9] Given that Lien was not an economic leader and that the precedent was a deviation from the line of the Seoul MOU, the aforementioned statement was indeed to reassert China's decisive role in approving Taiwan's participation. If Beijing and Taipei initiate a consultation on advancing Taiwan's participation in APEC, the signing of a new memorandum of understanding to reflect current dynamics of cross–strait relations would bring about win-win-win outcomes for Beijing, Taipei, and APEC. Two of the possible agenda would be: (1) the extension of the 2008 Peru model, which welcomes Taiwan's former national leaders to represent Chinese Taipei in APEC Summits; and (2) the removal of restrictions on Taiwan being a host of APEC ministerial meetings and informal summits. The former not only benefits both Beijing and Taipei, but also represents a convergence of interests among diverse opinions of the pan-blue and pan-green camps in Taiwan. The latter advances Taiwan's APEC participation on a genuinely equal basis and, at the same time, enables Taiwan to make a greater contribution to regional processes.

INDIRECT PARTICIPATION IN PAN-ASIA–PACIFIC SECURITY COOPERATION

ARF and CSCAP

ARF was initiated at the 26th ASEAN Ministerial Meeting and Post-Ministerial Conference held in Singapore on 23–25 July 1993 to promote open dialog on political and security issues of common interest and concern between ASEAN and non-ASEAN member states. The first ARF Ministerial Meeting was launched a year later. There is no pre-condition regarding the regional boundaries for the ARF's membership. Thus, its membership and participation cover geographical regions of East Asia, South Asia, America, and Europe.[10] The ARF process, as stated in the Concept Paper adopted in 1995, would continue a gradual *evolutionary approach* to sustain and enhance the peace and stability in the region. Although this definition indicates the incompleteness of ARF's institutional design at the time of its establishment, three stages of this process — the promotion of confidence-building measures, the development of preventive diplomacy mechanisms, and the development of conflict resolution mechanisms — were specified in the Concept Paper.

In 2002, a list suggesting the Future Direction of the ARF was endorsed by member states in the 9th ARF Ministerial Meeting as a reference of strengthening ARF's institutional-building efforts. In July 2004, the ARF Unit was established at the ASEAN Secretariat[11] to provide administrative support for enhancing the role of the ARF Chair.[12] Following the decision of the 12th Ministerial Meeting in 2005, the ARF Inter-sessional Group on Confidence Building Measures was replaced by the ARF Inter-sessional Group on Confidence Building Measures and Preventive Diplomacy. The change signaled that members were more willing to discuss substantive issues of preventive diplomacy than before. Despite criticism and limitations, nevertheless, ARF remains the only multilateral security mechanism in the Asia–Pacific.[13]

According to the ARF membership criteria, new participants must be sovereign states with commitment to ARF's main goals and have impacts on the peace and security of the geographical footprint of key ARF activities. Members also agreed to control the membership number to ensure the effectiveness of the ARF process. Applications for membership must be submitted to the Chairman of the ARF, who then consults with all ARF participants at the Senior Official Meeting (SOM) to ascertain whether a consensus exists for the admission of the new participant. Actual decisions on participation are approved by the Ministers. Apparently, the "one-China" principle hampers Taiwan's membership in ARF, and thus excludes Taiwan from direct participation in the pan-Asia–Pacific security cooperation mechanism. Pragmatically, Taiwan strives for joining informal security networks in which statehood is not required.

The Council for Security Cooperation in Asia–Pacific (CSCAP) was established in 1993 to network leading think tanks in the region for promoting security dialogs. CSCAP has been defined as a multilateral track two processes in which academics, researchers from think tanks, journalists, and former and current officials participating in their private capacities explore policy issues concerning regional security (Capie and Evans, 2000: 233). The Steering Committee, co-chaired by a member from an ASEAN member committee and a member from a non-ASEAN member committee, is designated to plan CSCAP activities and meetings with balanced views across the region.

At the nascent stage, working group meetings were the main instruments to facilitate exchanges on common security concerns. Five working groups were formed to cover issues of maritime cooperation, North Pacific security, comprehensive and cooperative security, confidence and security building measures, and transnational crime (added in 1996).[14] In 2004, the working group format was changed to studying groups aiming at issuing memoranda to effectively respond to current debates and concerns of regional security issues. Study outcomes would be reviewed periodically and delivered by co-chairs of the CSCAP Steering Committee in regional intergovernmental processes for official considerations. Studies concluded in the first two years included subjects of capacity building for maritime security cooperation, multilateral security frameworks in Northeast Asia, drug-trafficking, peace-keeping, and peace-building in the Asia–Pacific area.[15]

The overlapping members of the ASEAN Institute of Strategic and International Studies (ASEAN-ISIS) and CSCAP founding members[16] played a crucial role in helping launching ARF. In April 1994, CSCAP members drafted a memorandum and submitted it to the first ARF Senior Official Meeting. Subsequently, the document was raised in the first ARF Ministerial Meeting for ministers' consideration to advance regional security cooperation. Since then, the CSCAP Steering Committee has occasionally presented reports and memorandums jointly adopted by CSCAP working/studying group participants to the ARF Chair. Such documents have been adopted on ad hoc case-by-case base. In 2006, when ARF adopted a Concept Paper on *Enhancing Ties between Track I and Track II in the ARF, and between the ARF and Other Regional and International Security Organizations*, the relations between ARF and CSCAP were strengthened noticeably. For instance, co-chairs of the CSCAP Steering Committee are now eligible to be invited to ARF meetings and directly participate in the ARF process.

The Beijing Factor and Taiwan's Participation

To Taiwan, participation in the CSCAP process has become an indirect way in pan-Asia–Pacific security diplomacy. When CSCAP founding members reached a consensus that inviting China into the process was essential to making CSCAP relevant in regional security given the security uncertainties stirred up by a rising China, Taiwan's full participation in this process could hardly be free of obstacles. To Beijing, only state governments are eligible to discuss external security issues in the international arena. Taiwan's participation in the discussion of regional security, even at the track-two level, may still represent the risk of sending wrong messages implying the recognition of Taiwan's sovereignty. CSCAP founding members fully realized the sensitivity of Beijing's attitude, but also saw the importance of including all security stakeholders in the dialog process. Thus, the inclusion of delegations from China and Taiwan in the CSCAP process has been an issue from the very beginning.

After three years of discussion and communication, arrangements of cross–strait participation were temporarily settled in December 1996. The China Institute of International Studies, a think tank closely attached to China's Ministry of Foreign Affairs, took China's seat at the CSCAP with full membership while Taiwan's participation was accommodated under specific conditions. Under the "one China" principle, member committees agreed that invitations to meetings at working levels could be extended to scholars and experts from Taiwan as long as the arrangements did not imply "two Chinas" or "one China, one Taiwan". Without a formal membership, Taiwanese delegations are considered "other participants" in meetings and are excluded from the CSCAP Steering Committee. Moreover, members agree that security concerns across the Taiwan Strait are China's internal affair, which should not be discussed in the CSCAP process.

Beijing has been less receptive to the idea of track-two diplomacy. Most of the time, China's delegation at the CSCAP working group consists of a retired ambassador, the project coordinator, an issue expert, and a lower rank official from MOFA. Views of Chinese participants follow their official lines and are less flexible than other intellectuals in the meetings. Participants from Taiwan are intellectuals and academics. The Institute of International Relations at National Chengchi University is currently coordinating Taiwan's participation in CSCAP-related activities and meetings. The names of the Taiwanese delegations are pre-agreed upon by the CSCAP Steering Committee. In practice, under the consensus rule CSCAP China has veto power over the names.

The original limitations on Taiwan's participation have been eased. Participants from Taiwan now have no role-playing limitation in the working/studying group meetings, and they are now allowed to make contributions to CSCAP-related publications. The category of "other participants" is no longer exclusively designated to Taiwanese participants. Those who do not belong to any national committee of CSCAP members but are invited by the host member of working/study group meetings are also listed as "other participants". In the first few years, sitting arrangements with a tag of "other participants" puzzled many new individual participants. More recently, the co-chairs or the host of each meeting have allowed more flexible arrangements, such as free sitting or sitting in alphabetic order of names.

The above arrangements have been mainly documented in correspondences between CSCAP Secretariat and CSCAP China or Taiwanese scholars. In December 2004, the *Procedural Guideline for the Participation by Scholar/Experts from Chinese Taipei in CSCAP Study Group Meetings*, drafted by CSCAP China, was adopted in the 22nd CSCAP Steering Committee Meeting in Kunming without Taiwan's knowledge. The document stipulates conditions for Taiwan's participation based on what has been agreed upon and practiced since 1996 except two points. First, members agree that Chinese Taipei will be used to refer to Taiwan in CSCAP documents. Second, Taiwanese scholars who are not on the pre-agreed list can be invited to the new meetings after prior consent from CSCAP members. The latter gives Taiwan more flexibility to organize its delegation. But in practice, CSCAP China retains its veto power over the names of the new participants proposed by Taiwan.

Prospects

According to the CSCAP Charter,[17] membership in CSCAP is on an institutional basis and consists of member committees. Admission of new members to CSCAP shall require the unanimous agreement of the Steering Committee.[18] In addition, CSCAP also accepts applications for associate membership, which may be granted to an institution or consortium of institutes in a country or territory. Associate members are eligible to participate in meetings at the working level and CSCAP General Meetings. Upon being invited, associate members can observe CSCAP Steering Committee meetings.[19]

Noticeably, the criteria of CSCAP membership seem to suggest the founding members' intention to find a way of accommodating Taiwan's membership. First, it is a "Member Committee", not a "National Committee", that a Candidate member must establish. Avoiding using the term "national" was an intentional design to ease the political sensitivity of inviting institutions from controversial countries to join the dialog process. Second, making institutions in a "territory" also eligible for associate membership allows the CSCAP process to accommodate institutions from territories with ongoing sovereign disputes. The founder members of CSCAP believed that such arrangements would help accommodate both memberships of China and Taiwan (Hernandez, 1997).

Currently, the capacity of Taiwanese participation is equivalent to associate membership. Institutionalizing the ad hoc arrangements agreed in the 2006 Procedural Guideline according to the CSCAP Charter could be in the mutual interests of Beijing and Taipei. It will result in more predictable patterns of cross–strait interactions in the CSCAP process and facilitate cross–strait dialog in common trans-boundary security concerns. Moreover, a stable development of cross–strait participation in the process of pan-Asia–Pacific security dialog would certainly be among the interests of the region as a whole.

NO PARTICIPATION IN EAST ASIA INTEGRATION PROCESSES

APT and EAS

When the forum model of APEC failed to effectively respond to the imminent financial crises in 1997–1998 and the economic distresses in the aftermath of the crises, regional economies began to search for more safeguard measures of preventing future crises. ASEAN member states sensed that trade and investment liberalization within ASEAN alone was not sufficient to ensure economic recovery, while China, Japan, and South Korea also realized that increasing economic interdependence required tighter regional governance to contain the spread effects. The launch of the APT process, formally connecting Southeast and Northeast Asia, was not only important in order to bring back the trade and investment flows necessary for economic recovery, but was also critical to the management of the spillover effects of political and security externalities in East Asia. The APT was deemed a state-led collective project to tackle comprehensive security concerns caused by economic crises.[20] When the U.S.-led IMF solutions were unfavorable to devastated countries, the APT process, in contrast, gained momentum.

Some of the most noticeable progress in regional integration through the APT process has occurred in the financial cooperation realm. In 2000, the Chiang Mai Initiative (CMI) was proposed to prevent another financial hit. On the basis of the existing ASEAN Swap Arrangement (ASA) and Bilateral Swap Arrangement (BSA), CMI established a network of bilateral swap arrangements under the APT framework and suggested a surveillance mechanism to monitor potential destabilizing factors. In 2005, APT members agreed to multilateralize the original bilateral network.[21] In 2009, the Agreement of Multilateralization of Chiang Mai Initiative (CMIM) was utilized in response to the 2008–2009 global financial tsunami. Members agreed to increase the initially agreed level of emergency funding from US$ 80 billion to US$ 120 billion, with the designated proportional contributions between ASEAN and non-ASEAN members at the ratio of 20 to 80 percent.

Other progress in the APT process included the disclosure of the Vision of East Asian Community by East Asia Study Group (EASG) in 2002. To a region with short history of multilateralism, sharing a vision of community building indicated a big step in the integration process. The targeted members of the East Asia Community were debated among APT member states. China preferred an APT model, while Japan suggested a community to cover wider geographical area in response to the emerging market of India. In 2005, the issue was temporarily settled, and the East Asia Summit was launched in 2005. Participation in EAS is open to ASEAN's dialog partners who hold substantive ties and are legally committed to the ASEAN Treaty of Amity and Cooperation. Inclusion of Australia, New Zealand, and India in East Asia community building implied that EAS is defined not only by geographical or economic factors, but also by strategic and geo-political concerns.

The Beijing Factor and Taiwan's No Participation

Since the establishment of the WTO in 1995, China voluntarily reduced tariffs substantially to the level suggested in the APEC's Bogor Goals. The reduction not only facilitated China's accession the WTO[22] but also successfully mitigated fears of the 'rising China' in the Asia–Pacific. In the wake of the 1997 Asian financial crisis, the failure of APEC's response to the economic distress pushed for more state-led regulatory and preventive measures in regional economic governance. Given a lesser degree of openness in its financial market in the 1990s, China was less affected by the turmoil and, thus, gained a relatively better position to use its economic leverage over new regional dynamics. Although APT was not initiated by China, it soon became a convenient platform for Beijing to exercise its leverage and promote its geo-strategic interests.

The APT has moved de-facto economic regionalization in East Asia toward policy-led integration processes. The more state-led integration projects in the region proliferate, the less chance Taiwan will join in the dynamics given the prevailing one-China policy. As a result, Taipei's leverage over regional development would become marginal, and in turn, Taiwan's inquiry for regional participation will hardly be taken into serious account.

In regard to participation in EAS, three preconditions set in 2005 have discouraged Taiwan's intentions of joining. Even when Taiwan has strong substantive ties with individual ASEAN member states, Taiwan is neither a dialog partner of ASEAN nor an eligible signatory party of any treaty under the one-China policy of ASEAN. The latter two impediments cannot be overcome without considering the Beijing factor.

Prospects

In the rapid trend of East Asia economic regionalism, it is understandable that Taiwan's concern with isolation would increase when it is excluded from the ongoing state-led ASEAN-centered integration processes. In the new dynamics of cross–strait relations, how

Beijing can help to mitigate Taiwan's fear has become a critical step not only in forwarding Taiwan's ASEAN policy but also in facilitating cross–strait economic integration.

In the 1970s/80s, when Taiwan's economic strengths far surpassed China, Taiwan missed the chance to develop a dialog partnership with ASEAN. The strategic environment now is less favorable for Taiwan to take any initiative to formally institutionalize its ties with ASEAN. Nevertheless, given the special status of United National Development Program (UNDP), a non-sovereign ASEAN dialog partner, special institutional arrangements for Taiwan to provide economic and social aids might still be tenable. Apparently, accumulation of bilateral ties with individual ASEAN member states would be necessary for Taiwan to gain the overall support. If China could refrain from interfering in Taiwan's efforts in enhancing bilateral ties with individual ASEAN member states, including negotiating preferential trade and investment arrangements, Taiwan would have had a better chance to join the East Asia integration process. At the regional level, with a special arrangement in membership, the APT process can accommodate Taiwan's participation without necessarily provoking the one-China policy. An APEC model can be an interim consideration.

CONCLUSION

In general, Beijing's policies toward Taiwan's international participation aimed at blocking any intent or activity that possibly encouraged or suggested Taiwan's de jure independence. After the resumption of cross–strait consultation in the second half of 2008, optimistic observers believe that as long as the goodwill of the leaders from both sides continues, pursuing a win-win solution allowing Taipei to send delegations to international organizations may become possible. Nevertheless, agreeing on the "1992 consensus" as a precondition of resuming negotiation might suggest a way to begin but can hardly ensure a risk-free process. Apparently, cross–strait negotiations in the near future will be conducted under a structural asymmetry in which Beijing enjoys overwhelming strategic leverage over both regional and bilateral agenda. Thus, understanding Beijing's perspective becomes critical for Taiwan to accurately define a policy balance in which the expansion of Taiwan's international space does not come at the expense of the stability of cross–strait relations.

To Beijing, negotiating Taiwan's international spaces is a political issue. From mid-2008 to early 2009, scholars and experts from leading think tanks and research institutions in mainland China have seemed to suggest at least three difficulties in formally setting the negotiations in motion and thus called for a cautious pace to move forward.[23] First, although recent developments in cross–strait relations have suggested a positive trend, the resumed trust seems insufficient to support a risk-free process of political negotiation. Any slight difference of opinion might turn into political incrimination and undermine the hard-won trust. Second, as China moves toward a pluralist society, public opinions matter. So far, leaders' goodwill at the national level has not been converted into public consensus at the local level. Taking domestic stability into account, Beijing has only minimum flexibility of concession on this issue. Third, positions of different departments and agents in the Chinese government are still too diverse. It is understandable that the Office of Taiwanese Affairs takes softer positions than the Ministry of Foreign Affairs and People's Liberalization Army on Taiwan's international participation.

Exchanges at the official/semi-official level suggest that from Beijing's perspective, dynamics in political negotiations should be subject to structural realism. That is, the rationales of give-and-take would have to be based on a power structure reflecting the capacities of involved parties. Novel ideas and solutions are encouraged but cannot be raised without a reality check. Emphasizing structural realism in the early stage of cross–strait détente indeed implies the limitation of Taiwan's strategic choices.[24] Beijing also referred to Article 7 of the Anti-Session Law adopted by the National People's Congress in 2005, to circumscribe its possible offer. Accordingly the two sides of the Taiwan Strait may consult and negotiate on the matter of Taiwan's international space that is compatible with Taiwan's status as a region.[25] In the Shared Vision of Peaceful Development across the Taiwan Strait jointly declared by Hu Jintao and Lien Chan after their first KMT–CCP meeting in 2005,[26] both sides agreed to facilitate talks on Taiwan's participation in international activities under the 1992 consensus. Noticeably, the possible issue to be negotiated, as suggested in the document, was indeed the "activities", not "membership", for Taiwan's participation in international organizations.

Therefore, détente of cross–strait relations is critical to improve Taiwan's policy environment but not sufficient to institutionalize Taiwan's participation in Asia Pacific regional processes. Until the principle of "mutual non-denial",[27] which is now well taken in cross-strait functional negotiations, can be applied to the handling of the trans-boundary issues involving Beijing and Taipei in international society, advancing Taiwan's participation in Asia–Pacific regional processes remains a challenge.

REFERENCES (SELECTIVE)

Aggarwal, VK and CE Morrison (eds.) (1998). *Asia–Pacific Crossroads: Regime Creation and the Future of APEC*. New York: St. Martin's Press.

Ball, D (2000). *The Council for Security Cooperation in the Asia Pacific: Its Record and Its Prospects*. Canberra: The Australian National University.

Beeson, M (2003). ASEAN plus three and the rise of reactionary regionalism. *Contemporary Southeast Asia*, 25(2), 251–268.

Capie, D and P Evans (2000). *The Asia–Pacific Security Lexicon*. Singapore: Institute of Southeast Asian Studies.

Feinberg, RE (ed.) (2003). *APEC as an Institution: Multilateral Governance in the Asia–Pacific*. Singapore: Institute of Southeast Asian Studies.

Funabashi, Y (1995). *Asia Pacific Fusion: Japan's Role in APEC*. Washington DC: Institute for International Economics.

Hamilton-Hart, N (2006). The Chiang Mai initiative and the prospects for closer monetary integration in East Asia. In *Regional Integration in East Asia and Europe: Convergence or Divergence?* Fort B and D Webber (eds.), New York: Routledge.

Henning, CR (2002). *East Asian Financial Cooperation*. Washington DC: Institute for International Economics.

Hernandez, CG (1997). Governments and NGOs in the search for peace: The ASEAN ISIS and CSCAP experience. The Alternative Systems Conference: Focus on the Global South. Bangkok, Thailand. March 27–30 (www.focusweb.org/focus/pd/sec/hernandez.html).

Hidetaka, Y (2005). Political leadership, informality, and regional integration in East Asia: The evolution of ASEAN plus three. *European Journal of East Asian Studies*, 4(2), 205–232.

Hund, M (2003). ASEAN plus three: Towards a new age of pan-East Asian regionalism? A skeptical appraisal. *The Pacific Review*, 16(3), 383–417.

Kawasaki, T (2006). Neither skepticism nor romanticism: The ASEAN regional forum as a solution for the Asia–Pacific assurance game. *The Pacific Review*, 19(2), 219–237.

Ravenhill, J (2002). *APEC and the Construction of Pacific Rim Regionalism*. New York: Cambridge University Press.

San, KH (ed.) (1998). *The Future of the ARF*. Singapore: Institute of Defense and Strategic Studies, Nanyang Technological University.

Stubbs, R (2003). ASEAN plus three. *Asian Survey*, 42(3), 440–456.

Su, C (2009). *Taiwan's Relations with Mainland China: A Tail Wagging Two Dogs*. London: Routledge.

Woods, L (1993). *Asia–Pacific Diplomacy: Nongovernmental Organizations and International Relations*. Vancouver, Canada: UBC Press.

Yang, P (1997). Taiwan's approaches to APEC: Economic cooperation, political significance, and international participation. International Conference on Canada–Taiwan Relations in the 1990s. National Chengchi University, Taipei, Taiwan, November 14.

ENDNOTES

1. For discussions on dynamics of cross–strait relations since the early 1990s, see Su (2009).
2. During the first year of the Ma administration, the Chairmen of SEF and ARATS have met three times in the so-called Chiang-Chen talks. Agreements reached cover issues of direct cross–strait air transport, postal cooperation, food safety, joint crime-fighting, and financial cooperation, among other issues.
3. For the full text of the speech, see http://www.gwytb.gov.cn/zyjh/zyjh0.asp?zyjh_m_id=1683.
4. For discussions on APEC institutional evolution in the first decade of its establishment, see Aggarwal and Morrison (1998); Ravenhill (2002); Feinberg (2003).
5. *Joint Statement of the Seventeenth APEC Ministerial Meeting*, Busan, Republic of Korea, 15–16 November, 2005. http://www.apec.org/apec/ministerial_statements/annual_ministerial/2005_17th_apec_ministerial.html.
6. ESC was further transformed into the SOM Steering Committee of ECOTECH (SCE) in 2005.
7. Taiwan often argued that "Chinese Taipei" is not recognizable in international postal services.

8. Comments here were based on interviews with individual representatives of Chinese Taipei to APEC meetings from 2000 to 2002.
9. Comments made by the spokesman of Ministry of Foreign Affairs, PRC on November 3, 2008. http://www.chinareviewnews.com/doc/1007/8/8/4/100788467.html?coluid=7&kindid=0&docid=100788467.
10. As in 2008, ARF participants are Australia, Bangladesh, Brunei Darussalam, Cambodia, Canada, China, European Union, India, Indonesia, Japan, Democratic Peoples' Republic of Korea, Republic of Korea, Laos, Malaysia, Myanmar, Mongolia, New Zealand, Pakistan, Papua New Guinea, the Philippines, Russian Federation, Singapore, Sri Lanka, Thailand, Timor Leste, the United States, and Vietnam.
11. *Terms of Reference of ARF Unit* can be found in official Web site of ARF. http://www.aseanregionalforum.org.
12. The ARF Chair is the Chairman of ASEAN Standing Committee. Views of *Enhanced Role of ARF Chair* were documented in May 2001.
13. For discussion on country's perspective on ARF's early development, see San (1998). For more recent discussions, see Kawasaki (2006).
14. For discussions on early developments of CSCAP, see Ball (2000).
15. For updates of topics and activities of CSCAP studying groups, please refer to the official Web site of CSCAP <http://www.cscap.org>.
16. Members of ASEAN ISIS at that time were Institute of Strategic and Development Studies (ISDS), in the Philippines; Center for Strategic and International Studies (CSIS), in Indonesia; Singapore Institute of International Affairs (SIIA), in Singapore; Institute of Security and International Studies (ISIS), in Thailand; and Institute of Strategic and International Studies (ISIS), in Malaysia.
17. The CSCAP Charter was adopted at a meeting of the Steering Committee Pro Tem in Lombok, Indonesia, on 16 December 1993. The Charter was subsequently amended in August 1995.
18. Article III of CSCAP Charter.
19. Article IV of CSCAP Charter.
20. For discussions on various issues of APT, please see Stubbs (2003); Beeson (2003); Hund (2003); Hidetaka (2005).
21. For background and evolution of CMI, see Henning (2002, 109–128); Hamilton-Hart (2006).
22. China filed its application for WTO membership in 1986. After concluding 37 bilateral agreements with its trading partners in the WTO, China gained its membership on 11 December 2001.
23. Remarks highlighted here are based on author's on-site observations in several informal meetings held in Taipei from mid-2008 to early 2009. Delegations from mainland China included Party School of the Central Committee of CPC, Chinese Academy of Social Sciences, China Institute of Contemporary International Relations, and Tsinghua University.

24. Ibid.
25. The Anti-Session Law was adopted by the third session of the 10th National People's Congress on 14 March 2005. For the translation of full text, see: http://english.peopledaily.com.cn/200503/14/eng20050314_176746.html.
26. The Shared Vision was announced in Lien Chan's first visit to Beijing during April 26–May 3, 2005. Both Hu Jintao and Lien Chan presented themselves as party leaders. The KMT–CPC Forum thus was launched under their leadership. It remains an important Track II mechanism after the resumption of cross–strait consultation in 2008.
27. During Ma's presidential campaign, speaking at a conference in India, in response to a question whether he was seeking Beijing's recognition of "Taiwan", Ma responded by saying he wasn't looking for mutual recognition... but mutual non-denial. http://www.forumosa.com/taiwan/viewtopic.php?f=89&t=62784; After being elected, Ma reasserted the notion as a restarting point of improving cross–strait relations. http://www.chinapost.com.tw/taiwan/national/presidential-election/2008/03/24/148519/Ma-repeats.htm.

Index